ALSO BY LAWRENCE SCANLAN:

NONFICTION
- *The Big Red Horse*
- *The Horse God Built: Secretariat, His Groom, Their Legacy*
- *Harvest of a Quiet Eye: The Cabin as Sanctuary*
- *Grace Under Fire: The State of Our Sweet and Savage Game*
- *Little Horse of Iron: A Quest for the Canadian Horse*
- *Wild About Horses: Our Timeless Passion for the Horse*
- *Horses Forever*
- *Heading Home: On Starting a New Life in a Country Place*
- *Big Ben*

FICTION
- *The Horse's Shadow*

CO-AUTHORED
- *Healed by Horses: The Carole Fletcher Story*
- *The Man Who Listens to Horses* [with Monty Roberts]
- *Riding High: Ian Millar's World of Show Jumping*

A YEAR OF
LIVING GENEROUSLY

DISPATCHES
FROM THE FRONT LINES
OF PHILANTHROPY

LAWRENCE
SCANLAN

A YEAR OF

LIVING

GENEROUSLY

Douglas & McIntyre
D&M PUBLISHERS INC.
Vancouver/Toronto/Berkeley

Douglas & McIntyre
An imprint of D&M Publishers Inc.
2323 Quebec Street, Suite 201, Vancouver, BC, Canada V5T 4S7
www.douglas-mcintyre.com

Cataloguing data available from Library and Archives Canada

ISBN 978-1-55365-416-2 (cloth)
ISBN 978-1-55365-617-3 (ebook)
ISBN 978-1-55365-841-2 (pbk.)

Editing by Jan Walter
Cover design by Heather Pringle
Text design by Jessica Sullivan
Cover photographs © Ric Kallaher/Corbis (hands),
Seide Preis/Getty Images (burlap)
Printed and bound in Canada by Friesens
Text printed on acid-free paper
Distributed in the U.S. by Publishers Group West

We gratefully acknowledge the financial support of the Canada
Council for the Arts, the British Columbia Arts Council, the
Province of British Columbia through the Book Publishing Tax
Credit, and the Government of Canada through the Canada Book
Fund for our publishing activities.

For Dusty Rose Scanlan
(March 11, 1996—June 4, 2009)

"The best way to find yourself is to lose yourself in the service of others."
MAHATMA GANDHI (1869–1948),
humanitarian, spiritual leader, author

"An imbalance between rich and poor is the oldest and most fatal ailment of all republics."
PLUTARCH (circa 46–120),
Greek historian, biographer, philosopher

"The good we secure for ourselves is precarious and uncertain until it is secured for all of us and incorporated into our common life."
JANE ADDAMS (1860–1935), American civil
rights activist, Nobel Peace Prize laureate, 1931

CONTENTS

MY INTEREST in philanthropy as a phenomenon was fuelled by the death of my mother six years ago and our family's debates about ways to honour her memory. The five sons and three daughters of Clare Scanlan decided, in the end, to fund a nursing scholarship in her name at the University of Toronto (my mother had worked all her life as a pediatric and geriatric nurse). The experience triggered thoughts about my own mortality, of course, and about legacy—the mark we make in this world.

Toronto financier Lawrence S. Bloomberg later upped our ante. He gave $10 million to the same school of nursing, now named after him. His largesse was typical of an unmistakable trend: individual generosity on a fantastic scale. The Bill and Melinda Gates Foundation, for example, has emerged as the most powerful charitable foundation ever seen. With a $29-billion war chest (and that was before Warren Buffett tossed in another $37 billion), it has set breathtaking goals, among them the defeat of malaria throughout the developing world. The annual budget of the World Health Organization, at under $5 billion, looks puny by comparison.

A charity Olympics has been underway for many years, and the numbers are dizzying. Seldom, as was often the case in the past, is it a matter of one person writing a fat cheque and being done with it. Instead, there is a high personal stake in these philanthropic exercises. Bill Gates is typical of the new breed of "social entrepreneur": a rich benefactor who wholeheartedly embraces a chosen cause and works on its behalf.

The role demands hands-on involvement, knowledge of the issue and a focus on solutions, including travel to far-flung places to observe first-hand how the money is making a difference. Such zealousness is without precedent, and it isn't just the wealthy who are enlisting.

Helping others has become fashionable. The Nobel Peace Prize of 2006 went to philanthropist Muhammad Yunus, a Bangladeshi economist who, three decades ago, launched the revolutionary idea of the Grameen Bank and micro-credit loans to destitute people.

Steve Nash, Canada's own and the National Basketball Association's Most Valuable Player in 2005 and 2006, created his own foundation and built in his wife's native Paraguay a pediatric cardiology ward. On retirement, he intends to become a full-time philanthropist working on similar projects.

Jeff Skoll, the Montreal-born billionaire and first president of eBay, formed the Skoll Centre for Social Entrepreneurship at Oxford University in 2003 to teach and celebrate his philosophy "that strategic investments in the right people can lead to lasting social change." Movie stars and rock stars have their pet charities, and former U.S. president Bill Clinton seems to have put a sordid incident from his past behind him, largely through his clout as an energized AIDS campaigner.

Today the word *philanthropist* frequently pops up in obituary headlines. Many of the deceased, no matter their means, age or gender, were apparently notable for their benevolent acts. *Philanthropy* has come to be widely and almost exclusively understood as a word to describe the notion of prosperous people giving away their wealth, typically near the end of their lives. But I was interested in its original meaning—from the Greek word *philanthropia,* meaning love for humankind. With that definition in mind, I began to catalogue varieties of kindness, large and small, and gifts of time or money, even of spare body organs. It struck me that as much as greed seems to characterize our age, there is also a powerful impulse at work the other way, towards giving.

I could have used any number of words to describe these acts: benevolence, generosity, humanitarianism, public-spiritedness, altruism, social conscience, charity, brotherly love, magnanimity, munificence, largesse, bountifulness, beneficence, unselfishness, humanity, kind-heartedness or compassion. The grander goal of social justice belonged somewhere on that list, as did the humble notion of sharing.

Benevolence is as old as humankind: think of the Good Samaritan in the Bible, the rule of obligatory giving, or *Zakah,* that is one of the five pillars of Islam, and the *tzedakah,* or call to charity, from Judaism. The ancient Romans had their *panem et circenses* (bread and circus programs for the poor). And the Latin phrase *pro bono* (short for *pro bono publico,* "for the public good") has widely come to mean any sort of freely offered public service, especially by professionals.

Billionaires seeking to eradicate the scourge of malaria, twenty-somethings looking for adventure, or the newly retired choosing to volunteer overseas rather than settling into their rockers—these individuals should be applauded, and why not? We live in a world of individual celebrity and individual achievement in sport and culture, and it's only natural that solo assaults on human misery would mark our time.

But where does this leave collective action against poverty and suffering? Are governments right to trust that wealthy benefactors and armies of volunteers will pick up the slack if they step aside?

I have been involved in community work all my life, running charity campaigns as a university student, coaching baseball and hockey teams as a young father, and in past decades helping to raise funds for non-governmental organizations (NGOs) working in the developing world, but I had never really got my hands dirty, never worked on the front lines where the answers to these and similar questions might be found. For the year 2008, I decided I would volunteer with twelve charitable organizations and dedicate a month of hands-on involvement to each one.

Organizing and logistics presented the first challenge. Some outfits didn't want help for only one month, and some didn't need or want a writer poking around for that long. In the end, I secured twelve placements that reflect long-standing interests of mine, from serving at the soup kitchen a ten-minute walk from my house in southeastern Ontario to teaching journalism at a community radio station in West Africa; from helping out at a riding camp down the highway to joining a crew building houses in the hurricane-ravaged parishes of New Orleans.

I hoped to plumb issues that seemed to me central. In the face of human suffering, here and elsewhere, what, if anything, is my obligation or that of my community and my country? Is it good to be good? The euphoria that Ebenezer Scrooge felt when he stopped his penny-pinching ways: does it endure and can it be measured in some scientific way? What are the rewards and hazards of deep volunteering? How does it change you, or does it? Does helping actually help, or does it only serve to prop up the status quo?

Early in my research, I came across a quote from the Swedish playwright August Strindberg (1849–1912). "All charity," he wrote, "is humiliating." I was haunted by those words from his play *The Ghost Sonata*. His view was stark and harsh, and yet it seemed there was truth in it too.

I would do some good, then, or try to, and take some notes along the way.

A NOTE ON NAMES: Some of those interviewed for this book were content to have their full names used; others preferred their first names only or a pseudonym. Where obtaining consent was an issue, such as with mentally challenged individuals, the names were changed.

LIFE
at Vinnie's

JANUARY 2. Day one for the new volunteer at the St. Vincent de Paul Society-Loretta Hospitality Centre and the very first order of business is to free his old truck, mired in foot-deep snow, from the parking lot.

I am here to help (by pitching in to shovel the lot), but first I have to move my truck and now it looks like I am the one in need of help. Snow is not the problem. It's the ice below. Rocking the truck—from forward to reverse and back again—launches me no more than a metre in either direction. The red '91 Nissan King Cab is stuck.

Two men and one young woman, the latter coatless in the cold, a cigarette dangling from her lips, leap onto the back bumper and in unison begin to pump on it. No one has said anything to the others, so clearly they have done this before, and it works. The engine revs, the tires grip and I'm free.

While the wife and daughters of one of my rescuers "shop" in the used clothing warehouse at the back of the lot, he and his companion start to clear the parking spaces. There is a dearth of shovels, so I dash home, grab mine and return to join them.

The two men chat amiably about wind chill, the Toronto Maple Leafs, what kind of shovel works best. Canadian banter.

"Vinnie's"—the St. Vincent de Paul drop-in centre here in Kingston, Ontario—operates out of a one-storey, aluminum-clad white box of a building set amid marginal housing in the city's north end. In a previous incarnation, this house at 85A Stephen Street was headquarters to a small pest-control company. In the northeast corner of the lot is a former carport that shelters benches for smokers, and my first impression is that many of those who come to Vinnie's for a hot meal, groceries, warm socks or simple companionship also take comfort in the small pleasures of nicotine and caffeine.

As I shovel near the smokers, I hear folks talking about the Christmas they had, how busy it was, and I remember similar conversations with my own friends just days before. The helper and the helped are one and the same, or so I think. The writer Joanne Page, who has volunteered for years at Vinnie's, gave me some wise advice before I signed on for the month of January: do not assume, do not judge, do not accuse, do not patronize.

IN KINGSTON, Princess Street bisects the city from the northwest to the southeast and acts as the great dividing line. The stereotype has it that if you live south of Princess, you are either a professor at Queen's University or one of the typically privileged youth who study there. North of Princess is supposedly home to the working poor and families on welfare. Fine homes and not-so-fine homes exist on both sides of the line, of course, but the divide between the two worlds is as stark and plain to see as the million-dollar yachts moored next to the notorious jail, Kingston Pen.

One effect of the area's having so many prisons is that the families of convicts come here to live, swelling the numbers of the city's poor. Roughly thirteen thousand people in Kingston live on some sort of social assistance, with an annual average income of $6,500. An equal or greater number work at minimum-wage jobs that generate an estimated annual income of under $16,000. According to Bhavana Varma, president of the United Way in the Kingston region, some 3,800 children, from junior kindergarten to grade 12, arrive at school hungry and with no lunch in hand.

"As a proportion of total population, Kingston has a lot more issues, a lot more pupils at risk than Toronto does," says Varma. She points to a huge disparity in income levels and to shocking levels of poverty in some areas of town.

I know of two schools eight blocks apart: in one, there is no library, and in winter some children lack proper warm clothing; in the other, the pupils have access to a fabulous library—and to golf lessons. My own comfortable home is just south of Princess, but I can walk to Vinnie's in ten minutes, and to another hot lunch program, actually on Princess and called Martha's Table, in two minutes. The disparity is huge; the distance is not.

THE STREET-FACING door of Vinnie's is closed to all but those who use walkers or wheelchairs and the wooden ramp, so almost everyone enters by the aluminum side door and steps. To the left is the dining room with its dozen or so Formica-grey tables, straight ahead is the one washroom, and to the right is a tiny kitchen with most of the south wall cut out so the servers and served have a clear view of each other. When the doors open in the morning, chat between them is light and playful.

Sister Loretta McAndrews, who convinced the parish priests that the need was great for a place like Vinnie's, looks out on the dining room from an old black-and-white photograph, her face tightly framed by the modified habit and simple veil then worn by her order. My aunt, Rosemarie Scanlan, a nun in the same order (the Sisters of Providence of St. Vincent de Paul) helped start the food bank in nearby Belleville and would have known Loretta well.

In my experience, nuns are not afraid to ask for things, big things, and they often get them. What Loretta McAndrews lobbied for was a gathering place where people in Kingston who had little or no money could socialize and enjoy a good hot midday meal.

Twelve people came to Vinnie's on the first day it opened in March 1982, but that year the daily average was only four visitors, attended to by two volunteers. The concept of the food bank had been introduced in Canada just the year before (in Edmonton), and the country's hard-won social safety net was still years away from its slow and tortured unravelling. For a time, Vinnie's operated just three days a week, then demand took it up to five. In 1993, an average of twenty-five people a day came in for a meal. In 2007, it was sixty-eight a day.

The 2008 data breaks down like this: 15,442 three-course hot meals were served at a cost of 70.4¢ each. An average of seventy-five guests arrived daily; some 5,714 clients received emergency groceries; and $31,857.75 was given out to help people with their electricity, rent, transportation, medical needs or other expenses. Volunteers gave 10,494 hours of their time and expertise. Had those volunteers been paid the minimum wage, their labour would have cost $91,826.88. Vinnie's actual budget in 2008 was $158,882.30.

Whether these higher figures are due to Vinnie's becoming better known or due to rising need is anyone's guess. Likely both factors have come into play.

WHEN THE shovelling is done (it takes about an hour and leaves me with apple cheeks, icicles on my beard and, later, a sore back), I duck inside, get outfitted with an apron and a baseball cap (to meet health regulations) and go to work in the kitchen. Throughout the month, I will come here two or three times a week, arriving in the morning and leaving around mid-afternoon. I feel awkward in the beginning, especially that first day. This is not my usual tribe, and I feel like I have "volunteer" stamped on my forehead, just as those coming to eat have "client" marked on theirs.

A calm and seemingly unflappable young woman named Jenn is today's head cook. Sully, a trained chef who has managed restaurant kitchens all over the city, is another paid staffer who fills in for Jenn on occasion. And while many volunteers show up through the week to prepare and serve meals and to wash dishes, Thelma is the one volunteer who is here every day of the week, from the moment Vinnie's opens to the moment it closes. Thelma is in her mid-fifties. She has a strong nose. She wears her hair pulled back in a ponytail. Her mouth is almost always on the verge of a smile. She seems intimately connected with this kitchen, the day's list of jobs and what to do when. There is chat between Jenn and Thelma, but it's casual and polite. No need to say "do this" or "do that," because each easily anticipates the tasks of the other.

Thelma knows where to find every pot, pan and plate in the kitchen; knows where to search for the missing broom. At one point I am holding a big serving tray and she sees my lost look and wordlessly points to the cupboard the tray calls home. If this place has a Mother Superior, it is Thelma. Jenn and I start to call her Thelma Smartypants, and you can see the smile spread across her face. She loves to be teased.

"It makes me feel useful to be here," she tells me. "I miss being here when I'm not."

Today's meal comprises homemade turkey-vegetable soup and crackers to start, one hot dog in a bun, a small side of fries, a dollop of cabbage-and-carrot coleslaw and pumpkin pie for dessert. Jenn has tried serving more elegant fare than this high school cafeteria menu. She once prepared beef stroganoff, another time tuna casserole, but the clientele turned up their noses at these offerings. They prefer basic beef and chicken, uncomplicated lasagna and stews, and hold the spices. Grilled cheese sandwiches, says Sully, still draw the biggest crowds.

The food is cooked on two stoves: a large gas model and a smaller electrical one. A small island in the centre of the kitchen is both prep area and plating station. Once the action starts, so too does Vinnie's industrial dishwasher, racing through its complete cycle in about five minutes, belching steam when its doors are opened. Any volunteer between jobs can always find work cleaning pots or putting away piping-hot plates. My first assignment is to use a broadsword of a knife to carve through sturdy cabbages and break them into ever smaller chunks so that Thelma can then persuade them into the food processor. Jenn boils water in a forty-litre pot for the hundred or so hot dogs. I serrate carrots and transfer pie onto plates, and when those jobs are done I ask Jenn or Thelma to give me something else to do. They cheerfully oblige. At 9 a.m., opening time, half a dozen or so people come in for coffee. For many of them, it's warmer here than in their draughty, under-heated apartments.

Vinnie's can accommodate forty-eight guests at a time. "It should be a quiet day," says Jenn. She's predicting twenty or thirty for lunch, with lots of take-home hot dogs left over. But by noon the place is packed and as some leave others take their places. The sated walk down the stairs and out the door; the hungry pass them on the way in. In the end, seventy come to be fed.

"It means," says Jenn, "that they've spent their money for January over Christmas. There's no money left for food. It's going to be a busy month."

Before anyone is served, Thelma rings a large brass bell that hangs above the kitchen entryway, then she goes to the end of the small dining room and asks for a brief silence—the equivalent of a traditional grace, though sometimes there is both silence and grace. Thelma knows every person in the room, how each comes to be here, and treats all with dignity and respect. While I was cutting cabbage, Thelma had set me straight. "This is *not* a soup kitchen. You line up at soup kitchens. People don't line up here. This is a hospitality place. You have to make people feel comfortable."

I am struck by how pleasant the atmosphere is, the smiles of gratitude when a plate is put down, the cheery hellos and goodbyes. The sincere thank yous. Vinnie's turns no one away, unless it becomes necessary, which sometimes happens when a guest turns unruly.

"That's the hardest," agrees Jenn, who works half-time here and half-time at a women's shelter. She is a woman in her thirties with fine skin and teeth, and the earrings she wears suggest that she takes her work seriously—but not too seriously. Otherwise, I'm sure, her two hard jobs would undo her.

Jenn is trained as a youth-care worker and is self-taught as a chef. She tells me, proudly (rubbing the fingernails of her right hand on her chef's whites), that Vinnie's was inspected by the health department just before Christmas and passed with flying colours. The dishes that come out of the sterilizing machine are steaming hot, too hot to be touched, and they dry in seconds.

7

"Too hot" also describes the odd guest ("client" or "participant" are other words that staff and volunteers use to describe those who come). Some here have been abused by their parents in the past or by their partners more recently. Some face unresolved mental health or addiction issues. A few are bitter and angry and it doesn't take much to set them off. More are simply worn down by the daily and perhaps decades-long grind of poverty. What must it be like, always, to have your hand out?

Poverty cannot be disguised. At Vinnie's, there are obvious giveaways: bad or missing teeth, lifeless skin, ill-fitting clothes and, the kicker, sad shoes, more apt to be plastic than leather, past their prime and wrong for the season. Often it's running shoes all winter long.

Anyone who causes a disturbance at Vinnie's is given a warning. One strike, two strikes, three and you're out. But even then, Jenn or Thelma will fill plastic margarine containers and glass jars with food that can be passed on by friends to that errant man or woman.

I see a teenager, no older than seventeen, leave with a jar of soup, her slice of pie inside a plastic tub, a large garbage bag full of clothes from the warehouse and coffee in a Styrofoam cup.

"You need a horse," I tell her. She laughs. My God, I think, she's young, too young to be a guest at Vinnie's. I try to imagine what home is like for this waif.

I have never worked in a restaurant in my life, so serving is new to me. I am taken aback when a thin woman in her sixties tells me that she has asked other servers four times for pie, and would I mind, when I get a minute, to attend to her? I bring her back a small plate containing, as it happens, two slices. She is thrilled.

At another table sits a woman with three sons, all teenagers, all with the same sallow complexion. They look unwell and discomfited and they seem not to be talking much. As one volunteer put it, coming here is not the kind of childhood memory you want to hold dear. How, I wonder, does a mother explain to her children where they are going when they set out for this place? Vinnie's is decidedly not a restaurant, for no money changes hands. Maybe that is why Thelma hates the phrase "soup kitchen." It's demeaning, and it conjures Depression-era line-ups.

There is a charm to Vinnie's and a deeply felt sense of community here. But no one comes to Vinnie's out of choice; they've come by default. Given their druthers, everyone here—and that includes the volunteers—would be elsewhere. The clients, of course, would rather have money to spare and their choice of a meal at home or, on occasion, at a restaurant in town. As for the volunteers, some, like Pat, a retired neurological nurse, just shake their heads, especially when they see mothers in the dining room with kids in tow.

"We shouldn't be here," Pat says. "There shouldn't be a Vinnie's and a Martha's Table and all these support services." It should never have come to this.

To say that clients have no choice is not quite correct. One woman calls Vinnie's every morning to find out what's on the menu. No doubt she calls around to Martha's Table and the other places in town that offer free or heavily subsidized meals (Martha's charges $1) and lets the bill of fare determine where she'll eat lunch that day. Vinnie's staff have come to expect her call and find it amusing.

Not so amusing is the brochure that Jenn gives me the first day. Published by Volunteer and Information Kingston, the six-page pamphlet lists all the shelters (six), the places offering hot meals for free (ten, all with varying hours), food banks (five), used clothing and furniture depots (thirteen) and drop-in centres (five). All these helter-skelter parts of an infrastructure are run mostly by volunteers and all of them compete with each other for the charity dollar. There was a social safety net in this country, but it appears to have been replaced by something thinner, weaker and hastily patched together.

FEW WHO come to Vinnie's are actually homeless, but it's because they spend so much of their income on rent that Vinnie's and the other agencies on this list are so critical to their survival. What the poor need, desperately, is decent and affordable housing.

Calgary journalist Gordon Laird has done the math and he figures it's cheaper to house poor people than to let them fend for themselves on the streets. In a 2007 report, *Homelessness in a Growth Economy: Canada's 21st Century Paradox,* underwritten by a foundation-funded fellowship, Laird cites a 2001 study in British Columbia which found that the average homeless person costs the Canadian taxpayer $30,000 to $40,000 a year in front-line emergency services—hospital care, motels for homeless families and shelters. A more recent study done in Calgary put the figure far higher, at $132,000. And in some American cities, the cost exceeds $200,000 a year.

Better, says Laird, would be a flexible housing strategy that offers a blend of affordable housing, rent supplements, higher welfare rates and changes to municipal bylaws that would free up rental units in existing homes. Given the numbers (an estimated 200,000 people are homeless in this country, though some say the true figure is 300,000), Laird argues that the government could save itself $4 billion a year by spending $2 billion a year on such a strategy.

Senator Hugh Segal, a self-described Red Tory who lives in Kingston, grew up in Montreal and has boyhood memories of poverty: food baskets arriving at his family's door around Passover, a bailiff coming to take away furniture. He has long been a champion of the poor in Canada. "Poverty," he says, "is not having enough money to get by. By any definition of poverty, five to eight million Canadians are poor. For a welfare family, this means they have $11,000 to $15,000 less than they need for basic housing, food and clothing." Segal and many others have pushed for an end to the current welfare system (which he calls punitive) and its replacement with a guaranteed annual income supplement.

Why the government does not do this baffles me. Is it short-term thinking? Is it because the poor have too few lobbyists barking at politicians? Maybe some of us are suspicious of the poor, seeing them as freeloaders. Maybe some of the poor, in turn, mistrust all those who have so much more than they do. Here and everywhere on this planet there is a gap between those with the means to live comfortably and those without, and that gap grows ever wider and more toxic.

BY MID-AFTERNOON the last lingering diners have left, the remaining pots and plates have been put away and a quiet falls over the place. It's Kenny time. A Vinnie's regular in his uniform of blue Leafs jacket and Leafs ball cap, Kenny is the self-appointed clean-up guy. He sails around the dining room and begins spraying the tables with antibacterial cleanser and flipping chairs upside-down and onto tables to ready the floor for the mop. Later I spot him outside, walking down the middle of the snow-covered street. Kenny is bow-legged and running-shoed; his gait is tippy-toed and purposeful. Like the white rabbit in *Alice in Wonderland*, he looks late for a very important date.

There is a note on one of the kitchen cupboards, attributed to someone whose name I do not recognize. "There are no unimportant jobs," it reads. "No unimportant people, no unimportant acts of kindness." The author of that adage, it turns out, is H. Jackson Brown, Jr., an ad man from Tennessee who gathered simple words of wisdom and gave the collection as a going-away present to his college-bound son. The success of *Life's Little Instruction Book* led to *P.S. I Love You* and *A Father's Book of Wisdom* plus a score of bestselling spinoffs. Homespun homilies are good business: millions of copies of these works have been sold around the world, and Mr. Brown is a very rich man.

Another sign, this one in the warehouse at Vinnie's, reads:

What you can expect from us:
1. A hot meal Monday to Friday.
2. Groceries once a month.
3. Clothing, linens, household items, boots and toys.
4. Help with your expenses if finances allow.

What we expect from you:
1. Respect for yourself, for us and our space.
2. To understand that we are here for everyone and to not take more than you need.

A like-minded sentiment from Bob Dylan has been framed and hung on the wall in the dining room at Vinnie's. "You are better than no one," it says, "and no one's better than you." The lines are from a love song called "To Ramona," which was released in 1964. These are the mantras that will guide me through my days at Vinnie's.

JANUARY 7. Everything at Vinnie's operates according to a schedule. An erasable board tells volunteers how and when the meal is to be set out. Jenn, Sully and Thelma need no such guidance.

11:15 Place soup bowls on island (in the kitchen).
11:20 Put bread in baskets.
11:25 Soup in bowls and on trays.
11:30 Welcoming prayer/birthdays/announcements.
11:35 Serve soup/bread on tables.
11:40 Serve main meals.
11:45 Serve dessert.

Thelma rings first the large bell at 11:30 to get everyone's attention and then a delicate dinner bell before offering her welcome. (A volunteer bought the dinner bell at the children's memorial in Hiroshima, Japan, and presented it to Vinnie's on her return.) I have learned that little separates Thelma from the eighty or ninety people who come here daily for warmth, food and company. Twenty years ago, she arrived at Vinnie's looking for groceries. She was a single mother of five and she needed help. More recently, she became a volunteer, sorting clothes in the warehouse, then assisting in the kitchen.

Five years ago, Vinnie's indefatigable administrator, Deb Greer, approached Thelma and asked her if she would take on another task. Deb had always offered the welcome, said the grace, wished the happy birthdays.

"Would you do it?" Deb asked Thelma.

"Oh, no," was Thelma's first response. She was too unworthy, too shy.

No longer. Thelma dispenses hugs and cheer, and I have no idea where this wealth of goodwill and kindness comes from or just how deep it is. I know only that her partner is very ill (his job was to spray-paint cars before protective masks came into vogue) and that she is not much better off than those she serves. And make no mistake, Thelma serves. She has, says

Deb, the same reputation in her Division Street neighbourhood as she does at Vinnie's.

"We have all different walks of life here," Thelma tells me. "We try to treat everyone as a somebody."

But isn't it sad, I ask her, to see that teenage mother coming into Vinnie's with her two-year-old son? Thelma turns the question on its side.

"At least she's coming in," Thelma says. "She's not keeping it all bottled up." By "it," I take her to mean the rage that must follow all the indignities inflicted by chronic poverty in a land of plenty, the frustration that comes with being an inexperienced mother with no partner to help out. Thelma's father worked at a golf course and tended bar. Her mother cleaned houses and made lunches for men working in the rail yards, then located downtown. "They made sure we never did without. They never hurt us." Implicit is that Thelma saw or knew kids who went without and suffered at the hands of their parents.

Today, she has fourteen grandchildren. She is also a granny figure to the children in her neighbourhood, bringing home food and cookies to give out. My own grandmother, who also lived for a time in the north end on nearby Markland Street, did the same. Thelma is fifty-seven, almost two years younger than I am. In my head, she is far older, and wiser.

"Everyone needs a little tender loving care," says Thelma. "I grew up with many of these people's parents; I got to know them too. I've seen people come in here so scared."

When I ask Thelma about seeing the same faces every day, about how hard it is to break the poverty cycle, she again refuses to be pessimistic. "I look on the bright side," she says. "Right now, some of them are on the down slope. But there are better days ahead." She gives the example of Dean, one of the men who helped me free the truck that first day. He's at work painting now.

Does she have a favourite volunteer? If she does, she is too polite, too genuinely considerate to say. "They all treat me like an angel," she insists.

Thelma receives a disability pension, like many of "the people," as she calls the clients at Vinnie's, but she believes that those who can work should work. She knows individuals who turn up their noses at jobs in restaurants or as city labourers. "Excuse me," says Thelma. "You take what you can get." Work, she believes, can cure a lot of woes.

Later, while I am alternately cutting apple turnovers in half, cleaning pots and layering margarine onto bread, I spot tattoos on Thelma's arms.

"What's the story?" I ask her, expecting to hear a tale of wild youth and recklessness.

"My grandkids," she says. The tattoos are paste-ons.

When a child comes in, Thelma goes right to the freezer and brings out a Popsicle. She sets aside cookies for that child, wants to meet and greet and coddle that child. One day it is the little two-year-old boy in sunglasses, there with both his grandmother and his mother who cannot be more than eighteen. Deb later tells me their story: the grandmother, just fifty, was assaulted numerous times by her various partners, and now her self-esteem "is in the toilet." The young mother has likewise been assaulted by her husband, father of the child. The poverty and the abuse are passed on like a virus from one generation to the next. Victim and perpetrator seem drawn to one another.

Some, though not all, who come to Vinnie's believe there is a pecking order here, with violent people at the very bottom.

Drug users rank just above them, with alcoholics a little higher on the ladder. It's not hard to identify who's who. The angry ones are those most likely to raise their voices and use rough language in the dining room; they seem to be on a constant low boil. The drinkers have missing teeth from all the sugar in the booze and blood in their eyes from the night before. The drug users are pencil-thin.

For some reason, the very young and the very old trouble me most. Early on, I serve a meal to a little old lady who wants salad only and passes on the stew; she looks lost and forlorn. The young men who come in often wear backpacks and strike a casual pose, as if they've just come from class. And maybe they have.

JANUARY 9. "Morning everyone," says Thelma, on the dot of 11:30. "Nice to see you all. Any birthdays today?" There being none, she tells them how good it is to see so many smiling faces. Thelma asks that we give thanks, that we remember the troops, everyone here and all our families. She asks that we be thankful for the nice weather (a thaw has melted the snow), and then she asks for a minute of silence, which she cuts off closer to fifteen seconds.

The volunteers—three women and me—swing into action. Little sandwiches (Wonder Bread "buttered" with margarine) are set out on the tables in plastic baskets lined, like nests, with paper napkins. Next comes the soup, then the main course, a meat and vegetable concoction that Thelma labels "stewp"—too thick to be called soup, too thin to be called stew.

The three paid part-time staffers, Deb, Jenn and Sully, manage this whole operation. The United Way provides some funding, as do the Sisters of Providence, but Vinnie's relies heavily on private donations from Kingston's churches and synagogue. Schools undertake food drives for Vinnie's, two big food companies deliver goods regularly and four stores pass on clothing and shoes every week. Those days when the need is greatest, the line-ups longest and the prospects for help most unlikely seem to be the very days when grandiose gifts materialize. One winter day a man came in and asked Deb, "What's the one thing you require most?"

"Warm clothes for men," she replied without hesitating. The man went to the local discount department store, S&R, and told them he wanted $2,000 worth of winter coats, toques and gloves. Told of their destination, the store manager gave him a 10 per cent discount.

This heartening tale has only one wrinkle, a postscript that bothered Deb Greer. One of those brand new coats was later found on offer at a second-hand store on nearby Montreal Street. Someone had accepted a coat and likely sold it for food, booze or drugs. To Deb, that's tantamount to stealing from the poor. If the recipient had no intention of actually using the coat, then leave it, she argued, and let it warm someone else.

Deb, who has a degree in sociology from Queen's University (class of '85), insists she learned more about life working the midnight shift at Mister Donut than she did studying at university. She worked for more than eighteen years at Interval House, a women's shelter, a long posting that somehow left her spirit intact and where she first met Jenn. Deb has the manner of a bartender you've been telling your secrets to for years. Everybody is "darlin'" and "honeybunch" and "sweetheart." She doesn't sit down much, just long enough to write out the cheques for those looking for emergency money to keep the electricity coming or maybe for bus tickets to get to a job interview. All these transactions are recorded in her blue book. Double-dippers beware. Somehow I can't imagine anyone but Deb doing this job, as she has been since 2002.

While she is adamant that no one coming to Vinnie's be judged or dismissed, she also hates being lied to. If mutual respect is one of the Ten Commandments at Vinnie's, "Thou shalt not lie" is an equal imperative, for to lie is to show disrespect. Deb hates "playing God," but occasionally she has to. Sometimes a man or woman selecting items in the clothing warehouse will help himself or herself to too many items, and Deb has to admonish the visitor, "You've taken too much. Share the wealth." Not an inappropriate term, given some of the brand new clothes and household goods that are occasionally donated. But for the most part, the community is what Deb calls "self-policing."

The folks who come to Vinnie's most days, "the regulars," are sweet and honest in her opinion. But they are also poor. Parmesan cheese put out on tables is distributed in small quantities, as is relish. Full containers disappear and so will toilet paper when more than one roll is left in the bathroom. Milk for coffee would likewise be swiped, so that awful whitening powder made in some chemical laboratory must suffice. Most folks here actually prefer it to milk or cream. Here it's always margarine, never butter. "Marg" is cheaper, and it's what they're used to, I'm told.

The majority have bank accounts, and Deb counsels them to direct-deposit their rent money. "We can always feed you," she tells them, but if misadventure or other circumstance leads to a missed rent cheque and eviction, their problems become much more serious.

Affordable housing in Kingston (formally called Rent-Geared-to-Income Housing) has a three- to four-year waiting list that is more than a thousand applications deep as I write. According to the United Way, one in two in my city (students excluded) spend 30 per cent or more of their income on housing; for one in five, the figure is 50 per cent. Since the poverty line is defined as spending more than 30 per cent of income on housing, half of all Kingstonians living in rental accommodation are poor, some terribly poor. It's numbing to write that truth, numbing to ponder it.

This calls for desperate measures—on the part of the poor, if not yet on the part of those in power. It may explain why Deb Greer doesn't always get the straight goods. She reminds me that some people can only get what they do by lying. Deb once wrote a cheque to a local gas station because someone had come to her pleading for gas money to make a critical out-of-town court appointment. She had her doubts about the tale, and she was right. The client went to one of Kingston's many quick-cash joints and managed to cash the cheque even though his name was nowhere on it. The next time Deb saw him she lit into him. Not only had he ripped off Vinnie's, he had surrendered 8 or 9 per cent of their money to the quick-cash company, which typically feasts on the poor by charging usurious cheque-cashing fees.

JANUARY 10. At the end of my fourth day at Vinnie's, I sit in Deb's chair in the warehouse. My back is still iffy from the shovelling and I am glad of that chair. She perches on a box of clothes nearby and tells me more about her clientele.

"The people we serve," she says, "often can't work. They have physical or mental problems, learning disorders or huge addiction problems. No job means no money. Few of the people who come here are actually homeless, but they are underhoused. I hate certain phrases, like 'the needy.' They imply that these people are responsible for their fate. They're not."

Ideally, says Deb, there would be another storey on this building, there would be a proper office, there would be enough money to pay people. "We do all this," she says, "with 1.5 people"—and the volunteers.

Deb, who has a mane of unruly black hair she habitually tames with her hand and a cigarette habit I'm sure she would love to quit, works five days a week at Vinnie's. The sixth is spent tending bar at Rhea's, a watering hole near the university. The money is good at the bar, but clearly it's subsidizing her hours at Vinnie's. Sully is a regular at Rhea's. He doesn't drink but his buddies do, and Rhea's is where they sort out their sports pools. That's how Sully met Deb and signed on at Vinnie's.

"Do we resent the poor?" I ask Deb. "Do we even hate them?"

"They're an easy target, for sure," says Deb. "It's a way of making yourself feel better, by dumping on others."

In fact, the gap between being able to pay for lunch at Tim Hortons and being forced to accept a free lunch at Vinnie's is perilously thin. One change in circumstance—job loss, rent hike, an illness requiring treatment you cannot afford—and suddenly Vinnie's and places like it become essential to survival.

Some believe that Vinnie's and its denizens are a world away, and they cannot accept the fact that good health, skin colour, inherited money, intelligence and much else that is often not their doing have helped make them comfortable. Even their charity is delivered with smugness. Deb bristles as she speaks about the donors who want to drop off couches with holes in the upholstery ("You can put a cover over it," one told her). People bring in dirty laundry, food-encrusted dishes, broken mirrors and even, one time, a pail of dirty diapers.

I read into such acts clear contempt, a way of thinking that says beggars can't be choosers. So prevalent is this thinking that on weekends the St. Vincent de Paul Society truck is parked across the entrance to their parking lot. Without such a barrier, the lot would become a dumping ground.

That said, Deb ducks into a closet near her desk and pulls out a dubious item that some well-intentioned matron has bestowed on Vinnie's: a mink stole. "Part of the deal here," says Deb, "is making people feel good." It's why Thelma will sometimes wear a goofy hat, a Stetson, toque or beret, in the kitchen, and it's why Deb in the warehouse occasionally sports a bridesmaid's dress. Maybe one day the mink stole will be pressed into service. At Vinnie's, it's not wieners and beans but "cowboy casserole." If they can send clients away a little lighter at heart than when they came in, that at least is something.

There is a contract at work in this place, and as my days here mount, I'm not sure who benefits more: the providers or those being provided for. What I'm starting to understand is that by mingling with people who have no choice but to dine here, I may be offering some hope to them. Look, someone does care. And whatever worries or aches I bring to this place seem small and unworthy when I leave. There is at least contact between those of us with careers and vacations and plans to renovate the bathroom and those of us who have never had them, or, if they did, have lost them along the way.

When I first came to Vinnie's, my focus was on the work itself and on getting to know the other volunteers and Deb and her crew. But after a few weeks there, when I became more comfortable in the company of the clients, and they seemed more accustomed to my presence, I felt the barrier between us drop just a little. I could sit with the smokers on the carport bench and was included in their conversations.

I also got curious. Who were these individuals? And how did they come to be here?

ROB "ROBBY DOODY" (as in Howdy Doody) Morrison used to be a clown for Garden Brothers Circus; now he works summers as a ticket-taker, concession stand worker and carnie. He's fifty-two, though he looks much older, tall and gaunt and lanky, with dark shadows under his eyes and a bird's nest beard. He wears a hoodie, almost always up. If you saw him on the street, you would peg him as a down-and-outer.

Yet there's a playfulness about him. One sunny day in mid-January I am sitting with him outside while Thelma smokes beside me. Rob is explaining that Thelma doesn't like to hear swearing, so every time Rob wants to say damn, as in "Where did I leave my damn bag?" he says instead, "Where did I leave my Hoover bag?" As in Hoover Dam.

"What did the composer's chicken say?" he asks me another day.

"Bach-Bach-Bach-Bach."

All those years of clowning have had their effect. He shows me a photo of him taken decades ago in what he calls "whiteface," a thick layer of white makeup over the entire lower half of his face. Plaid jacket and cap, blue plaid pants, red running shoes, tie almost down to his knees, a huge red cherry on his nose. He and another clown are leaning into one another in a circus ring set up inside a school gymnasium; the basketball net is directly behind them. On the edges of the circus ring are clown tools: bicycles, percussion instruments, juggling pins. You can't really tell if he's happy, but I'm sure that he is.

I ask Rob the same question I put to everyone who drops into Vinnie's for a meal or a coffee and who agrees to be interviewed: if I could change your circumstances, grant any wish, what would you ask for?

Rob does not hesitate. "Give me back my health so I could go back to clowning. No question."

The adopted son of two lieutenant colonels in the Salvation Army, he remembers how often his preacher parents were relocated. They would arrive in a new neighbourhood, and young Rob would go knocking on every door. "You got kids I can play with?" he would ask. This peripatetic childhood almost certainly gave him wanderlust. Rob's father took him as a six-year-old to the circus, a move the father would later regret. The preacher regarded the circus as a den of iniquity and insisted that the carnies and jugglers, acrobats and clowns were all alcoholics and drug addicts. Some were, Rob concedes.

Naturally, he ran away from home at the age of sixteen to join the circus. He made some "mistakes" along the way, like robbing a bank in the late 1970s, a move that put him in William Head Institution in British Columbia for three years. But it was chance that did him the most harm. One afternoon in 1991, he was travelling in the back of a pickup truck with the carnival caravan near Rockford, Illinois. The driver had been drinking, more than Rob realized, and caused an accident that almost cost Rob his life.

He woke up in the intensive care unit of a hospital with a broken jaw and shoulder and several teeth missing. A companion died from a broken neck, and only Rob's superior physical fitness—from all that clowning around—had saved him. He spent ten years recuperating. A stroke that followed ended his clowning career and left him with limited use of the left side of his body. Between summers as a carnie, he has worked as a hospital porter, janitor and short-order cook. These days he gets by, though barely, on a disability pension of $999 a month.

Many at Vinnie's have some sort of medical disability and are paid according to the severity of their injury. On hearing this, I think of the insurance forms I filled out when I started various jobs in my life. Someone had calculated what a foot or hand or leg was worth if lost on the job, and I was always struck by how little value was attached to my appendages. A bureaucrat in the Ontario Disability Pension office apparently believes that Robby Doody the Clown can actually live on $999 a month. His rent, he tells me, is $600. Vinnie's does more than soften the blow of having to live on so little. The staff and the regulars are, says Rob, "my adopted family." He spends all of his mornings here and a good part of his afternoons too.

Back in a little anteroom near Deb's desk in the clothing warehouse, Rob reaches into his bag, a kind of purse, and hauls out the other things he has promised to show me. Apart from pictures from his clown days, each preserved in a battered and scratched plastic sleeve, there is a 2005 touring schedule. The circuit can be exhausting: week 9 in Manitoba, for example, shows five cities in six days. When did you rest? I ask, aware that erecting, striking and travelling all have to be squeezed into those days. "I once went three days without sleeping," Rob tells me.

There is, too, the Garden Brothers Circus Blessing on a blue pamphlet that commemorates an appearance at Toronto's Sky-Dome. "LET US PRAY," it begins (and I have reprinted it here exactly as it was in the original, complete with typo), "The God of Abraham, Isaac, and Jacob, Yahweh, Mohammed, Buddha, and Jesus. We pray as members of the Garden Bros. Circus a company of troubadours sharing our gifted talents with the people who come to this scared place our temple the Circus."

For a man like Rob, raised by clergy, such a prayer can bring a tear to the eye. He says he has turned his back on religion, but not on God.

Rob's spirit seems intact. It's his body that's been ravaged. "Three years ago," he says, "I was messed up with drugs and booze. I did AA, but it never worked."

How did he defeat addiction, then?

"I think I just grew up," the former white-faced clown replies.

Rob does not look forward to old age, when health issues and finances will pinch even more than they do now. His legacy to his children and grandchildren, for the moment, is a collection of Hot Wheels model cars, Beanie Baby stuffed animals and McDonald's action figures. Somehow, that makes sense. A clown will be remembered by his toys.

JOAN'S LONG and stringy grey hair is parted in the middle, her eyes are a pale blue, and her body is so thin she looks to be swimming in her jacket. "I've had a hard life," she tells me, revealing a gift for understatement.

Joan grew up in a north-end house where she was abused as a child. She would arrive at school exhausted from whatever was going on in that home at night. Joan failed grades 3, 7 and 8 and finally, at the age of sixteen, quit school to work as a house cleaner, a job she still does today at the age of forty-nine. But the work is slowing down, especially since her employer hired an illegal worker.

It's difficult to know where Joan finds peace in her life. Just weeks before we spoke, she was told she has cancer that will require five weeks of chemotherapy and radiation. But she is reluctant to proceed with treatment until two key matters are dealt with. One is a place to stay. Joan did have a room in a house, with a shared bathroom. But the filth—the stacks of dirty dishes, the clumps of dog hair—drove her to her sister's place, which has its own tensions. Worried about theft, Joan's sister is loath to allow Joan's friends in the house. "I do know thieves and I do know drug addicts," Joan admits, "but they would never steal from me." The sister remains unconvinced.

The second issue concerns Joan's twenty-six-year-old daughter. The daughter's boyfriend twice beat Joan in front of her grandchildren when she told them that their "daddy" was not, in fact, their daddy.

Joan has put her cancer treatment on hold until she has assurances from her sister that her friends—whom she will count on as caregivers—are allowed in the house. Joan also wants her daughter's abusive boyfriend gone. These are two tall orders and, meanwhile, the tumour presses on her kidney. She's working when she can and she's trying to find the time and energy to apply for a disability pension.

In such a life, Vinnie's is a ray of light. For about five years, Joan has been coming here several times a week, more to clothe her friends and relations than herself. "Vinnie's is gold," she says.

MEET GEORGE, a 1.9-metre-tall, long-haired man with precious few teeth. The whole time we talk he looks down and fusses with his name tag, the one that all volunteers at Vinnie's are supposed to wear. He picks at that name tag like it's a scab, until I want to plead, "George, can you leave it be?"

George is one of the small cadre of clients who, for whatever reason (to help, to make the time pass, to alleviate boredom), both dine and serve as volunteers here. Like Kenny and Thelma, they know what to do without being told.

George is forty-four and has a grade 9 education, but he can neither read nor write. Teachers just kept passing him on, like a bad penny. He comes every day and sorts clothes, mops the floor, does what he can. The dishwasher jobs he applies for never seem to materialize. "I'm a good worker," he asserts. "Ask Deb."

George lives in the Heights, a rundown part of Kingston. He has a heart murmur and has suffered memory loss since a traffic accident, which entitles him to a disability pension of $835 a month. Rob's stroke got him $999, so who knows? Maybe some other ailment will come along to boost George's income. In the world of disability pensions, medical calamity pays. He is also, like so many here, estranged from his family—in his case, from twelve siblings.

Were I to wave my magic wand and give George what he wants, he would be grateful for teeth and $135 more a month. It breaks my heart to hear him ask for so little, a telling indication of how George perceives his place in the world. With the extra money, he says, he would see the odd movie, maybe go to a restaurant, pleasures I take for granted.

George views himself as a community activist fighting for the poor. An illiterate man, he is nonetheless eloquent on the subject, and I can feel some anger rising in him as he speaks.

"We're a rich city," he says, the name tag twirling now, "a rich country. There are so many empty buildings while we need shelters and apartments."

JUDY'S STORY is a reminder, and I need such reminders, that not everyone here was born into poverty. A starkly thin woman with watery blue eyes and hair drawn back tight in a ponytail, this fifty-two-year-old mother of four once lived a middle-class life, with a home and gardens and a husband who owned his own roofing business. Then, after twenty years of marriage, everything fell apart.

Divorce led to depression and self-medication, and within three years she was hooked on drugs and alcohol and living on the street. Judy slept in shelters and, on occasion, in the old horse barns at the Memorial Centre grounds where the fall fair takes place. "It's not safe in there," she says. I thought she meant she felt vulnerable to attack by thugs, and she agrees that risk was there, but it was seeing a marten that scared her most.

27

Judy has been clean for several years, and a letter from her minister got her into subsidized housing. "Thank God for public housing," she says. "We need more of it."

She also has a message for people who judge addicts. "We're not bad people. We just got lost." A twenty-one-day treatment program plus time with Narcotics Anonymous and Alcoholics Anonymous helped her. Now she's looking for work and she wonders if Walmart has openings. In the meantime she volunteers at Martha's Table, which is closer to her apartment.

"I'm not embarrassed to come to Vinnie's," Judy says. "In a way, I'm proud to be here."

THE NUMBER crunchers at Ontario Disability have decided that Dave, a.k.a. "Stretch," merits only $550 a month. His knee problems, exacerbated no doubt by his two-metre height, and kidney woes curb his ability to work yet don't seem to count for much in the eyes of what Stretch calls "the system."

Stretch, forty, sounds like a neo-con when he voices his opinions of the poor. "It's a war down here. People take from Vinnie's to sell. Watch the yard sales around here come spring. I have four people in my building, with kids, on welfare. They should be working. Some are lazy. They grew up in a welfare home and they have no family morals."

Stretch wears an old leather jacket and a Montreal Canadiens ball cap. Like Rob, he left home at sixteen and abused drugs and alcohol. He spent eleven years working as a cook at Denny's, where his specialty was stir-fry. Seeing his father die of alcohol poisoning got him off the booze.

His fondest wish is to be rid of his aches and pains. His kidney problems, he admits, are self-induced from smoking marijuana. He would smoke seven "bongs" a day while watching video games, then feast on junk food, to which he is still addicted. His homemade solution is to eat barbecue wing chips, which are so wickedly hot that one bag may last him five days.

Like George, Stretch needs serious dental work. The cost of making his smile more presentable and therefore more attractive to employers: $1,263. My genie would have to conjure that sum as well. Stretch has a student loan (from courses in cooking at the University of Toronto), which is why he doesn't have a bank account. The collection agencies would soon scoop up his money. That means he has to bank at the quick-money joints.

But our chat always returns to his theme of making the poor responsible for themselves, of not just throwing a little cash at them. Stretch has seen too many people drink away their rent money. His answer? Force them to take drug or alcohol counselling as a condition of living in subsidized housing.

Strikes me as paternalistic. But on one thing Stretch and I agree: the status quo is untenable.

SOME SIXTY-FIVE volunteers work in the kitchen or warehouse at Vinnie's, and it's not all that hard to replace the dropouts. It's keeping them for the long term that challenges Deb Greer. "Some don't realize how hard the work is," she says. "Sometimes there's a culture clash between those who live in suburbia and our clientele. But the diehards are diehards. People like Earl really get it."

Earl McDonald has served Vinnie's as board member and/or dishwasher for sixteen years. He disappears to Florida during the winter (his wife has a medical condition that makes Canadian winters impossible to bear), but the rest of the year he's there five days a week.

Earl is retired now, but he was once vice-principal at Regiopolis-Notre Dame, which calls itself "Canada's oldest English Catholic high school," just up the street from Vinnie's.

When a colleague organized trips to Colombia or the West Bank so students could experience other realities, Earl tagged along. He's also made four trips to Calcutta to work for Mother Teresa's Missionaries of Charity. In another time, Earl would have been called a do-gooder, a phrase we don't much use any more.

There are Catholic underpinnings to Earl's acts of kindness, but if the soul points him to Vinnie's, so does the body. Earl's sensibilities are bred in the bone. One of eight children, the son of a miner who lived in a town near Sudbury, he remembers his home as a drop-in centre. He never knew who he'd find sleeping on the couch in the morning. Earl's parents set a good example.

He is aware of all the advantages he had, how well he was paid as a vice-principal, how his seven children have made successful lives with careers or businesses of their own. When you wash dishes at Vinnie's, Earl says (and I know the view), you look out the window towards the warehouse and you see the traffic entering and leaving. When young women pass by, he can't help but compare their lives with his own daughters' and acknowledge that they are worlds apart. This angers him. He thinks a system that perpetuates the gulf between those who have and those who have not is a disgrace.

He tells this story. "In Florida, farm workers from Latin America pick the tomatoes. No one else wants the work. It's too hard, too hot, the wages are too meagre. Workers were trying to get Burger King to pay one cent for every pound picked. McDonald's had said yes. Burger King at first fought it."

That's just greed, says Earl, and tampering with the tax system to deal with inequity is just fiddling. "I deeply believe our present economic system has to be changed. There's enough food and wealth on the planet to go around, but it's not being shared."

30

A WOMAN I'll call Dawn has been volunteering four days a week at Vinnie's for the past four months. A tall, striking woman with a warm smile, she's not like so many here who have stories to tell and want to be heard. She's more cautious, less forthcoming. All she will say is that her reason for being here is a long story.

In the food pantry, I watch her load groceries into boxes. The routine goes like this: a person in need of emergency food sees Deb, explains his or her situation and receives a ticket, the kind of tag you see in the movies tied to a toe in the morgue. On the ticket is written a number in black—1, 2 or 3—to indicate whether it is a single person, a couple or a family who requires help. Clients may apply for groceries no more than once a month.

Some clients walk brazenly into the pantry as if entitled. "I was surprised," Dawn tells me. "Some are quite stroppy and demanding. They'll say 'Don't give me that shit!' Others are so grateful."

A single person receives a no-frills selection: soup, pasta, pasta sauce, tomatoes, pork and beans, tuna, peanut butter, tea bags, Kraft Dinner and Jell-O. Soap and shampoo are also routinely tossed into the plastic bag—one bag for those with a car, doubled bags for walkers.

Dawn has worked with developmentally handicapped people in the past, but Vinnie's is her first up-close exposure to those who rely completely on government help and social agencies to get them from one day to the next. She likes the fact that desperate people are being helped, but their desperation has begun to wear her down. "I feel helpless," she says. "I keep on seeing the same faces. There's no progress. The neediness here bothers me." It's especially heart-wrenching, she admits, to give out baby food and diapers, to see children starting life at such a huge disadvantage.

GORD IS a big man with a big heart who formerly worked as a receiver-shipper with an old north-end family-run grocery store. A ten-year veteran of Vinnie's, he is one of those volunteers who needs Vinnie's as much as Vinnie's needs him. He's the driver of the truck that makes the rounds to pick up donations, groceries and other volunteers, to deliver bank deposits and to take Thelma home at the end of her shift. For Gord, the glass is always half full at Vinnie's. He sees people who are just "down on their luck" getting food, clothing and some human company. Is there abuse? "Every system has abuse."

Gord has osteoarthritis in his knees and lives in a seniors' residence, subsidized housing that he is grateful to have. A bitter divorce (is there any other kind?) means little contact with his five children and three grandchildren. "My wife," he says, the emotion surfacing in him, "poisoned them against me." If I could grant him anything, it would be a reversal of that calamity. "Unite my family again."

"Vinnie's is the only good thing I've got going in my life," he says. "I'm in at 7:45 every morning. I give Thelma and Debbie a ride here, then I make the coffee. Vinnie's fills a huge hole in my life. The people here have kept me alive." He hates weekends and summers, when Vinnie's isn't open.

AS THE end of January draws near and my time at Vinnie's winds down, I try to understand why I so like this place and yet why I share a little of Dawn's apprehension that time spent here has the power to darken my spirits. Now and again I'll catch someone out in the dining room staring at me. There can be no confusion of clients with volunteers: my uniform—ball cap, name tag, green apron—proclaims my identity. Sometimes I stare too. We are all creatures under the sun, but I go home to a nice three-storey house that I own on the south side of Princess. They go home—to what?

I am struck by the genuine affection that people like Earl and Gord feel for those they meet at Vinnie's. Maybe this is the true definition of a civil society, that there is no judging of another's history or habits or shabby dress. The hand is extended, day after day. Still, I find the level of medical and psychological damage of some of these men and women almost too much to bear, especially when I think that the poverty goes back generations.

Charles Dickens visited Kingston in 1842 and pronounced it a "very poor town," and Robertson Davies once wrote that the social divisions in this city were "as sharp as you could cut them." I am told that some houses in the north end lacked water and sewer services as late as the 1960s. When is this going to stop? And who will replace Thelma when she "retires"?

JANUARY 23. I sit with Gord and Jean, another volunteer regular. Behind me, Kenny is spraying the tables with water and bleach, a job I have done not five minutes before. Kenny is a whirlwind, ignoring or dismissing the possibility that someone has usurped him.

As Kenny wheels about, Jean beckons him over, but her voice is too feeble for him to hear over the clatter. Finally, I call out.

"Kenny, you're needed over here!"

"Turn around," Jean says to him. "Look, your coat's torn." And it is. Kenny has caught it on something sharp and the white insulating material is now exposed. "Come on into the warehouse," she tells him. "We'll get you a new coat."

That's Vinnie's for you. They look out for each other. Some volunteers here contribute up to a hundred hours a month.

Sister Mary Ellen Killeen, eighty-three years old, never misses a day. Jean is ninety-one.

At the same time, the place exacts a toll. My friends Diane and Joanne each volunteered here for a long time and then pulled back, though Joanne drops in at least once a month, "just to see everyone and make sure nothing too terrible has happened." Dawn will take a break not long after she speaks to me. As Deb will so graciously put it, "She needs some time."

JANUARY 30. On my last day at Vinnie's, we serve about forty people, half the number I helped serve on January 2. The welfare and disability cheques have come in. Thelma knows the dates. "The people" are feeling a little flush, but there's no escaping the fact that they live from cheque to cheque.

On January 31, I receive an e-mail from Deb about a car wash being organized to help a woman make up a shortfall on her rent. A kind north-end car mechanic has loaned his workspace to the woman in question, and she and her ex-husband will wash my Corolla and leave me wondering at what some people have to do just to pay the landlord. This is true hand-to-mouth existence. Thousands of people live this way in my city.

A few weeks later, I buy two sink stoppers and an electric frying pan for Jenn. Hang around Vinnie's a while and you come to know what they need in the kitchen. I drop them off on February 13, just before Valentine's Day. "I love you," says Jenn.

Pure instinct had compelled me, that and the sign in the kitchen reminding me that there are no unimportant acts of kindness.

·   ·   ·

[THE HORRORS OF HOMESTEAD]

ANDREW CARNEGIE is the father of modern philanthropy, the man who set that ball in motion. Between 1883 and 1929, he and those he employed built 660 libraries in Scotland, England and Ireland; 1,689 in the United States; and 156 in Canada—2,505 libraries in all. Carnegie's name rarely appeared on the buildings, but his motto—"Let there be light"—was inscribed over each library's entrance.

The Carnegie Library of Pittsburgh houses a photographic portrait of Carnegie. He is wearing a heavy woolen suit and he is leaning over a studded leather chair, no doubt a very expensive chair, and his left hand is clasped lightly over his right. His nose is broad, his look thoughtful. His cheeks are Santa Clausian. Anyone would see kindness in those eyes.

In his lifetime (1835–1919), he gave away $350 million (the equivalent of $8 billion today). Carnegie's book, *The Gospel of Wealth*—a set of essays, with the lead essay offering the book its title—sets out the obligation of the rich to share their fortune. He once said, famously, "The man who dies... rich, dies disgraced." Almost mythical in his generosity, he hovers, like an angel some would say, over every dot.com millionaire, every moneyed matron, every ordinary soul looking to make a resounding gesture in the face of death and taxes.

When Warren Buffett enriched the Bill and Melinda Gates Foundation by $37 billion in 2006, he said he was simply following in the footsteps of a certain simple Scottish steelmaker. Buffett had read *The Gospel of Wealth* and gave a copy to Bill Gates. There is a model in Carnegie's bountiful impulse, but there was also something deeply flawed in his philosophy.

Carnegie was born to an impoverished family in Dunfermline, Scotland, in 1835 and was still a child when they arrived in Allegheny, Pennsylvania. Unlike his contemporary, John D. Rockefeller—who believed that a higher power had chosen him to sit among the ranks of the very rich—Carnegie took a more humble view. He believed that timely and fortuitous investments, not financial cunning or divine intervention, led to his fortune.

At the age of thirteen, he got his first job as a bobbin boy, changing spools of thread in a cotton mill twelve hours a day, six days a week, for $1.25 a week. Two years later, Carnegie became a telegraph messenger boy, then operator. Smart, hard-working, self-motivated and drawn to books, he was soon employed, first as a secretary and then as a superintendent, for the Pennsylvania Railroad Company. Someone there took a shine to him and offered him advice on investing. His rise was nothing short of meteoric.

He also, and this is a curious thing, leaned hard to the left in his political thinking. He told *The New York Times* in 1885 that "socialism is the grandest theory ever presented, and I am sure some day it will rule the world." Carnegie called for steep estate taxes as a way of punishing the rich for holding onto their millions and not redistributing it before death.

When he was seventy-three and ten years from dying, Carnegie had already given away vast sums of money, yet he worried that he continued to retain too much wealth. He wrote to people he greatly admired, including Theodore Roosevelt, and sought their advice. "If you had, say, five or ten millions of dollars to put to the best use possible," he asked them, "what would you do with it?"

Carnegie seemed genuinely uncomfortable with his wealth, and by then he had good reason to feel uncomfortable. Most of us know his name and his good works, but many know nothing of the Homestead Strike of 1892. This was the defining moment in Carnegie's life. "Nothing," he would later write in his autobiography, "in all my life, before or since, wounded me so deeply. No pangs remain of any wound received in my business career save that of Homestead."

Homestead was a steel town on the banks of the Monongahela River, eleven kilometres east of Pittsburgh. The factory and indeed the town were, in many ways, part of Carnegie's domain. When the contract of the Amalgamated Association of Iron and Steel Workers expired on June 30, 1892, the owner of the Carnegie Steel Company left for Scotland, leaving contract negotiations in the hands of his partner, Henry Clay Frick. Carnegie's instruction to Frick was to shut down the plant and wait for the union to cave in. Later, writing from England the words he would always regret, Carnegie told Frick, "We... approve of anything you do. We are with you to the end."

The bloody end, as it turned out.

Frick brought in the Pinkertons, the private police who were the favourite tool of that era's so-called robber barons. At midnight on July 5, 1892, tugboats began pulling barges carrying three hundred Pinkerton agents, all of them toting Winchester rifles, up the Monongahela River. Thousands of workers, their wives, their children and sympathizers, all converged on the pier at 4 a.m. The men warned the guards not to step off the barges, and, when they did, gunfire erupted from both sides.

History does not record who fired first. The battle raged for fourteen hours. Strikers rolled a flaming freight car towards the barges, tossed dynamite at the Pinkertons and poured oil into the river before trying to set it on fire. When the guards finally surrendered, three of their men were dead and nine workers were dead or dying, with many more wounded.

The events at Homestead would rank among the bloodiest moments in the history of American labour, and Carnegie would take the memory to his grave. The British statesman William Gladstone wrote Andrew Carnegie a sympathetic letter, but Carnegie seemed beyond consoling: "This is the trial of my life (death's hand excepted)," he wrote back. "Such a foolish step—contrary to my ideals, repugnant to every feeling of my nature... The false step was made in trying to run the Homestead Works with new men. It is a test to which workingmen should not be subjected. It is expecting too much of poor men to stand by and see their work taken by others... The pain I suffer increases daily. The Works are not worth one drop of human blood. I wish they had sunk."

Six years later, he went back to the town of Homestead to dedicate a building that would house a library, concert hall, swimming pool, bowling alley and gymnasium. Carnegie's great library-building project began the same year as the Homestead Strike. But some communities of the day declined his largesse. They said his money was tainted.

As for Frick, an anarchist named Alexander Berkman tried to assassinate him in the wake of Homestead, and while he was recovering from that attack, his fourth child died shortly after birth. Those two events seemed to soften his image somewhat, and he is remembered today as an industrialist, arts patron— and philanthropist.

John Steinbeck, author of *The Grapes of Wrath,* a novel about the terrible poverty of American migrant workers during the Great Depression, was a champion of the poor. Carnegie and Frick may have been in his mind when he wrote in one of his essays: "Perhaps the most overrated virtue in our list of shoddy values is giving... One has only to remember some of the wolfish financiers who spend two-thirds of their lives clawing a fortune out of the guts of society and the latter third pushing it back." Steinbeck called their philanthropy "a kind of freighted restitution" and he wondered whether acquiring wealth and giving it away were simply two sides of the same coin. "Giving," he wrote, "can give the same sense of superiority as getting does, and philanthropy may be another kind of spiritual avarice."

Steinbeck may be judging too harshly. But Frick, for his part, had no illusions that eleventh-hour generosity would somehow save him from his fate. Frick received a note from Carnegie during the latter's last days. Carnegie was urging a meeting between them, for their once fabled partnership had dissolved and they hadn't spoken a word to each other in years. Frick's reply fell into legend: "Tell him I'll meet him in hell, because that's where we're both going."

Carnegie, though, was pretty sure he was going up, not down. "The gospel of wealth," he wrote, "but echoes Christ's words. It calls upon the millionaire to sell all that he hath and give it in the highest and best form to the poor by administering his estate himself for the good of his fellows, before he is called upon to lie down and rest upon the bosom of Mother Earth. So doing, he will approach his end no longer the ignoble hoarder of useless millions; poor, very poor indeed, in money, but rich, very rich, twenty times a millionaire still, in the affection, gratitude, and admiration of his fellow men... This much is sure: against such riches as these no bar will be found at the gates of Paradise."

MEAN
Streets

FEBRUARY 4. Cathy Crowe, one of about a hundred "street nurses" working among Canada's homeless and certainly the most feisty, has agreed to meet me in a downtown Toronto coffee shop along with two of her compatriots from the Toronto Disaster Relief Committee (TDRC). They want to look me over before agreeing to my request to work alongside them for a month, to parachute into their world.

My first impression: they all look tired. Not beleaguered, not beaten or defeated or ready to give up the struggle, but showing evidence of battle fatigue. I'm starting to realize the stark difference between volunteers like me and workers like Cathy who live and breathe the fight. If I am the militia, they are the front-line troops.

The TDRC advocates for the poor. With a friend, Beric German, Crowe helped found the organization ten years ago in hopes that logic and political pressure would convince politicians and citizens to respond to the crisis of poverty in Canada, and especially in its big cities. To her immense disappointment and frustration, little has changed. If anything, the crisis has deepened.

Crowe's short blonde hair comes down to her eyebrows, calling attention to intelligent blue eyes. She's a woman in her mid-fifties who strikes me as someone who can make small talk if called upon, but this morning she is eager to get right to the point. She arrives with Andrew Mindszenthy, the TDRC's Housing Not War outreach coordinator. A slight and reserved man in his mid-twenties, Andrew is a whiz at political strategy and brings his youth, technical savvy and experience working in refugee law to antipoverty activism. Beric ("he's brilliant," Cathy assures me just before he arrives) speaks and looks like a scholar, with his bald pate and salt-and-pepper beard. His eyes seem sad, but when he's about to speak of mischief, he can't help winking. When I ask him about his training, he just smiles. "High school dropout," he says, then adds that he has spent time as an aid worker in Bangladesh and has experienced poverty himself.

One of the first things Cathy tells me at the Second Cup roundtable is that four to six homeless people die every month in Toronto. The TDRC tracks these numbers and issues cold alerts in winter and heat alerts in summer. Cathy, Beric and Andrew have long done front-line work on the streets, and they continue to do it, all the while trying to raise funds for, and consciousness of, the poor.

In 2007, Crowe published *Dying for a Home,* a book that paints a scathing picture of street life in the big city and the horrors of homeless shelters. To this point in my life, I have never been inside a homeless shelter (I have truly led a sheltered life) and seldom contemplated what one might be like. Shelter from the storm? The storm, Cathy Crowe argued in her book, rages *inside* the shelter.

Crowe wrote about a man who had undergone heart surgery and was then discharged from the hospital into a shelter, about an elderly man who was raped outside a shelter, about a woman who died in the car that doubled as her home. And she reported the routine and unrelenting abuse that some police, physicians and welfare workers heap on the homeless.

"My experience as a street nurse," Crowe wrote, "has forced me to rely less on nursing theory and nursing research and more on economics, truth, power and politics." She explained about having to "leap into the fray to grab what should be given. For if politics is about the distribution of limited resources, I learned that nothing is ever freely given. You have to fight for it."

In the process, Cathy Crowe became a convert to political action. Whenever I walk with her in downtown Toronto, and we walk a fair bit in my time with the TDRC, I am struck by the purpose in her stride. Fit and fierce by times, she is a woman on a mission. She tells me that whatever naiveté she once possessed, whatever faith in the system she once had, has given way to something else: a determination to end the suffering that she sees all around her on the streets and in the rooming houses of one of the wealthiest cities in the world. The TDRC has scored many victories in past years, and these keep her in the game.

In 2004, Crowe received the Atkinson Charitable Foundation Economic Justice Award and the cheque that went with it. The foundation renewed her funding for several years, allowing her to continue in her new calling as a public speaker and advocate. She still collects romance nurse novels dating from the thirties to the sixties, written in the Harlequin style and bearing titles such as *Cruise Ship Nurse, Nurse With Wings* and *Mountaineer Nurse*. None of those titles describe her. *Social Justice Nurse*, more like it.

JUNE CALLWOOD, the author and journalist who wove the fight for social justice into every day, led an exemplary life. A sublime social activist, she founded more than fifty groups and institutions, including Nellie's, a shelter for women and children, and Casey House, an HIV/AIDS hospice.

"Very little in this increasingly nutcase world makes sense to me," I once heard her say. She was speaking in a church in Lakefield, Ontario, on the subject of generosity. "But I am convinced that altruism is not just a virtue but a necessity. People naturally tend to cultivate interdependence because they know they can't survive without it."

"Do you believe in God?" CBC-TV host George Stroumboulopoulos had asked June just two weeks before she died in April 2007.

"I believe in kindness," she answered, in the last interview she gave. "I believe that when you hold a door open for someone, you change them—just a little bit."

Callwood counselled us to give to people on the street, to look them in the eye, to make contact when we drop a loonie into another person's hand. But more and more, we look away—as individuals and as a society.

WHAT CATHY Crowe and her cohorts were experiencing in 2008 was not just the averted gaze of politicians but a strategic diversion of society's attention. Crowe agrees with Naomi Klein's thesis, laid out in her bestseller *The Shock Doctrine: The Rise of Disaster Capitalism,* that the new capitalism invents threats, just as Hitler did, to distract and intimidate its citizens. How can we possibly fund medicare, public housing, unemployment insurance, union wages and other hard-won benefits of a just society when the War on Terror is so pressing? A war on poverty, the preservation of a civil society and the ideal of social justice simply fade from the front pages and the national agenda.

Here's a section from one of Cathy's 2008 newsletters: "Our military spending will reach $18.2 billion in 2007–08, the highest annual amount since World War II. Much of this is being spent on military equipment intended for the war in Afghanistan... The military budget now represents 8.5% of all federal spending. *The Toronto Star* reports that Prime Minister Harper intends to boost the Canadian Forces' budget to $20 billion by 2010."

Cathy Crowe and the TDRC have long called for the dedication of a mere 1 per cent of federal spending, approximately $2 billion annually, to a new national affordable housing program. "What we're asking," Cathy tells me, "is this: you've got money for war but not for housing?" She quotes Gandhi: "'Poverty is the worst form of violence.'"

ANDREW HANDS me a small poster announcing a rally for the following Thursday. It will gather homeless advocates, the antiwar movement and the agencies (mainly churches) that attempt to supply the needs of the homeless. Some 141 organizations have signed on to this coalition. But is there much of an antiwar movement at all in Canada?

I have a theory, and I share it that morning in the coffeehouse. What's under way in this country is a casual militarization of the culture. Don Cherry has been saluting dead Canadian soldiers in his "Coach's Corner" segments of *Hockey Night in Canada* for years, and the CBC has been content to let him wave that flag. The Ottawa Senators have a Tickets for Troops campaign through which soldiers attend games at a reduced rate and fans are urged to wear red as a sign of support. Feb Fest, my town's winter festival, features armoured vehicles from the army base for children to play in and on. Both the Grey Cup and the Stanley Cup finals have become occasions for showcasing the military. The Canadian armed forces never had the money for this in the past, but they do now. Sport and war have buddied up. They were always cousins, it seems to me—I remember watching the 48th Highlanders on the ice at Maple Leaf Gardens before a Leafs game in the fifties—but now they are brothers.

Beric German notes another change in the atmosphere. Funded agencies are now seeing strings attached to government money coming their way. Any whiff of criticism, any hint of politics, and the tap could be turned off.

Outfits like the TDRC, which make a lot of noise about the politics of poverty, face continuous funding challenges. Andrew Mindszenthy works full-time for the committee, not on a yearly or monthly contract but a weekly one. With an annual budget in the $40,000 range, the TDRC receives financial support from unions, principally the Canadian Auto Workers Union, and from individuals. The committee would never dream of asking government for money, nor would government dream of giving it to such a thorn in their side.

Committee members have been known to bring hidden cameras into shelters to measure the spaces between beds and to count the number of toilets, all to puncture the myth that Toronto has adequate beds for the homeless and that its shelters meet the loftiest of international standards. The result is that when some shelter staff see Cathy and her cohorts coming, they quickly shut the door.

The city of Toronto's Streets to Homes website carries the proud declaration that "Toronto's own world-class housing program... has been given the nod as one of 12 finalists for the World Habitat Awards. The awards, which carry a £10,000 prize, recognize innovative solutions to homelessness." Problem is, says Cathy, that some of the homes that street people are being moved into have been declined three times by families waiting for public housing. "The conditions are inhumane." The cheerleading out of city hall makes her want to spit.

It galls her too that up to twenty-five churches and many hundreds of volunteers in Toronto have been conscripted to feed the poor. "This whole pool of people end up feeling good about helping poor people," she says, "but none are walking into the mayor's office and complaining." Hers was a crusty comment but an insightful one. Few dare to criticize well-meaning volunteers, but Cathy Crowe was doing just that.

FEBRUARY 7. A Housing Not War rally at King Street and University Avenue, in front of an office tower that houses the Toronto office of James M. Flaherty, the federal minister of finance, draws a hundred souls at noon on this bright cold day.

"End the occupation, troops out now," they chant. "There's no business like war business," the Raging Grannies sing. Protestors hoist signs, speakers take turns shouting their indignation into a megaphone, and the whole scene harkens back to my student days. I'm there to take photos and scribble notes, but my pen soon stalls in the cold. A provincial opposition politician tells us that Canada, alone among major Western countries, is without a national housing program, but I'm afraid this peep of protest won't change hearts and minds. Flaherty isn't home, and even the cops look bored.

FEBRUARY 11. Cathy, Beric and Andrew give me the all-clear via e-mail to work alongside them for the rest of the month. I am to offer research for their website, do some organizing work (phoning people on their list to tell them about forthcoming meetings

46

and rallies) and cover the trial of three soldiers accused of beating to death a homeless man, Robert Croutch, in a downtown Toronto park in 2005. The trial, though, is delayed.

Meanwhile, Cathy's remark about the conscription of volunteers to feed the poor stays in my mind and I look into the history of food banks. The notion originated in Phoenix, Arizona, in 1965 after a man named John van Hengel, a volunteer at a St. Vincent de Paul Society soup kitchen who also ate there out of need, spoke to one of the clients. The client, whose husband was in prison on death row, told him she fed her ten children with food she routinely collected from grocery store garbage bins. Food with damaged packaging or nearing its expiry date was regularly tossed, but there was nothing wrong with it. The woman told van Hengel that there should be a place where such food could be temporarily stored, much in the way that money is deposited and withdrawn at banks.

Van Hengel acted on the idea. He persuaded local grocery stores to give him the food they would otherwise throw out, and he convinced a local church to donate an empty building. The first food bank was born. Van Hengel was apparently a very jovial man, with no hint of self-righteousness. University-educated, he had worked as an ad man, a publicist, a restaurant maître d' and a beer truck driver. He spent weekends at the racetrack, and whatever he won he gave to the food bank. Today, the network of food banks he helped create in the U.S. distributes 900 million kilograms of groceries to twenty-three million Americans every year. John van Hengel died at the age of eighty-three in 2005, but not before receiving an America's Award, an honour established by Norman Vincent Peale and often described as "the Nobel Prize for Goodness."

Canada likewise has thousands of food banks and meal service programs. And just as a nun figured in the creation of

Vinnie's in Kingston, another nun helped launch a Toronto scheme called Out of the Cold. It got its start in 1987 when students at the downtown St. Michael's College School came to know a local homeless man. When the man died, the students were moved to respond to the plight of others like him, and with the help of Sister Susan Moran (her order is Our Lady of Perpetual Sorrow), they did.

Out of their discussions evolved a plan that would see churches and synagogues all over the city open their doors to the homeless once a week in winter. Eventually nineteen religious institutions, from Holy Blossom Temple to St. Michael's Cathedral to Chinese Gospel, came on board, establishing rotating and volunteer-run sanctuaries that offer food and hospitality. A few provide a warm bed for the night. It was all supposed to be temporary.

This is a commendable thing that the churches do, although each is open only one night a week, forcing the homeless who use their widespread services to become nomads. These men and woman pay for their bad luck, their medical disabilities and, yes, sometimes their addictions.

HOMELESSNESS IS deadly business in Toronto. In the past two decades, some 550 deaths of homeless people have been documented. But one of Canada's leading authorities on homelessness and health, Dr. Stephen Hwang at St. Michael's Hospital, believes the number is closer to 1,800 deaths, and even that, he says, may be an underestimation.

The TDRC holds a vigil at the Church of the Holy Trinity on the second Tuesday of every month to honour the homeless who have died on Toronto's streets. Aside from a plaque at the church, the deaths of the urban homeless are by and large not reported. The numbers seem to carry no weight.

Cathy Crowe suggests that I take a walk to check out for myself what Toronto offers its homeless population—the largest concentration of homeless people in the country. Beric has the idea of me visiting shelters and church basements, and Cathy urges me to check out their washrooms and showers. The first thing to suffer when shelters start to feel the squeeze is hygiene.

FEBRUARY 18. Accompanied by Beric German and Gaetan Heroux, I carry what the poor carry—a small backpack. I walk into shelters and ask for a bed. There was a time when people like Beric and Gaetan had easy access to the shelters, but over the years they've raised too much of a stink about conditions and no longer feel welcome.

Using moles like me, they do occasional spot checks. This is all part of the dance that goes on between the two sides in the poverty reel, the activists and the administrators. Beric is based at Street Health, a non-profit agency that offers nursing, counselling and other health care services to the homeless, the poor and the marginalized. Gaetan is based there, too, but he works for another agency called Neighbourhood Link, helping individuals replace lost and stolen ID.

A Québécois with a hint of a French accent still, Gaetan once managed the drop-in centre at Central Neighbourhood House (CNH), an inner-city community centre and service provider, for ten years. The work, the politics (including a prolonged internal battle with CNH's board of directors) and the sheer magnitude of the need finally led to burnout. Some four hundred people a day would come in, all with the same complaints: no food, no money. His administrative position at Street Health puts him one step removed from the front lines, and he prefers that.

49

Gaetan and Beric see themselves as advocates for the homeless, and they are concerned with how the clients are being treated at shelters and whether the shelters are full. It's important to know because when shelters reach 90 per cent capacity or more, the city is obliged by law to open another facility. Tonight, with temperatures just below freezing, we'll visit five places within easy walking distance of each other: the Good Shepherd (the Queen Street shelter widely viewed as the best in Toronto's system), two shelters run by the Salvation Army (the Maxwell Meighen Centre at Sherbourne and Queen, and the Gateway on Jarvis), the city's referral centre on Adelaide Street and, finally, Seaton House (the city's biggest homeless shelter and, by some accounts, its worst).

First stop, the Good Shepherd. No beds. And, says a man smoking outside, this night no hot water either.

As we walk the streets, I am approached three times by panhandlers. We pass pizza joints and bars, one with a gaggle of men outside singing and smoking grass. Some of these men are shelter regulars.

Outside the Maxwell Meighen Centre, a tall man with a staccato patter tells us this shelter is full, as is one at Downsview in the north end, and another, St. Brigid's, in the east end. It's 9 p.m. and he has no idea where to find a warm bunk.

"The homeless are getting the runaround," he complains. "They send you here, they send you there, and then when you go to Out of the Cold, no beds. It's 'Come in for a sandwich and get the fuck out of Dodge.'" Several years ago, he says, he could call Street Helpline's toll-free number and explain his circumstances. "I'd get a lift to where I needed to go, a sandwich, a bowl of soup, a sleeping bag and a bag of tobacco. Now I get zero." You can still dial for help, says this man, but help won't be forthcoming.

The city council's resolution directing staff at city hall to open up more space when the system reaches capacity should address this obvious need, but far from opening new shelters, the city keeps closing existing ones. The city had replaced just sixty of the 312 hostel beds lost in the previous eighteen months. We pass a shelter on Parliament Street once operated by a First Nations agency but closed when the administrators and the city clashed. An old United Church on Jarvis Street that housed a shelter has been sold to make way for a condominium development. Now *there's* a metaphor for the times.

We talk as we walk, with Beric telling me that he sees a pattern. Small towns have no infrastructure to deal with masses of poor people, so those "down on their luck" come to Toronto, where, he says, the authorities are determined to discourage them. Keeping the shelters full and allowing police harassment, he argues, sends a practical message. "Don't come here."

That is a problem. The city knows full well that if new shelters were opened or old ones refurbished, they would rapidly fill up. A national housing program would tend to keep poor people in their home towns and provinces, but in the absence of such a program, all roads for the poor lead to big cities like Toronto. So there's plenty of blame to pass around for the disgrace—there's no other word for it—that is the assisted housing mess in this country. Says Gaetan, "The poor know the system. They're forced to use the system to survive and they know it intimately, in a way that we never will."

They know, for example, that even when the better shelters are said to be full, it's best to wait outside until the 11 p.m. curfew and the bed checks are done. Some patrons with assigned beds don't show due to circumstance or misadventure, and there's always another candidate among the men lingering outside late into the night.

Behind a wide counter at the Salvation Army Gateway shelter on Jarvis Street, two men wrestle with great bags of sheets. The welcome smell of fresh laundry wafts everywhere as one of them informs me that the place is full, with fifteen men on the waiting list. The referral centre on Adelaide Street, he says, will help me find a place for the night. He seems sympathetic to my plight and draws me a map so I can find the centre.

The referral centre is nothing more than tables and chairs in a cavernous room where the eight men inside have staked out spots as far as possible from one another. Only two men sit facing, the one quiet, the other berating him loudly. At one point a homeless man is asked by a staff worker if he wants a snack.

"What did you say, sir?" the sitting man asks, rising in deference. This is a man with little self-respect left.

At the centre, I am asked a few questions by staff, such as "Are you Native?" "What's your date of birth?" "Where did you sleep last night?" I am told that the only bed available this night—just one—is at Seaton House. Men on the street have a saying: "There's always a bed at Seaton House." Satan House, some call it. At midnight, twenty men are waiting at the referral centre. One bed remains, the one at Seaton House, and there are no takers.

FEBRUARY 19. Mid-morning I register at Seaton House on George Street, near Sherbourne and Dundas in the lower east end of the city. I get a pink emergency admission card and on it a white adhesive sticker that bears my name, date of birth and my bed number: 2-B039.

Built in 1959 and capable of sheltering up to 580 men, Seaton House is as cozy as a prison. At 3:50 p.m., I return, go upstairs to check out the dorms and find a man walking the halls and murmuring softly to himself, "Open the dorms, open the dorms, open the fucking dorms." He'll have to wait another ten minutes. In the hallways, I see row after row of heavy square lockers, many bearing dents and each padlocked.

One street-facing dorm seems bright and airy, with about ten single metal beds a fair distance apart. But the dorm across the hall holds some forty two-tier bunk beds. The washroom upstairs seems fairly clean, as do the showers, but the washroom downstairs off the big TV room features a sodden brown-stained towel in the corner of one cubicle and paper on the floor. Thanks but no thanks.

In the TV room, about thirty men are following a very loud, death-filled Charles Bronson movie. Some have taken off their shoes to rest their feet; almost all wear running shoes. There is a smell about the place, hard to define, but my guess is an elixir of stale cigarette smoke, unwashed bodies, old booze and despair. The only people laughing and appearing to enjoy themselves are some black Caribbean guys in the front room playing backgammon. I stay about an hour, then bolt for my Toronto home—my mother-in-law's three-storey house in an affluent central neighbourhood known as the Annex.

That night I come back to Seaton House for another hour and watch a bit of the Leafs game in the smaller TV room. Big screen, Leafs versus the Columbus Blue Jackets (the former win 3 to 1), and behind me an animated conversation over whether hockey was better in the days of the "original six" teams than it is now. I could be in a sports bar among lots of good-looking, fit young men. What, I wonder, are they doing here?

I decide to get a breath of fresh air. Outside, men are smoking. One is talking about falling off a roof and breaking his back and how a neighbour attended to him faithfully. He says he could scarcely believe the kindness, and his listeners seem rapt, like children hearing a fairy tale. A man who panhandled me on Queen Street the night before stoops to pick up cigarette stubs, though each cigarette has been smoked to the filter.

I am sitting on a wooden bench while staring up at high black metal fencing. A turnstile lets you out, but not back in. To do that, you must use the central door and show your pink card. For security's sake, I presume, thick glass separates guests from staff. A five-centimetre-diameter hole in the glass allows for the passing back and forth of ID and cards. Upstairs and downstairs, forbidding signs trumpet the rules. "No weapons allowed in this building. This includes the following: scissors, knives, razors, sticks, metal objects, guns, screwdrivers, bottles, etc."

Down the street is Filmores Hotel, whose billboards beckon with $5 lap dances "European style," which begs the question: is Canadian style not good enough? Some call George Street "crack alley," and I will witness an exchange of crack pipes on my way home.

This is one reason that people avoid shelters. Men fear for their safety, never mind their health. The hot airless dorms may or may not pose other risks: bedbugs, scabies, lice, flu, cold germs, tuberculosis. The man sleeping a few feet from your face may have been arguing with a lamppost earlier on, and he may continue that discussion into the night. The man on the other side of you may have soiled his pants.

Seaton House is a virtual warehouse for alcoholics, drug addicts, the mentally ill, the aged and the marginalized. I leave taking deep breaths and thanking my stars I have a better bunk, a much better bunk, than this. I had thought only briefly about staying, but the notion soon left me. Someone else needed bed 2-B039 more than I did, and the medical risks of staying seemed genuine.

An image that stays in my mind is of a man on the second floor who has hauled a chair out into the hallway. The dorms are all dark, downstairs is cacophonous, so he has found the one place where he could do what he wanted to do: read a book in quiet and privacy. I like my privacy. I like quiet. This man does too.

I leave Seaton House feeling what I can only describe as grief, and it's there yet.

FEBRUARY 20. I want to experience Toronto's Out of the Cold program, and on Wednesday evening there are three options available, including Yorkminster Park Baptist Church on Yonge Street north of St. Clair.

It's a bitter cold night. The red digital sign outside the church reads −10°C, but the wind howling down Yonge Street has far more bite than that number suggests. Two men walking ahead of me, Inuit I am almost certain, look wobbly from drink. The one is tall and he shuffles along, while his impish shorter companion eggs him on and urges him to walk faster. You would think the smaller man was a boy on his way to a birthday party, anxious that he might miss the loot bags.

At the door, a man with a German accent welcomes us, genuinely. At the sign-in downstairs, there is no demand for ID, just the same pink form I signed at Seaton House—name, date of birth, social insurance number and signature. In return, I am given an adhesive sticker with my name on it and a blanket. The drill is this: pick out a rubberized mattress in the gym (I choose a beige mat near the basketball net, though navy and wine are also available), lay down your blanket and affix the sticker. Your spot is thus reserved.

The website for Yorkminster indicates that places are available for sixty guests, but I count sixty-five mats on the floor, and when I leave an hour or so later I am told that they are at capacity—seventy mats. It's pretty much cheek by jowl in the gym, the mats just inches apart in some areas, a foot or two apart in others.

One floor below is the basement, where supper is served: macaroni and cheese plus rice and salad, yogurt, bagels and fruit, pastry, coffee and juice. Beside me is a burly man who reaches into his pack and places on the table a wrinkled paper towel, one packet of sugar and one of aspartame, and his reading material, a thin novel by crime writer Ed McBain. The man opposite, a young fellow in a checkered shirt with his name tag upside-down over his heart, asks me if I have a subway token I'd like to sell. I do have one in my pocket and I give it to him, and we begin to chat.

My time at Vinnie's was supposed to imprint the "never assume" rule, but apparently not.

"When you worked," I ask the man in the checkered shirt, "what was your work?"

"I worked today," he replies. He's not bunking here at all. He has only come for the food, and several servings at that. The rent he can manage on his wages but on food he comes up short. I think back to the smart-looking young men watching the Leafs game at Seaton House. I wonder how many of them have jobs but can't manage rent or are taking a break from the circuit of friends' couches.

As for the big fellow beside me, he is initially gruff and there is food at his mouth. He doesn't look too bright. Wrong again. This guy has a degree in psychology from Queen's University, a four-year degree he did in three years because he had a little time on his hands: he was in Kingston's Collins Bay Institution.

He has been on the street for thirty-eight years. I tell him this marks my first time on the street and that I'd be grateful for some advice. He gives me both good news and bad news about church-run shelters. There isn't the "attitude" that privately run shelter staff sometimes display, the volunteers are usually friendly and kind, there is no checking of ID, no exhaustive interviews about financial status, and the food is often excellent. He raves about some shaved beef he ate at St. Patrick's Church downtown the previous week. However, he says, church-run facilities typically lack showers, they're often full and you have to roam the city to find the ones that are open.

"So how do we clean up this mess?" I ask him, referring to the thousands of homeless, the jammed shelters, the long waiting lists for affordable housing.

"For starters," he says, "give back to the poor what Mike Harris took away." In 1995, the then Ontario premier slashed social programs, cuts in the 22-per cent range that have yet to be restored and that inflation since has ratcheted up to 35 per cent. It was as though the government said, "We're going to screw the poor and give the rest of you a cheque in the mail. You okay with that?" And overwhelmingly, the people of Ontario said yes.

On the other side of a partition that runs the length of the room is a temporary clinic operated by reflexology students, and there is no shortage of customers. Feet are being bathed, massages given. "It will really relax you," one of the organizers tells me. "Guaranteed."

Back on this side, a volunteer who has been wrestling for half an hour with the TV finally gets the movie going. The little Inuit guy claps with delight as the familiar theme song of *Titanic* begins to roll. Not a bad choice in the circumstances.

I walk away, up the wheelchair ramp and into the gym where, despite high ceilings, the smell of man's inhumanity to man is starting to kick in. I beckon to a volunteer, show him my mat and tell him I won't be needing the bed after all. I leave the church, as I left Seaton Hall, grateful to be going somewhere else.

FEBRUARY 21. About a dozen people, including Gaetan Heroux, Beric German and Cathy Crowe, make deputations on homelessness before city council's Community Development and Recreation Committee. Every one of the sixty or so chairs set out for the public is occupied.

Heroux quotes from a *Globe* editorial published on February 27, 1874: "Promiscuous alms-giving is fatal... It is true mercy to say that it would be better that a few individuals should die of starvation than a pauper class should be raised up..." Heroux argues that the city is moving back to "those old prejudices and discriminations."

His anger is palpable as he tells the committee that the police are ticketing panhandlers under the Safe Streets Act and burdening them, in some cases, with thousands of dollars in fines. One homeless man who speaks after Gaetan says he has a hundred convictions and is looking at two years in provincial jail. "I've been 'uploaded' to the province," he says, earning laughter and applause.

"As for shelters," Heroux tells the committee, "I don't know where to start." He describes his findings from our Monday evening walkabout and how a dispatcher with the 24-hour community services hotline told him she had no idea where to send callers seeking beds, some of whom were screaming at her in frustration. "No room at the inn," is the message of Gaetan's one-night survey.

Phil Brown, the city's general manager of Shelter, Support and Housing Administration, assures committee members that "we have not been at capacity" and that "we monitor this very closely."

Committee chair Joe Mihevc is left scratching his head and asking, "Which numbers are the right numbers?"

This much I do know. Had I been genuinely in need of the one bed at Seaton House that was available on the night of my grand tour, I—like the twenty men waiting patiently in the Adelaide Street referral centre—would have declined it. Every night through the winter, untold numbers of homeless people in Toronto the Good sleep under bridges and atop grates rather than take refuge in particular shelters. Meanwhile, the church basement shelter program run by volunteers and launched twenty-one years ago by a conscientious Catholic nun as an "emergency measure" has been forced to expand.

FEBRUARY 27. Another TDRC meeting in another café, this time at Lettieri Bar Victoria on Adelaide Street. Cathy thinks out loud about what their next strategy should be; Andrew glides over his computer, listening and taking notes. Beric, ever the lecturer, has long answers to everything. The federal budget has just come out and every constituency from middle-class families to students to cattle farmers to artists is polled in today's *Globe and Mail*. The one constituency missing is the poor. Who speaks for them?

The four of us kick around ideas. Certainly we will add quick hits on the Housing Not War website so people can understand why the TDRC opposes the war in Afghanistan and what it's really costing us. Should the TDRC go after the NDP and try to force a hardening of its position on the war? Or should the TDRC focus on the upcoming federal by-election in Toronto-Centre that former Ontario premier Bob Rae will contest?

Cathy grows increasingly agitated at Beric's ramblings about the war. The two are old friends, but this is a tense time for the antipoverty movement in Toronto and in Canada. Finally Cathy stands up, declares "it's not working" and leaves the meeting. Andrew, too, soon departs for the cramped TDRC office at Trinity Square.

Cathy, Beric and Gaetan have all at one time or another spoken about the price of the work they do. In a forty-five-minute video, called simply *Street Nurse,* Cathy describes being set to speak at a press conference in Ottawa but breaking down with fatigue before going on. Gaetan left his job managing the drop-in centre at Central Neighbourhood House when the stress got to him. Beric refers obliquely to a past hospitalization when the strain of the fight felled him. When Cathy said, "it's not working," she could have been referring to that strategy session, the poor turnout at recent rallies or the decades she has devoted to this cause.

Alone in the café with Beric, the disco music playing, I ask him, "What keeps you going? What sustains you?"

"It's partly," he replies, "that we know that the work of activists pays off. You saw what happened with deputations at city hall. Without protests and these other dynamics, we can't have change." The worst is when people are not active or lose faith. "We know there will be times like this."

"If you're going to do something serious," he continues, "you can't expect it to be given to you. There is struggle for great things; you have to suffer. But there will be great victories too. It's not a straight path."

Beric's cellphone rings. It's Cathy. She's at the corner of Sherbourne and Dundas, the epicentre of Toronto poverty and addiction, where seven squad cars have converged and police are arresting people. Drug raid? Harassment? Hard to say. Cathy wants Beric to come, and he says he will, soon.

For two more minutes, he continues to talk about today's "new world order," where poverty is never the priority. Profit is.

There's a cutting wind this day and it's in our faces as we walk to Sherbourne and Dundas. By the time we arrive, Cathy has gone and the police have done their work, so we join Gaetan and a Street Health worker for lunch at the corner. Gaetan says he's been arrested twice by the police simply for witnessing an arrest like those that just happened. Twice he took the police to court for wrongful arrest and assault. Twice he won. The constabulary settled before the matter ever went to court.

FEBRUARY 28. Police find a man sprawled at the bottom of some stairs in an underground parking garage near Yonge and Bloor. An ambulance supervisor at the scene tells a reporter that the man has no pulse and shows "signs of hard living." His crutches are found at the top of the stairwell. Temperatures that day dipped to −18°C, or −27°C with the wind chill. The man's name was Robert Maurice.

ON THAT same day, one of the coldest of the year, provincial NDP housing critic Cheri DiNovo holds a press conference at the Ontario Legislature in Queen's Park and announces her intention to introduce a private member's bill in March that would amend the Ontario Human Rights Code to enshrine adequate shelter as a right. DiNovo says she understands full well that the bill stands no chance of passing, not least because the amendment would allow the homeless to sue the province. Hers is a gesture meant to give a little prominence to a barely flickering issue.

At the same press conference, Brice Balmer of the Interfaith Social Assistance Reform Coalition says the churches are embarrassed by their long-running basement programs. "They can't go on much longer. Our people are burning out."

In answer to a reporter's question about how this year compares with other years on the street, Cathy Crowe says there are fewer city-run outreach vans and the ones available to help the homeless are no longer allowed to dispense "survival supplies" such as food and sleeping bags. "The city calls it 'enabling,'" she says. In almost two decades as a street nurse, Crowe has never seen it worse. "The system is a mess."

There's a larger issue too. Cathy fears that the coming economic recession will bludgeon what remains of government-supported services and cripple those agencies that depend on private donors. When the job losses mount and the inevitable cutbacks are made, those who live so precariously now will be joined by the newly desperate and the streets will be even meaner than before.

FEBRUARY 28—29. Out with Toby Mullally and two of his staff, all from an outreach program called Street Survivors, run out of Central Neighbourhood House. During cold-weather alerts their job is to approach people lying on the streets at night, ask if they're okay and offer them gloves, invite them into the van to warm up or transport them to the all-night referral centre and then on to a shelter, if that's what they want.

We start around 8 p.m. when the van picks me up in the Annex. I'm glad of the van's heater, for it's already −18°C. Driving along Rosedale Valley Road through a midtown forested ravine, Toby points out a locked wooden box off the road. This is evidence of a home for someone, "an encampment," as the city calls it. I learn other terms. "Opportunists," also known as "survivalists," burrow under fallen trees and branches in the Don Valley and make a home there. "Amateurs" are self-appointed charity dispensers who hand out sleeping bags and sandwiches. "They're not a solution," says Toby. "Neither are we. We're just making sure people don't freeze to death." A Street Health survey found that almost half of people living on the street are using crack cocaine, a habit that dramatically jacks up the levels of stress, violence and isolation that all homeless persons must endure.

We drive around the downtown core, sticking mainly to an area bounded by Queen Street, Lakeshore Boulevard, John Street and Jarvis Street. Toby stops to talk with a man and a woman, both in their sixties, sleeping on a grate on wide and prestigious University Avenue, sometimes called Hospital Row. "They're fine," Toby says when he comes back to the van. "It's amazing how warm it is by that grate." The problem is that in severe cold, steam can freeze—with deadly result.

I have brought my tape recorder with me and when I replay the tape later I am struck by how much fun we had that night, which ended for me around 3 a.m. when Toby dropped me off back in the Annex. One old guy, sleeping near the Art Gallery of Ontario with a grocery cart beside him loaded with his possessions, insisted he was fine. Toby was returning to the van when the fellow called him back.

"What did he want?" I asked Toby.

"He wanted to know if the Leafs won tonight." The man was delighted to be told that the Leafs had won 4–3 in a shootout over the Florida Panthers.

At Bay and Queen, three of six people sheltering inside a heated TD Bank machine enclosure accepted our offer of a ride to the referral centre and they piled into the van. Carl was a drug addict; Jeremy, a furniture mover and alcoholic; Mike, the Aboriginal comedian, was from Manitoulin Island.

"Why were the Indians here first?" he asked me.

"Don't know."

"Because they had a reservation."

The mood in the van was lighthearted. Toby said that in seventeen years of working on the street he had never felt himself in danger. Those who sleep on the street, he said, are in crisis mode all the time. They don't necessarily want to be on the street as much as they don't want to be in a shelter.

Next day, I get a call from Beric. Toby's in hot water, and it's my fault. One of the three men we picked up at the bank machine asked me what I was doing in the van, and I told him I was both a volunteer and a writer doing research on homelessness. That information has found its way to Toby's boss.

I e-mail him hastily, worried that I have put his job at risk. He writes back: "Although I may not have followed the chain of command in getting approval to have you along with us, I think it gave you an unrehearsed window. As far as what I said, I guess I'll have to take the heat. I may not get promoted."

"Take the heat," refers to a story that Toby told about Gaetan while we stood in line at a Tim Hortons on Bloor Street at 2:00 in the morning. Someone had once come to Gaetan with a conundrum: he wanted to help a street person but feared he would have to break the rules to do so. Gaetan's advice: "Take the heat."

Later, Toby sends a follow-up note: "I'm not in any hot water. For the most part, they recognize that we are all on the same side. Any attention drawn to the plight of the homeless keeps the issue alive. I was being sarcastic when I said I may not get promoted. I forgot to mention that I am the luckiest guy in Toronto. Man, I should be paying my clients for this experience, and Gaetan and Beric for their wisdom and sacrifice."

FEBRUARY 29. On the phone this morning, Cathy tells me that the death of Robert Maurice, the man found in the garage stairwell, has given the TDRC a jolt. Someone from the TDRC called the coroner's office, as they always do when they hear of someone dying on the street. The person who called was given the runaround, told to phone another line at another time.

"They hate us," says Cathy. "To them, we just mean paperwork." The TDRC wants to know about the autopsy. Did the severe cold and, by implication, the apparent dearth of adequate shelters in this city play a role in the death of Robert Maurice?

Cathy is able to tell me a little more about him. He was a Cree from Meadow Lake, Saskatchewan, aged fifty. He shifted back and forth from the streets, shelters and rooming houses for almost two decades. He was known to the folks at Sanctuary, a nearby drop-in centre that Cathy describes as "faith-based but progressive." Staff and clients there were taking his death hard.

Even if inevitable—maybe Robert Maurice died of a heart attack—he did not have to die in a cold stairwell. Someone must call his relations and tell them the news. They will want to know the circumstances. Did he suffer? For how long?

Cathy had apologized to me at Queen's Park for bolting the coffeehouse meeting the morning before. She spoke of fatigue, of designating another TDRC member to speak for her at an upcoming event, about taking some time off and getting some rest. But not now. There will be a protest at city hall. Even before I board the train back to Kingston, she sends me a copy of an angry letter she has dispatched to city councillors about Robert Maurice, reminding them of the deputation just a week before. The warnings of the downtown agencies had been ignored, and now this.

In one newspaper report, a policeman speculated that Robert Maurice fell on his way home from work—home being a rooming house where he had shared a room. But the man had a bottle of cheap sherry in his pocket and he looked every bit a homeless man. He had spent the better part of nineteen years on the streets, in shelters and, at the end, in a spartan rooming house. Even though he had a bed, he apparently often slept outside, where he was free to socialize. Gaetan goes to see the man's room and he tells me it has a bed and a tiny cupboard for clothes, nothing more.

If he had a bed in a private boarding house, did that matter? It seemed to matter a great deal to the Toronto press and to the authorities. If Robert Maurice was sleeping on a friend's couch, he was homeless. But if he had the option of sleeping in his own bed, though rarely did so, he wasn't homeless. Gaetan and Cathy were beside themselves with rage and exasperation.

NO ONE really knows how many Canadians qualify as homeless. Estimates range from a low of 200,000 to a high of 300,000. Most bunk on friends' couches or in rooming houses and run-down hotels, with only 10 per cent actually living in shelters or on the street. It has also been estimated that the cost to the nation of homelessness, in shelters, social services and to the justice system, is about $6 billion annually. Of homeless people, 25 per cent to 50 per cent suffer from some form of mental illness.

Ottawa Inner City Health, which provides medical care to an estimated six thousand homeless people, has been monitoring deaths of homeless people in the nation's capital since 1998. Compiled by front-line health care workers and simply called "Homeless Clients' Deaths, Ottawa-Carleton," the document is stunning to behold. First of all, the numbers stagger belief: in that nine-year span (the most recent data end in 2007), some 332 homeless people died either on the street or after a long time living there. The document lists the date of death, the person's name and age, and something of the circumstances.

February 28, 1998, Maureen Bluecloud, 35, exposure, lived on street, found dead by police, alcoholic and sub-stance abuse...

September 2, 1998, Barry Loveless, 39, seizure, died in shelter, alcoholic...

December 2003, Marco Monzon, 40s, abandoned building fire...

July 16, 2007, Dan Cullen, 39, found at war memorial, alcoholic...

April 2004, Sheilah Scanlon, 45, fell off balcony...

October 2008, Danny Craig, 20s, suicide? train tracks...

The number of Aboriginal names is striking, likewise the many young people (Tammy Couture was stabbed to death in November 2007 at the age of seventeen). There is ample testi-mony to the savagery of their lives and deaths: suicide, drown-ing, murder.

What gives the document its power is the naming of names (the name Sheilah Scanlon, so close to my own, had no more and no less impact than all the others). As I read them, I felt obliged to pause at each one, to give the deceased at least a moment of acknowledgement. I had the feeling that those who maintain this grim ledger operate out of that same sentiment. That and who knows what other emotions.

Wendy Muckle has been executive director of Ottawa Inner City Health (OICH) for eight years and has worked with that city's homeless people for twenty-five. She observes that the data on deaths of homeless people are as elusive as street people themselves (thus the OICH tally is "unofficial"), but that the world medical literature does agree on one thing: the mortality rate among homeless people is four times that of housed people.

Eight years ago, OICH began to put names and photos on a plaque to honour the homeless dead, much as the Toronto Disaster Relief Committee does in that city. The Ottawa Mission shelter has bought cemetery plots for the homeless dead to spare them the indignity and ignominy of being buried by city workers in unmarked graves.

In Los Angeles, the L.A. Coalition to End Hunger and Homelessness published a study, *Dying without Dignity,* that documented the deaths of homeless people in that city between January 2000 and May 2007. In that time, 2,815 street people died, an average of one a day. Los Angeles is the homeless capital of the United States, with 73,000 street people. The average age of death was 48.1, a far cry short of the national average of 77.2.

In Canada, Dr. Stephen Hwang has looked at mortality figures for those living on the street or in shelters and he found the same stark difference. For men, the odds of living to age seventy-five are forty percentage points lower than for the richest one-fifth of the population. Cold in winter, their diabetes and high blood pressure often untreated, the risk of violence near constant and their bodies pummelled by their addictions, they do not live long.

All over North America, it's the same. People die prematurely outside or after years outside, on Hastings Street in Vancouver's Downtown Eastside and on Brunswick Street in Halifax, and mostly the deaths go unremarked.

Wendy Muckle's prescription for these early deaths is simple: housing and support programs. "We all require support," she says. "The homeless require more care but they get less."

AS I drove around downtown Toronto with Toby, what struck me were the contrasts in close proximity. The "encampments" in Rosedale Valley a stone's throw from the mansions above. The tent hidden in the brush near a vast and gleaming BMW dealership at the bottom of the Don Valley Parkway. The six people using a TD Bank entryway to warm themselves in the heart of the financial district. These contradictions left me deeply ashamed for a city I grew up in, and for my country.

I am angry that Robert Maurice died, angry that the shelters are so few and so ratty, angry that churches have been forced into the food bank and soup kitchen and shelter business, angry at how few politicians at every level take notice.

Back in Kingston, a friend sends me a quote from Anatole France's novel, *The Red Lily,* published in 1894.

"The law, in all its majestic equality, forbids the rich and the poor alike, to sleep under bridges, to beg in the streets, and to steal bread."

.   .   .

[TWIST OF FATE]

IN APRIL 2009, the Kingston Community Roundtable on Poverty Reduction and the Limestone and Algonquin Lakeshore District School Boards hosted a one-day event called the Poverty Challenge. The idea of the conference—a day of theatre more like it—was to use role play to cast community volunteers as social service bureaucrats and high school students as poverty-stricken individuals forced to rely on the system. The goal was to teach both what it's like to try surviving without money or to be a bureaucrat handcuffed by rules and budgets.

The venue was the Faculty of Education at Queen's University on a day when a late-season snowstorm had blanketed the city. Some 120 students from Kingston and area were bussed in and then coached to play one of eleven roles. "Grace," for example, suffered from depression and drug addiction, and her partner was also a user. "Greg" had been slashing his wrists after being thrown out of his house. "Molly" bore a child at the age of fifteen, had her baby taken away for a time and was then accused of welfare fraud. Every character was based on a real person.

The volunteers, who numbered eighty, were mostly older and retired, though among my group were a musician with the Kingston Symphony, a city councillor and a student at Queen's. Twenty-two agencies, among them a women's shelter, a health centre, the welfare office and Vinnie's, were represented in this massive pedagogical exercise.

"Be firm and officious," Jamie Swift, one of the organizers, advised us in our training seminar. We were taught to say things like, "Rules are rules, and if we make an exception for you, where does that leave us?" We were told that people receiving social assistance are bound by law to reveal that fact to potential landlords, which effectively legalizes discrimination against them. As a bureaucrat working at the health centre, I had to tell a client that the Ontario Disability Support Program would pay for the drastic dental work required to extract all her teeth but not the $1,200 cost of dentures.

This was the wacky world the students were asked to enter, one in which teeth are deemed optional. Rents are sky-high in Kingston (a small city with two post-secondary institutions competing with low-income people for housing), but if you're on social assistance and spend most of that income on rent, welfare detectives could well be on your case. You can try spending most of your income on a decent apartment and rely on food banks and soup kitchens for food, but they close on weekends, so what do you do then? And how, with nothing in the bank, do you muster first and last month's rent?

To mimic the real system, we bureaucrats were told to spend no more than five minutes with each client. Not quite the bum's rush, but close. City councillor Vicki Schmolka had participated in a similar exercise before the last municipal election, and she said that playing the role of an impoverished individual trying to navigate the system really affected her. "I felt ground down by the end," she told me. "It was amazing how powerfully fatiguing it all was. I was diminished by it."

When Judi Wyatt, a retired English teacher and a key conference organizer, set out to gather profiles for use in the experiment, she found that poor people's lives are characterized by chaos, disorganization and anxiety. In a brilliant stroke, all the students who played, say, "Molly," got to meet the real Molly at the end of the day.

"The reaction [to the exercise] was quite dramatic in some cases," said Wyatt. "There was complete surprise, even shock." Some of these actors began to identify and sympathize with their characters, a sentiment that only deepened when they met their characters in the flesh.

A videographer chronicled the students' thinking before and after the exercise. Complacent about poverty in the morning, the students by the afternoon were angry and indignant—not at us bureaucrats, but at the system that made life a hell for those who work in the maze and those who must navigate it. The same students who had been asked earlier in the day to list adjectives to describe the poor ("lazy," "stupid," "irresponsible," "mooch") now had a completely different list ("strong," "resourceful," "persevering," "underestimated," "misunderstood"). Shown that first list of adjectives early in the day, one of the eleven welfare clients had said she was wounded by the comments ("Is *that* how they see us?" she had asked) and almost bolted the conference. But she stuck around and was pleased by the transformation in attitude.

"The kids loved the role-playing," said Jamie. "They saw that poverty was not just a World Vision commercial on TV. They had the definite sense that something was wrong, that food banks were not enough and that there should be more awareness of the problem." Every high school in Canada could benefit from this exercise.

One of the characters profiled, a woman known as "Megan," had arrived in Kingston as a PhD student. Tops in her class, she had come on a scholarship, but when this single mother of three lost her housing and had trouble finding work (temp agencies said she was overqualified), she turned to food banks and suffered a blow to her self-esteem from which she is still recovering. Judi Wyatt observed that it was good for students to meet her, so they could see that intelligence alone is sometimes not enough to ward off poverty. "Only a twist of fate," said Wyatt, "separates us."

AMAZING
Grace

MARCH 4. I can't recall a game of euchre like it. Pat has eaten chocolate beforehand and it seems to have made her light-headed, almost goofy. Margaret deals a hand, turns up the last card and we all pass before Pat picks it up or turns it down, as if she herself has dealt. She does this twice, a violation of euchre etiquette akin to reaching over and taking food from someone else's plate.

We all have the giggles. I try calling a play-by-play to keep Pat straight, but I muddle it. Vivien, lurking in the reeds as always, does the best job of playing a real game. Margaret, normally the sharpest knife in our drawer, needs to know what was led, what's trump, as if Pat's goofiness is catching. Mario, a new client at the day program run by Hospice Kingston, has never played euchre before and he looks on in an attempt to learn. I doubt he is learning anything from our shenanigans.

What may have launched the silliness was Pat's tale of going to her clinic the day before to have her medications injected and how the attending nurse had botched the job. Blood and meds sprayed everywhere, and Pat had to call another nurse to arrest the flow. The first nurse later complained that more blood landed on her than landed on Pat, as if she were the injured party.

The three women just howl at this story.

"Really," says Margaret, who sometimes spends whole days at the clinic offering support to her fellow patients, "you could make a film of what goes on down there."

Before the euchre game, twelve elderly gentlemen in matching black pants and golf shirts with "A-Men" embroidered over their hearts, sang to us, barbershop-quartet style. "Amazing Grace," "Swing Low, Sweet Chariot," "When the Saints Go Marching In." Mario tells me that this last number brought back a dear memory of a family reunion in Italy in 1974 when a happy-go-lucky cousin—on hearing that same song—grabbed Mario's hand and they danced round and round a table. "I could see us dancing as they sang," he tells me.

Mario has been sick only since December, but already he is weak, using a walker and taking many drugs. How many pills? I ask him. He just holds out one hand, palm extended and facing down, and lifts it high in the air. I understand instantly that he takes pills by the pailful.

After lunch, he and I chat for half an hour, about how he was born in Egypt to Italian parents, about having his picture taken in the 1960s with then President Gamal Abdel Nasser ("I just trembled the whole time; the threat of assassination was constant," he says), about his friendship with a man in Brazil that dates back to 1932, about his love for language and his fluency in Italian, French, Arabic and English.

I feel a kinship with him. He wants to talk, and it gives me pleasure to listen. I say I will pick him up the following Tuesday. "Call first," says Mario, who lives as we all should, one day at a time. I have a notion to take Mario to meet Pat Vecchio, a friend who happens also to be my barber and who came from

Italy as a teenager. Mario can sit in Pat's big red chair, they can speak Italian together and reminisce about the old country.

But Mario isn't well enough for an outing in the weeks following and he never returns to the day program. This is one feature of volunteering at Hospice Kingston. Some clients attend for years, others only briefly. Sweet chariots keep swingin' low, comin' for to carry them home.

THE IDEA behind hospice programs is profoundly simple: it is better to die at home than in hospital. My own mother succumbed to brain cancer on April 14, 2003, but she died in her own bed as she so much wanted, attended to by her sprawling family. Her illness and surgery had coincided with the SARS crisis, and all of us—my father, my siblings, our partners and our children—had grown weary of the hand-washing with antibacterial soap, the line-ups at hospital entranceways, the phalanx of clipboard-wielding nurses who sometimes let us through to visit, sometimes not. Occasionally our numbers were curbed and we had to see Mom in shifts. We could not wait, she could not wait, to get home. Once she was there, our task was to make her as comfortable as possible, and partly because there are so many of us, we managed pretty well.

Someone had the idea of putting up a whiteboard in the kitchen, with the hours of the day listed across the top and our names down the side. That way, our visits could be planned and spread out so there was always someone available to run to the pharmacy or homecare supply store, to make a meal or do dishes or clean the house. One of my sisters, a nurse, flew in from Vancouver, and one of my mother's sisters, also a nurse, drove down from North Bay. I showed up wearing an old grey fedora with the peak turned up at the front and VON stuck in the black band, and presented myself as the night nurse. There were tears all right, but laughter rang through that little brick house. My mother's family doctor thought the world of her and made house calls and patiently answered all our questions during team meetings held in the living room. The place filled up with caregivers and health professionals; neighbours and friends dropped off a steady supply of casseroles and pies . . . so many oars in the water.

But what happens when all these tasks fall to an elderly spouse or a few friends of like vintage? Death may come quickly or take its time, and caregivers are soon exhausted. Hospice Kingston is a non-profit charitable organization that offers several kinds of help. One is a day program held each Tuesday at St. Mary's Parish Centre for patients who have been diagnosed with a terminal or life-threatening illness. While the caregiver at home gets a day off, the patient gets a ride with a volunteer driver, conversation over coffee and snacks at the centre, maybe some entertainment, a game of cards and a hot lunch. Therapeutic touch or foot care might be offered. Patients return to their homes with flowers provided by the program, the one I am volunteering with during the month of March.

Had I completed a thirty-hour palliative care course, I could also have visited patients at home. Here again, the aim is to provide comfort to the dying and relief to the caregiver. While the latter is freed to run errands or maybe just go for a long walk, the volunteer may do what the patient requires—prepare a favourite snack, read aloud from books, newspapers or magazines, or take the patient shopping or to medical appointments. Sometimes the volunteer does no more than sit and listen.

A brochure prepared by Hospice Kingston includes two quotes. One is by French philosopher Simone Weil: "The love of our neighbour in all its fullness simply means being able to say to him, 'What are you going through?'" The other is from author George Eliot: "What do we live for, if it is not to make life less difficult for each other?"

The organization's own simple motto is "We can help."

IN THE mail this month comes a book, *The Joy of Kindness*. "Kindness, like cruelty and indifference," says author Robert J. Furey, "is contagious. The more we encounter it, the kinder we become." Furey also quotes Aesop. "No act of kindness, however small, is ever wasted." Didn't I see something like that taped on a kitchen cupboard at Vinnie's?

Along with the book is a letter from its sender, Joan Levy Earle, a writer, painter and devout Catholic who finds the subject of generosity a compelling one. She worries that "the world no longer hears the promptings of its spirit," yet she finds many examples close to home of extraordinary generosity. Like a couple she knows who spend some of their weekends cooking and freezing meals for a housebound elderly couple (first driving three hours to get there). "What an example of kindness I have learned from them," writes Joan. She says she once helped a family in need, without telling her husband, with money she didn't have to give. "It stretched my faith and changed my life forever and I continue to reap the rewards from that gesture. When I did finally tell my spouse, he simply smiled and nodded his head in agreement. It was a turning point in our relationship as I realized that his heart was just as open to the promptings of the spirit, and I no longer needed to do these things in secret."

MARCH 11. The St. Mary's Parish Centre is almost the size of a basketball court, with a lofty ceiling and a bank of windows on the west that lets the light pour in. The walls are robin's egg blue, and there is a small crucifix at the south end of the room overtop a painting of Christ praying in the Garden of

Gethsemane the night before he was set upon his cross. This is far more room than the twelve of us need, but a Canadian can never have enough space.

We sit in a wide circle in La-Z-Boy chairs and a couch, a gift from a local funeral home. I am reminded of that scene in the movie version of *One Flew Over the Cuckoo's Nest,* when the psychiatric patients are urged to contribute something to the circle. Our circle is much wider, though, as if the clients are desperate for breathing room. Only a few dare cross that circle with their voices, so most of the conversations are with those to either side of their La-Z-Boys.

Later, after morning coffee and cookies and euchre and a lunch of meat pies, we come back to our same deep chairs. I ask everyone what they have learned from their illness. What do they know now that they didn't know before? I am amazed by how at ease they are in their responses, but I should not have been surprised. Clearly, they had thought long and hard about this question.

Pat, to my left, is a forty-something blonde with a history of breast cancer. I have heard her say to another client as they pored over old photos from her albums, "Those were the days when I had boobies." She taught English and math at a local high school, before the double mastectomy and the radiation.

"I learned my strength," she tells the group. "I learned to live in the present and not to worry too much about the past and the future. I had always appreciated nature but now I find myself saying, 'Stop. Look.'"

She has also learned that "you must be your own advocate, even if you rub people the wrong way." She says that a part of her does not believe the CAT scan, which insists that the cancer has *not* metastasized. "Metsed," she called it. Cancer shorthand.

Jean, who has been battling ovarian cancer for years, wonders simply why she's still alive. "I've struggled with my survival when most people with my cancer do not. It's not guilt. There's no name for it. I call it bittersweet, my survival." She's fresh from the psychiatric ward at Hotel Dieu after suffering a bout of anxiety. Jean remarks on how many young people were there, and how they all wore the same uniform: hoodies. She's thinking of buying one herself so she'll fit in better next time.

Jean is a survivor in another sense, too. She was the founder, in 1977, of the city's Sexual Assault Centre. "What prompted you to create the centre?" I asked, both fearing and knowing the answer. "Because it happened to me," she says.

Vivien, a former public health nurse who grew up in a village in the St. Lawrence Valley, is adept at euchre. But she will take more enticing to open up. "No surprises," she replies curtly to my question on what cancer has taught her. Maybe, as a nurse, she has seen it all.

Roger, the husband of Carole Pensom who coordinates the hospice volunteers, has suffered a massive stroke and spent a year in rehabilitation. All that time, he understood speech but was not capable of it. He's more or less fine now (his right side is still partially paralyzed), but his road to recovery was long and arduous. Roger is also a volunteer for the hospice, driving clients to and from the day program, making in-house respite visits, taking photos for the website and, as Carole puts it, "anything else I can rope him in for."

Ron, a sparky eighty-three-year-old with a wry wit, was given a year to live by doctors five years ago. He's had prostate cancer, liver cancer, his knees are swollen and he uses a walker to get around. "I'm not a well-educated man," he says, "but my faculties are good." He says he gets excellent care at the hospital but he wonders each time he goes in if he'll get past the psychiatrist. What he learned, he says, is how devoted his wife, Dolores, is to him. "My right-hand man," he calls her. They have nine children.

At lunch, "Dol" fed him a spoon of something and he pretended to gag on it. She knew, before anyone else did, that he was putting us on.

Ron went to St. Mary's school across the street in 1932, a time when Catholics ("micks") got stones thrown at them. He served on a corvette in the Royal Canadian Navy during the Second World War.

As we chat, the university student volunteers sit in their own La-Z-Boys and knit. "Coach Betty's knitpickers," they are called, after another volunteer some sixty years their senior who taught them how to do it. They are making red and white scarves.

I had not expected to see blue-jeaned youth here. The business of attending the dying falls mostly to the elderly, and I expected that both those who avail themselves of hospice services and those who volunteer here would be men and women in their fifties, sixties, seventies and beyond. I am a bit taken aback to see young people barely into their twenties. But just as pain and suffering may strike at any age, so too may kindness and generosity.

Slim and pretty, dark-haired and mature beyond her years, Kaeli Johnson is a twenty-one-year-old student in biology at Queen's University. She tells me she belongs to the Hospice Club at the university. There are dozens of clubs at Queen's, everything from dance, archery and judo to more specialized organizations like the South Asian Law Students' Association. But a club that hooks up students with the terminally ill?

"We started it three years ago with four students," Kaeli explained. "Some of us had members of our own families in hospice. I volunteered in high school, starting in second year, so my work here is just a continuation of that."

What does she get from it? "The pleasure of interaction with these people. I give them support, but they give the same back to me. They ask about our lives, our families. Family is big in this room, also trips and new babies. What they teach me is that memories shape who we are and they go on shaping us until we die. And that there's meaning in simple things like card games or a meal."

Kaeli concedes that it's hard when someone who has been coming to the drop-in dies. "It's like losing a family member. It changes the dynamic of the group." She also admits that some-times pleasantries won't do, as when someone wants to talk about the loss of a loved one or a medical problem she knows nothing about. Kaeli is not always sure what to say or do. She knows only to listen, and to be there every Tuesday for the drop-in. In the end, she is guided by a simple rule. "It's about being civil and kind."

And there is an added bonus: "My euchre game," Kaeli says, "has improved considerably."

MARCH 18. I take a little poll at the drop-in. What brings folks here, overwhelmingly, is cancer.

My mother died of brain cancer, her brother of gastrointes-tinal cancer. Their mother died of leukemia. My father's sister died of cancer of the lymph nodes. Cancer may well lurk in my genes. My sister was treated last year for breast cancer, and I have had nine lesions removed by a dermatologist or surgeon, all smaller than a dime. "Warning shots across the prow," the surgeon called them. I remember what the dermatologist told me on the phone back in 1995. "You have a touch of cancer," he said. I was rocked, yet strangely reassured. I didn't have cancer;

just a touch of it. My cancers looked to be brush fires, easily doused.

For me and many like me, the enemy is the sun. That yellow orb—lifting my spirits when I see it rise, warming the room I read in, the very source of light and life—will kill me if given half a chance. When I was a boy, a freckled boy with Celtic blood, I was careless under the summer sun. Blisters the size of tapioca would rise on my arms and back; I could burn, famously in family lore, through cotton. Now I cover up. But have I closed the barn door after the horse has fled? There has been a reckoning from all my sunburns.

I'm not a full-fledged member of the cancer club, as many clients are at the hospice, but I've put in my application. I have at least acquired fluency in the language of skin cancer. Basal cell carcinomas are common and rarely life-threatening. Squamous cell carcinomas are less common but potentially deadly unless detected early. Keratocanthoma are nasty and tender little volcano-shaped lesions that mimic squamous cell carcinomas but typically heal on their own. I've so far been spared melanoma, the most dangerous. The tipoff is moles that change in size, shape, colour or feel. Actinic keratoses are dry, scaly patches of skin, which are easily treated, typically by liquid nitrogen. Untreated, they too can become dangerous.

In matters dermatological, I am what you might call a frequent flyer. I've been seeing a dermatologist at least every six months for seventeen years, and I have watched my file thicken to book-size in that time. A spray canister of liquid nitrogen has eradicated most of my hot spots. Biopsy is often both diagnostic tool and treatment. Twice, though, a surgeon went farther and excised some small part of me, a part I didn't really want anyway. On April 3, a surgeon will again have a go at me with his scalpel after my family doctor took a biopsy of a spot on my left eyebrow that troubled me. I am learning to trust my instincts. Sure enough, there were, as my family doctor put it, "findings."

Still, I feel lucky. I have so far been spared major surgery, radiation, chemotherapy and all the anguish they bring. Compared with the clients at the day program, I am a cancer dilettante. But I take a good look at their faces. This could be me one day.

So many of my friends and relations have succumbed to cancer, and there is only one good thing I can say about that hideous disease: it often gives its victims time to bid farewell, to set affairs in order, to make peace if need be. A heart attack or car crash may offer someone a painless death, but the pain has its own life. It gets passed on to the ones left behind.

There is a symbiosis at the hospice, where the living and the dying are brought together. The American writer Annie Dillard once observed that we are all dying, it's only that some are on a faster track than others. I think that all these volunteering stints may end up teaching me the same thing: that time spent with another tribe is almost always a good thing. Walls come down, prejudices are shattered, eyes are opened.

WHAT BOTH volunteers and participants at the hospice love about their gatherings, says Carole Pensom, are the stories. One day it was Mel talking about what it was like to drive a horse-drawn milk wagon for Price's Dairy in Kingston. Another day a client remembered the time that gypsies came around to her parents' farm and how fearful she was, for she had been told that gypsies stole little girls. You really could write a book, says Carole, and because ten is the maximum number of participants for these Tuesday drop-ins, no one feels pushed off the stage or thrust to the back. When numbers warrant it, Carole adds a Friday drop-in.

Back in the La-Z-Boy circle, Pat is talking about the awful choice that her cancer presented to her. The anti-estrogen drugs she took helped beat back the disease but left her vulnerable to arthritis. Yoga, she says, helps. All along her way, Pat has studied her illness. She still spends days at a time on the computer. "You know too much," a doctor once told her. "If every patient was like you, this institution would fall apart." One MD actually defers to her on matters of treatment.

Over another game of cards, a volunteer named Jean talks about how people seldom discuss their illnesses here. The drop-in serves both as a break from the medical and clinical part of their lives, which can seem overwhelming, and as a breather for the caregiver at home. Betty, another volunteer, speaks of how exhausted she was looking after her dying husband. "One day a week," she says, "a respite volunteer would come and take my husband to Providence Manor for a day. I could shop for groceries! I felt free as a bird."

AFTER A lunch of quiche, I sit down at the euchre table again and talk with Margaret. She walks with a cane because her cancer has spread to the bone. "My bones," she says, "are literally disappearing."

We spend most of forty-five minutes discussing the special needs of mentally challenged people and how those needs are often not met in this country. Margaret, whose own daughter suffered brain damage as an infant after reacting to a whooping cough vaccine, worked almost full-time as a volunteer lobbyist between 1968 and 1985. "My head is still sore," she tells me.

Forty years ago, the government of Ontario announced its intention to close institutions that housed mentally ill and mentally challenged people. Such institutions were seen as warehouses. "Some were," says Margaret, "some were not."

Trained as a primary school teacher, bright and eloquent, she found herself sitting on committees to better the lot of people like her daughter, now forty-four years old. Margaret's experience is that some challenged children do integrate well into schools, but not all do. For a time, she lived in England, and she marvelled at one school that featured the teaching facilities on one floor and a health unit directly below.

Margaret toured places for mentally challenged people in western Europe, and she remarked on how different the Dutch and Swedes are from North Americans when it comes to taxation. "They have a sense there," she says, "of the common good. Here, our focus is more narrow. It comes down to what sort of society we want. Are we all individuals clambering over each other to make money or are we somehow responsible for each other and our society?" Until more money is allotted to them, says Margaret, the mentally challenged will also remain poor.

Years of lobbying at the Ontario Legislature at Queen's Park taught Margaret another truth: politicians are only too happy to download responsibilities that were once theirs onto charities and non-profits. Not only does it allow politicians to brag that they're keeping taxes low, but when there are complaints, the politicians can say, "We fund the agency. We've done our job. Take your complaint to them."

Consider Meals on Wheels, the example Margaret gives. If the funding is low, the quality of the food will decline. Who gets the blame? Not the politicians. No, it will be the women and men who do the best they can with what they're given.

One volunteer, Hélène, has just returned from a long visit with her ninety-three-year-old father in Paris, France. He still lives at home, with meals prepared by Meals on Wheels, or Repas Livrés à Domicile as it's called over there. But this being France, what comes to his door is veritable gourmet food. As the French say, *c'est comme ça.*

Only at the end of our chat, when I ask Margaret what brings her to these Tuesday sessions, does she talk at any length about her illness. "I have terminal cancer," she says, and I have the feeling she has said that to herself and to a great many others so many times that the words have lost their sting. She might be talking about coming down with a cold.

"The drop-in," she says, "gives me a place to get out, have some fun. Most of us have different problems but we don't dwell on them. We all have our times," by which she means down times, physical and psychological.

Before a person can register for the hospice day program, he or she has to admit to having a terminal illness. And that's not easy for a lot of people. By coming here, says Margaret, "you have accepted that life does *not* go on." Euchre is a perfect activity for such a group. The game lacks the intensity of bridge or poker, allowing players to devote a small part of their brains to playing, and most of the rest to teasing and kibitzing. The group that gathers here are all members of the same club, as it were, and while it's not one that most would aspire to, we will all some day be eligible. Why not, asks Margaret, enjoy some company along the way?

I'M READING *Random Illuminations: Conversations with Carol Shields* by Eleanor Wachtel. In it, Wachtel asks Shields about her first novel, *Small Ceremonies.* Published in 1976, the book concerns a biographer who discovers the notes of a failed novelist.

Shields told Wachtel during their interview that goodness is "the main preoccupation of the book" and that she had been interested in the idea of goodness for years though she had trouble defining it. She wondered about people who send money to flood victims and why they do it. "I think people are happier when they perform acts of goodness," Shields concluded. "That's all I can say. They're happier doing something. And the amount of evil in the world that we read about all the time lately is, I believe, relatively insignificant. It's a wonder that so many people are good, not that so many people are evil." Later, Shields tells Wachtel this will be the century in which we finally figure out what she believes are the two great questions: human consciousness and the nature of goodness.

As if on cue, *The Globe and Mail* next morning carries an item on the front page of the business section. The headline: "Selling good feelings, one cup at a time." A young writer and art director at the big Toronto ad agency Ogilvy & Mather came up with the idea of convincing a client—in this case, Kraft Foods—to use advertising as a means of inspiring random acts of kindness as well as promoting Maxwell House Coffee.

The TV ads are stark and plain. Just a cup of coffee against a dark background and the words, "The average TV ad costs $245,000." The next frame, same cup, reads, "This one cost $19,000." Final frame reads: "Where should we spend the difference?" The campaign, called Brew Some Good, invites viewers to nominate causes for Kraft's consideration.

There's something unsavoury about this, one more corporation rebranding itself as philanthropic. Part of me wonders why they don't just give the $226,000 to a worthy cause and forget about the chest-beating. And yet another part of me welcomes the use of our most powerful medium to get people thinking about generosity in their own lives. All those other ads on TV have only one message: "Buy, buy, buy!" Here's one that says, "Give, give, give!"—while you buy, buy, buy.

WHAT'S STRIKING about the volunteers at Hospice Kingston is that there seem to be so few from the demographic middle ground. There are the fresh-faced kids from Queen's University and St. Lawrence College—Mark, Jordan, Kelsey, Brad and Kaeli—with their radiant smiles and clear complexions, and there are the oldsters—Bette, at eighty-three, is typical.

I imagine the youthful volunteers come because they have no children yet, no mortgages, a little time on their hands and goodness in their hearts. Some of them are bent on careers in medicine and want the experience and the notation on their resumés, but many genuinely enjoy the company here. Much separates the youngsters from the oldsters: age, health status, pep. And yet the two groups mingle easily and respectfully. If civil society needs a model, here's one.

The senior volunteers come because their mortgages are paid, their offspring are grown up and gone, their parents are deceased and they too have time on their hands and goodness in their hearts. Margaret observed that when she had travelled to the cancer clinic the day before for her chemotherapy, she had seen three volunteer drivers, all over the age of eighty. One was making regular runs with a patient to Princess Margaret Hospital in Toronto.

Last week the young volunteers held a bake sale at the university and raised about $65, enough to pay for the food they will need to provide next Tuesday's lunch. I'm staying for that day, April 1. I have some mischief planned.

IT CAN be hard for volunteers to deal with the emotions of dying people. But for the most part, these Tuesday drop-ins are about human companionship and not the nastier aspects of atrophy.

"I do feel an emotional connection with these people," says Mark McPherson, a twenty-two-year-old MSc student in epidemiology at Queen's. "It gets emotional once in a while and it's hard when people pass away." Mark always has a smile and he seems to take courtesy to some other level. "What do you get out of these exchanges?" I asked him.

"There is so much wisdom in this room," he replied. "They've taught me perspective. My own problems pale in comparison to theirs. They are so optimistic. It's inspiring. Sometimes I wonder if I would be so optimistic in their shoes. Coming here prepares me."

Mark came to Hospice Kingston for practical and idealistic reasons, which have nicely dovetailed. "I wanted to get out into the community, to get out of the Queen's bubble," he says. "And I'm interested in chronic disease and its effects on people." He has tried to recruit friends on campus for these drop-ins, but the notion of terminal illness spooks them, and the Hospice Club remains a small but tightly knit group. Some club members come once a month, but Kaeli and Mark rarely miss a Tuesday.

Sometimes the fit between this volunteer and that client is simply magic, says Carole Pensom. "It makes you cry." One of her volunteers speaks Dutch, and this lifts her visits with an elderly Dutch couple a greater degree of intimacy. Sometimes the man or woman facing mortality literally has no one in the world, and so the void that a volunteer fills can be immense.

APRIL FOOL'S DAY. Having set the hook last week by bringing in some of the horse books I've written, I hobble in this day with my horse-head cane (inherited from my father-in-law) and complain that I have fallen off my horse and sprained my knee. They all go for it, though one does wonder to herself how a man with a sprained right knee can cross that leg over the other. I limp all morning, lay it on thick. Then at noon, I rise from the lunch table, dance a little jig with my cane in the air and announce that they have all been had.

I'm a little like my father, who cannot help himself. He laughs at his own jokes. Still, the prank has legs, as it were.

MY EXPECTATIONS going into the hospice experience were not met, but happily so. I think I anticipated a more raw exchange between the living and the dying, not cards. What the volunteer has to offer here is what any member of this "club" seeks, and that is some kind of normalcy, respite from the storm. Understood and often unstated are the circumstances that brought everyone here, but when those circumstances are discussed it's with openness and forthrightness. In this club, Pat's spray-of-blood story is pretty damn funny apparently, if you've been there. The gift for the volunteer is the gift of inspiration: I too will one day—and who knows when—walk this path. And I can see how it's done, with class.

THE SPRING 2008 issue of *U of T Magazine* has a striking interview with Dr. James Orbinski, author of *An Imperfect Offering: Humanitarian Action in the Twenty-First Century*. He was head of the Médecins sans Frontières (MSF) mission in Rwanda during the genocide in 1994 and, as international president of MSF, accepted the Nobel Peace Prize awarded to the organization in 1999.

I admire a great deal about this man, including his humility and his take on generosity. He quotes the Leonard Cohen line, "Forget your perfect offering. There is a crack in everything."

That, Orbinski writes, is "the essence of my experience over the last twenty years as a physician, as a putative humanitarian, as a person who has tried in various ways to influence the political processes that determine who gets what, when. It's very much an imperfect process with equally imperfect outcomes, but it doesn't obviate the absolute necessity of trying. You achieve something, and sometimes just enough to go on."

In the book, his question is this: "How am I to be, how are we to be, in relation to the suffering of others?"

In Rwanda, he witnessed extreme poverty, malnutrition and diseases such as polio resulting in paralysis—a tragedy no longer seen in the Canadian health care system. Orbinski began to ponder the moral questions behind the unequal distribution of resources. What he knows for certain is that if he does nothing, nothing will change.

"Every moment in your life," Dr. Orbinski says, "is a choice"—a decision about how we see the world, how we see ourselves in it and what we will do. And whether a person's instinct to help culminates in that person going to a hospice close to home or to a war zone a world away, those instincts are all of a piece and should be both heeded and celebrated.

. . .

[FLOWERS FOR LIFE]

EVERY SPRING, a couple who live in the country north of Kingston plant a flower garden. Jane Good recently retired from career counselling at Queen's University; her husband, Peter, is a retired high school science teacher and avid birder. Their garden, called Avenstone, is at least an acre in size, row upon row of cutting flowers destined for local homes and hospices in the Kingston area. Flora Vita, or "Flowers for Life," the Goods call it. The thought was that everyone appreciates beauty, and maybe none more than those living with a life-threatening illness and the people who care for them.

In midsummer, when the garden is at its finest, about a hundred of their friends come to Avenstone and are encouraged over the course of several weekends to clip flowers, take home a bouquet (I can never resist the chest-high sunflowers) and leave behind a donation for Hospice Kingston and Hospice Lennox & Addington for non-profit palliative care in the region.

In winter, the garden lies under snow, of course, but the flowers keep coming to the hospices. For many years, Jane has had an arrangement with Pam's Flower Garden, a local business that donates bouquets from late fall until spring. What is notable about this act of philanthropy—and it is no small act, but many hours of work—is its simplicity. And, in this era of the grand and headlined gesture, its virtual anonymity.

WELCOME
Home

APRIL 9. Round and round we go in the vacant end of the parking lot at the psychiatric hospital on King Street, close by the lake. A workman wearing a hardhat and fluorescent vest crosses that space, smiling knowingly as he goes. He understands what's going on: someone is learning to drive.

The instructor is me, and the vehicle is my durable red jalopy. The body is badly rusted, but the engine is willing and the buggy not quite yet ready to retire.

The student is Dirce, an animated woman from Cape Verde, an island nation off the west coast of Africa. She has a twelve-year-old son, a husband who sells cars, and she herself works full-time as a waitress in a café at one of the Kingston malls. She has been in Canada three years and speaks a pretty capable English—remarkable considering that she arrived here with no English at all.

"I'm driving!" she shouts, thoroughly delighted and beaming a 100-kilowatt smile.

Back at the offices of Immigrant Services Kingston and Area (ISKA), I have listened to Dirce speak Portuguese, her mother tongue, with one of the women who works there, a native

93

Brazilian. I spent some time in Brazil in 1999, visiting Rio de Janeiro, São Paulo and the Pantanal, the largest freshwater wetland in the world. Pantanal is pronounced Pan-tan-OWWWW, and I learned to love the sound of Portuguese which, to my ear, is the tremolo of clever cats in deep discourse.

Dirce is so grateful for the time I spend with her, going through the driver's handbook, then taking her to the parking lot to get behind the wheel for the first time in her life. She worries that I am wasting my time, that she will somehow damage my vehicle. The only one in any possible danger is the workman crossing the lot with some two-by-fours over his shoulder, as if he might need weapons to fend off the truck that is stopping and starting, weaving circles and crazy eights, always in first gear.

On a gentle incline and with a pillar too close behind, I do fear that the truck might roll back while Dirce wrestles with synchronizing gas pedal and clutch. "Like an accordion," I tell her. "Clutch up, gas pedal down." And, when we come to a stop, "Clutch down, gas pedal up." As we drive back to the Immigration Services office, I tell her to imagine that she herself is driving and to move her feet as I am moving mine. Dirce is way ahead of me. "I *am* moving my feet," she tells me.

"*Brigado,*" she chimes happily as she steps out of the truck. "Ciao." Thanks and goodbye.

I step into the office, talk to staff and clients, and try to get a sense of what goes on here. ISKA is where people like Dirce, who have crossed oceans and all manner of cultural divides, take some of their first steps to integrate into Canadian society. Situated in a rather nondescript V-shaped strip mall with a pizza place at the hub, the offices of Immigrant Services meld with those of a sprawling health complex that serves both the north-end community and newcomers to Canada.

94

Carolyn Davies, who runs both operations (her formal title is director, Community Engagement and Health Equity) takes me on a tour of the back hallways leading to medical offices, meeting rooms and kitchens. "Without you," I tell her, "I'd have had to drop bread crumbs to find my way out."

A carved wooden mask on one wall (I'm guessing from West Africa) lends just the right touch to the commons outside her office, while ISKA office doors are decorated with posters celebrating multiculturalism and photo montages portraying young immigrants playing soccer, proudly holding a freshly caught pike or posing for group shots in the summer shade. Kingston remains a largely Caucasian community, so what strikes me about the photo montages are all the shades of black.

With funding from both the federal and provincial governments, ISKA employs nine people who collectively speak nine languages. Davies says that funding is adequate, though some expenses for youth programs, crisis intervention and transportation costs must be funded from other sources, and that remains a challenge. Demand for services is rising, reflecting a notable increase in the city's immigrant population.

In a pinch, staff here could call on the almost five hundred clients who use ISKA's services and find an interpreter for any one of thirty languages. The 130 volunteers who help at ISKA range in age from fifteen to seventy-eight, 10 per cent of whom are immigrants. Stephen Kirby, who coordinates volunteers here, says, "Newcomers helping newcomers doesn't always work. New arrivals want native speakers, so I have to be creative sometimes when those same new arrivals offer to volunteer." Stephen is a widely travelled man who strikes me as ideal for this job. He is warm and welcoming, he's keen to learn from other cultures and he seems entirely comfortable with difference.

"Many who come to these offices," says Carolyn Davies, "have no concept of the idea of services, and they're incredibly grateful. They're very good at sharing with each other and our own staff, to the point where boundaries can become blurred." ISKA's employees, for example, aren't allowed to accept gifts, yet the notion of a professional staff-client relationship may be foreign to those they serve.

Mistakes are inevitable when cultures meet. Brazilians, says Davies, are physically affectionate, while Asians are more deferential. Some Muslim women are comfortable shaking hands, others are not. Kirby says breaches of unfamiliar etiquette do occur at ISKA, but they're usually harmless. I'm hoping to avoid any faux pas.

TODAY'S *Kingston Whig-Standard* carries an op-ed page piece titled "Letter from Uganda" by John Geddes, a family doctor who teaches in the Department of Family Medicine at Queen's University. He spent some time in Uganda recently, in part as medical director for McGill University's Canadian Field Studies in Africa program. As I read his article, a light comes on. I have been trying for months to arrange a trip to Africa, but my first idea of working at an orphanage for Sudanese refugees living in Kenya looks unlikely due to the politically charged violence in that country. I've been in touch with Canadian Crossroads International too about possibly serving them in some way, but nothing is settled yet.

Dr. Geddes's column offers the prospect of doing useful work with long-term benefits. He calls it "educational outreach."

"Part of the problem in rural Africa," writes Dr. Geddes, "is that the people just don't know. They don't know how to save energy, what causes AIDS, how mosquitoes can spread malaria, how water that looks clean can contain viruses or bacteria that will make you sick if you don't boil it before you drink it. They have never been told."

APRIL 10. We gather in ISKA's largest meeting room at noon to hear a human rights activist from Africa. As she gets to the most wrenching part of her testimony, Justine Masika Bihamba begins to stroke the back of the translator sitting beside her, to offer support and to keep the translation coming. "Say my words," the hand urges. "I know they're not pleasant, but say them." When she gets to the most savage part of her story, it is Bihamba herself who needs support. She weeps openly as she speaks, buries her head in her hands and finally has to stop.

Bihamba, who is dressed all in black save for white running shoes and a blue-and-white ribbon in her dreadlocked hair, speaks French and Swahili. She looks to be in her forties, but the only wrinkles on her face are under the eyes, a hint of her burden. Her translator is Gaitree Oogarah, an ISKA staff member from Mauritius who is fluent in French.

The audience of forty or so comprises mostly two grade 10 civics classes from Kingston Collegiate and Vocational Institute, along with ISKA staff and volunteers. A poster describing the talk was headlined "Mining Women's Human Rights in the Democratic Republic of Congo (DRC)." But none of us are prepared for what we see and hear that afternoon.

Joseph Conrad wrote about the same part of the world in *Heart of Darkness*. The horrors he described in 1902 have largely disappeared in modern times, but hearing Justine Bihamba speak I am left wondering if that country has ever really recovered from the brutalities of colonialism and slavery. The DRC is a huge country in central Africa, with a population of 62 million. The message that Bihamba has come to deliver is that its political assassinations, civil war and four million deaths in the past five years are not rooted in tribal warfare. She argues that this is a war fuelled by greed, and amid all the turmoil, women suffer most.

The first thing we see is a five-minute clip of a documentary film. Gaitree Oogarah warns the students that even this brief excerpt might prove unsettling and some might want to step out of the room. Not one does. The black-and-white footage shows a gathering of Congolese women, all rape victims, demonstrating in protest. The next scene is a dramatization of a typical assault: a lone woman washing pots at a riverbank, being surprised by a man and thrown to the ground screaming—at which point the film is cut short. The voice of Justine Bihamba is one of the few being raised against these crimes, which she says happen with impunity all over her country and with staggering frequency.

The DRC, she tells us, is blessed with enormous wealth in the form of natural resources such as gold, oil, copper and coltan (the last an ore used in the manufacture of cellphones, DVD players and computers). Eighty per cent of the world's supply of the precious coltan is found in the DRC. Some four thousand mining concessions are busily extracting all of this bounty, but none of it gets back to the people. "If the mining companies," says Bihamba, "gave even one-tenth of what they took out in wealth, that would have a huge impact." Clearly, that's not happening. Worse, the very fabric of Congolese society has been torn apart.

One domino topples another, then another, starting at the mines. "Men working in the mines," Bihamba explains, "are not given enough money for their work, so less or no money is sent back to the families. Women are abandoned and forced into hard labour or sex work. Some women are given to miners without partners. Some women are shared." There is no hygiene at the quarries, so disease is rampant. Children, too, are drawn to the mines seeking jobs. Large numbers of children leave school, so the rate of illiteracy rises, as does delinquency. She paints the government as weak, corrupt or indifferent.

Bihamba is part of an organization, Synergie des Femmes Pour Les Victimes de Violences Sexuelles, that tries to secure medical and psychological treatment for raped women and accompanies rape victims to tribunals where the perpetrators are denounced. (Though hundreds of thousands of women have been raped, only a few hundred cases have been heard by tribunals and only very rarely are men charged or punished.) The victims, says Bihamba, range in age from ten months to eighty years of age.

For obvious reasons, her work is extremely dangerous. In September 2007, while Bihamba was away, six soldiers came to her house and tortured her daughters for forty minutes. They wanted the women, both in their twenties, to reveal their mother's location and show them whatever documents Bihamba possessed. One daughter lost teeth from blows to the jaw, the other had a knife inserted into her anus.

Since then, Bihamba has taken her daughters out of the DRC and resettled them in Kenya. She herself has only visitor's status in Canada, and while she was en route here, six of her Synergie des Femmes colleagues back home were killed. Bihamba plans to travel across Canada trying to raise awareness about what's happening to women in her country (she spoke to an audience at Queen's University later in the day), but that means retelling the story over and over again of how her own children were beaten and sexually assaulted. Once back in the DRC, Bihamba will face the short-term challenge of raising the $400 a month required to house and educate her daughters in

Nairobi; her long-term goal is to get herself and her daughters into Canada permanently.

In the Kingston audience today is Mimi Kashira, who now lives in this city but who comes from the same town in the DRC as Bihamba. In 2007, she courageously took a CBC-TV documentary crew into the DRC to make a film called *Blue Helmets: Peace and Dishonour*. The film explores allegations that peacekeeping soldiers from all over the world sometimes indulge in rape. At one point, Kashira has a question for her countrywoman, and both decide to bypass the translator in favour of something more comfortable. The room hears, just briefly, the music of Swahili.

"Many people are being killed in the Congo," Kashira tells the room, "so that we in North America can use cellphones. There's something unfair here. The world has to do something." She notes that the church she belongs to, Kingston Alliance Church, is linked to an aid program that works in the DRC. "For $80," she says, "you can allow a woman to be educated for one year; $50 will allow a woman to start up her own business."

Another obvious measure, suggests Cheryl Sutherland, a graduate student at Queen's who co-chairs ISKA's advisory committee and who is part of a network trying to help Justine Bihamba, is to make Canadian mining companies operating in the DRC accountable. "We have signed on to international treaties," Sutherland says. "Canada has a contractual and moral obligation to the DRC." If we own stocks or belong to a pension plan connected to mining in the DRC, we might want to send the mining company a letter or go to a shareholder's meeting. Ask them what they pay the miners and how they treat them.

Christinah Kutama, who grew up in Zimbabwe and is now an ISKA staff member, makes the point that extreme poverty makes everyone desperate. "Everyone is trying to survive.

People do extreme things—like attacking children. They're not necessarily bad people, but they're in a bad situation. They are talked into disgusting things, for even a tiny amount of money."

All the while, I am struck by Justine Bihamba's quiet dignity, her courage and her determination. She and the women of the DRC could use some help, and I do send a cheque to Mimi Kashira's church and write an op-ed piece on Bihamba's talk. But there's no denying the feeling of despair that filled the room, and I left numbed by what I had heard.

AS THE months unfold, the demands of the new volunteering meld and coalesce with the old. April brings a fundraiser for Horizons of Friendship, an event that is the epicentre of my normal volunteering life. Between ISKA assignments, I'm busy.

For thirteen years, I have helped draw celebrated Canadian writers to Kingston for a posh literary event we call Writers & Friends. Margaret Atwood, Michael Ondaatje and David Adams Richards have all kindly donated their time and talent to it. My job involves attending the organizing meetings that start eight months in advance, reading the authors' books, writing my introductions for the event, and picking up and delivering authors to and from their B&B accommodations and the train station. The same crew has worked behind the scenes for a long time, somehow arduously and effortlessly at the same time, and the sense of teamwork and accomplishment is quite sweet.

APRIL 13: I emcee the Writers & Friends event, which is a tremendous success. Some 140 tickets are sold at $110 each, and there is a record take in the silent auction. We may send $25,000 to support the work of Horizons in Central America and Mexico.

At the event is Canadian author Gil Adamson, who reads from her dazzling historical novel, *The Outlander*, which touches on a real-life disaster that struck the town of Frank, Alberta, on April 29, 1903, at 4:10 a.m. Some 82 million tonnes of limestone slid from the summit of Turtle Mountain and buried part of the town, killing seventy people and injuring scores.

Adamson has a phrase to describe how help was offered on that terrible morning in the mountains: "There had been much of this lately. One man tending to another's wounds; sometimes the injured one rising and going to a worse-off fellow. Goodwill flowing downhill." In a perfect world, goodwill *would* flow downhill, easily and naturally, and I like to think that this lovely phrase captures the true spirit of philanthropy: tending instinctively to the wounds of others worse off.

After the fundraiser, at the celebratory dinner with our artists, my friend Paul Gervan taps me on the shoulder. We need an emcee for our event in June. "Will ya do it?" he asks.

Robert Lovelace has been jailed for his protests over a proposed uranium mine north of Kingston. There is to be a benefit concert to help him with his and fellow protesters' legal bills. Bruce Cockburn will sing, as will David Francey. Michael Ondaatje will read; so, I am told, will Margaret Atwood. I feel a kinship with all these folks. I cannot say no.

APRIL 14. As a volunteer at ISKA, my jobs include joining in "conversation circles" that allow newcomers to this country to practise their English, attending potluck dinners where we can all savour the foods of our different cultures (I bring butter tarts to wave the Canadian flag), leading language classes and helping one-on-one in practical ways.

Today I have been paired with Joniross M. Yap, or Jon, as he calls himself, a young Filipino of twenty-three, here all of a month. Born in a village, he has the shy manners of a night creature unaccustomed to the light, but he wants a job, any job.

His resumé notes that he has worked in both the food and beverage industry and in health care. It took forty hours by air to get to Kingston, which must seem to him a great metropolis.

I take Jon to my two best bets. The Belvedere Hotel has for years offered free accommodation to authors coming to the Writers & Friends fundraiser. I saw co-owner Ian Walsh only this morning when I stopped in to pick up writer Sharon Butala and take her to the train station.

Four hours later, I am escorting Jon on his first job-hunting expedition in Canada. He looks hesitantly into the Belvedere's airy and antiques-filled lounge, then at the wide stairs and walnut banister capped at the bottom by the statue of a woman holding a bird. This is one of the grand old limestone B&Bs of Kingston. Ian takes the resumé and says all the right things. He tells Jon that he looks like a very capable young man but that a great many applications have come in, some from university students. They make the best employees for the Belvedere, since they can work full-time when the tourists arrive in summer and part-time when demand for rooms slackens in fall and winter. So, no job, but a painless introduction to the process.

Next stop, Pan Chancho (Spanish for Bread of the Pig), the sister operation to Chez Piggy (Home of the Pig). Zal Yanovsky and the woman he adored, Rose Richardson, opened Chez Piggy in 1979 and Pan Chancho in 1994, although the latter had been operating only a short time in its new location on lower Princess Street when Zal died of a heart attack on December 13, 2002. (I had seen him outside the bakery the morning before when I picked up the baguette we always have for breakfast on Saturday. He had noticed that my right front tire was low, and said so. I thanked him, and he waved goodbye.)

Zal (rhymes with Paul) was the lead guitarist for the Lovin' Spoonful, an American rock band of the 1960s, and he and

Rose set a fine example for the rest of us. Both were community activists who had travelled widely in Latin America and demonstrated great compassion for its poor. They were extraordinary volunteers, though I doubt that either used that word. Helping seemed to come naturally to them. Rose died of cancer not long after Zal, but something of them and their generous spirit lives on in the two establishments they created. Ongoing are two breakfast funds launched in their names, one in aid of local kids and another to feed impoverished children in El Salvador.

One year, my wife, Ulrike, taught an ESL class that included two Turkish men, both anxious for any kind of work. I mentioned them to Rose one day when we were serving together on the Writers & Friends committee (me working on the author component, Rose on the food). "Send them to me," she said. As if it was raining, they were wet, and she had umbrellas to spare. Of course, she hired them—as bus boy and dishwasher.

I have that exchange in my head as I take Jon to Chez Piggy in search of Nick Waterfield, who manages both establishments. I play hockey with Nick every week in the winter. Kingston is a village, really.

"We might need someone here as of Thursday," he tells us, "but Veronica at Pan Chancho needs a dishwasher right now." Away we go to Pan Chancho, where we meet Veronica who directs us to Anne who hires Jon on the spot. He will get a trial shift the next day, nine to five, and if he passes, the job is his. The pay is $8.75 an hour to start, but he will hit $10 before long.

Thinking about the sterling example of Rose and Zal and John Geddes and all the other altruistic people mentioned so far, I wonder if generosity is simply bred in the bone. You either have that gene or you don't. But no, it's not biological;

it's learned behaviour, passed on by parents and grandparents, by mentors and models. Culture, too, can help cultivate that instinct, some better than others.

Stephen Kirby and his family lived in Indonesia for eight years, working for a non-governmental organization (NGO) until 2006. What he observed was that in the Muslim culture there is a very strict tithing process, with 2 per cent of one's income given after the feast of Ramadan to community leaders, who then distribute the money to the poor. This didn't resolve poverty or diminish in any way the every-man-for-himself mentality that ruled the rest of the year, but it did force God-fearing people to give.

Some people in this country argue that generosity, the history of philanthropy, even the anthropological study of sharing should be taught at every educational level. I have a friend who works in a daycare, someone new to the country and struggling to learn English. One of the first words she learned at work, from toddlers as they squabbled over possession of toys, was "mine."

APRIL 15. As I write this, Jon is likely scrubbing his first pots and dishes of the day. It was easy getting him that job. Not exactly a career launcher, but a start. Jon sent me an e-mail: "Sorry for my late reply... i got the job... thank you so so much! my 1st day was good... i will get used to it... cause i need money so that i can buy anything i like :)"

Jon will soon learn how little his dishwasher wages will net him, but who am I to dampen his joy? He lives with his mother, stepfather and sister on a north-end street with crumbling pavement. When we got back to his house yesterday, he very much wanted me to see the look on his mother's face when he announced that he had a line on a job. She wasn't home, though, and Jon had no key. When I left him, he was sitting on the steps looking proud and pleased and waiting for his sister to return from school.

APRIL 16. I have an early meeting with Dr. John Geddes at Morrison's, the greasy spoon facing Market Square that has not changed since my days at *The Whig-Standard* when I would slip down now and again to the restaurant for a rejuvenating fries and gravy.

Over our breakfast, he tells me more about his work in Kenya, about going to a clinic there where they had no running water. He asked about the cost to drill a well; the answer was $950. He came back to Kingston, "beat up my friends" as he puts it, and raised that sum. His point: it takes so little to make a big difference over there.

(The story reminded me of a similar situation closer to home. A friend told me about a pal of his, a dentist, who does pro bono work among Native children in northern Ontario. It seems the province could not find the $1,800 required to fluoridate the town's water supply and thereby reduce cavities. The government preferred instead to wait for the caries to fester and then airlift out dental emergencies by helicopter, at thirty times the cost. Apparently we still prefer a pound of cure to an ounce of prevention.)

"A lot of my friends," says Dr. Geddes, "used to have this notion that retirement meant going to the cottage and fishing. But there are a lot of very fit sixty-year-olds out there and they want to *do* something, give back." And sometimes, it's a very simple thing, like bringing clean water to a village, that will have a profound impact on health outcomes in the whole community.

Dr. Geddes, through McGill's outreach program, has contacts in Uganda, Kenya and Tanzania. There he teaches classes in health and nutrition, water and sanitation. He'll do five weeks with Canadian Field Studies in Africa, then spend five weeks on his own.

Dr. Geddes tells me about Mama Nora Mlingi, a woman who lost her husband and started taking in children in Tanzania, near Mount Kilimanjaro and the town of Arusha. She receives some help from benefactors in the Netherlands and Switzerland, but Doc Geddes was drawn to her too. She needs money to pay the teachers at her orphanage, to buy books and uniforms.

"She's just one person," he says. "And I don't think this is an unusual story. She goes day to day. People there live day to day."

He suggests that Ulrike and I can go there to help out: teach, peel vegetables. "But you can't peel vegetables and walk away," he says. "You will *do* something. You'll get engaged." I have learned this already. By getting my hands dirty, I have become connected and want to stay connected.

Dr. Geddes is starting up his own charitable foundation, The CanAssist African Relief Trust, so that those who give will enjoy a tax break. He has spent $4,000 of his own money putting the structure in place. He concedes that it's a micro project, but the small scale, he argues, is a good thing. He worries that large-scale, government-to-government aid can be swallowed up in corruption. Keeping it small offers a measure of control.

"If you can go," he says, "you can make a difference to ten kids' lives. And if you get a hundred more helping in Canada, then it's a thousand lives."

I have the sense that this sort of work is simply a part of his fabric now, that there is no "home life" separate from "volunteer life." The two are interwoven, and increasingly I believe that this is how it should be.

APRIL 17. This morning I help teach an ISKA-run conversation class for Chinese mothers and one Russian mother. It is interesting to learn what they miss of home, and the things that are hard to find here: black rice, a certain spicy noodle, a flour-and-sesame concoction that is much loved in Shanxi province, a Russian yogurt-like substance called *kefir*—made, apparently, by inoculating cow, goat or sheep's milk with kefir grains. Traditionally, the concoction was made in skin bags that were hung by a door, and anyone passing through that door would knock the bag to keep milk and grains well mixed.

I love watching Aygul, Daniel's mother, hum to herself and dance a traditional Chinese dance. I imagine I am seeing something ancient, and perhaps I am. On the other hand, everyone in that English class uses Skype, an ingenious web tool combining video camera, phone line and computer, to talk with folks back home.

For anyone who has just arrived in this city from another country, ISKA is a lifeline. Mothers at home with children are offered the company of other women and daycare for their children while they chat. Through the parent organization, Kingston Community Health Centres, they can get boots and snowsuits and clothing for their sons and daughters, cooking lessons, and food in an emergency. Newcomers make friends and forge connections. They have help with their resumés or with finding a dentist, housing or work. There is a doctor on staff (an immigrant from the former Czechoslovakia) and a wide range of medical services.

At those potluck dinners, every continent and many of the

cuisines of the planet are represented. At ISKA, courtesies are observed and people seem naturally and easily gracious. It's like a mini—United Nations but one where everyone actually gets along.

However, lest anyone think that Kingston is home to only kind-hearted souls with consistently open arms, ISKA is also the place where the many problems facing immigrants are discussed over coffee. A black faculty member at Queen's University was subjected to racial slurs on the street late in 2007 by four students wearing engineer jackets. Muslim women in head scarves report waiting at bus stops and seeing the driver roar past. Muslim men with ample professional qualifications complain that they are screened out by potential employers on the basis of their unfamiliar names.

"Kingston is still a pretty white town," observes Carolyn Davies, one that is still suffering from its lack of exposure and awareness.

APRIL 24. At ISKA, I lead an ESL conversation class with a group of four: a Polish émigré named Slawek, a Chinese woman named Zua-mean or "Jamie," her three-year-old daughter, Song-yan, or "Christine," and Stephen. We talk mostly about food—our favourite desserts, and whether it is better to buy the cheaper imported fruit and vegetables or the more costly local produce. I make the case for the latter. A few weeks ago, our household signed a contract with Patchwork Gardens, run by a cooperative of like-minded men and women who have become organic farmers. They will provide all the vegetables for us and twenty-four others who have bought shares in their operation.

Jamie concedes gracefully that local produce is often more flavourful. But for all my arguments—environmental, social, economic—in support of buying local fruit and vegetables, I am forced to see her point. For a family of immigrants counting pennies, cost is king.

TODAY THERE is what they call an "international café," organized by a young woman from São Paulo working as a volunteer at ISKA. We form a circle and tell stories.

Noreen, a woman from Honduras, tells about how back home she and the other eleven children in her family sometimes had to vacate their beds and sleep in the living room when their mother took in foster kids for long periods. When they complained, her mother would say, "One of my children will be blessed by this." Elza, a Brazilian, says her mother would do the same. And she reminds us of the woman from Togo who comes in to ISKA once a week for a quilting bee. As is the practice in her homeland, she makes quilts to send to the poor. It strikes me: I know nothing about real generosity, which at its best, I'm starting to believe, is instinctive, habitual and lifelong.

ALBERTO DOMENECH has lived in Canada for only four months, and during all that time he has never stopped thinking about the folks back home. In Cuba, he worked as an adjunct professor of Spanish and literature and, for the past ten years, as a translator for the Cuban Institute of Friendship with the People (Instituto Cubano de Amistad con los Pueblos, or ICAP). I meet him at the offices of ISKA where he volunteers as a translator. He is also, as he puts it in his easy and fluent English, a "radio guy." Alberto's hobby, in other words, is radio-controlled model airplanes.

It was not long after arriving in Kingston that he discovered Kingston Radio Control Modellers (KRCM), a group of sixty-five local enthusiasts who fly their small craft at their home base just south of Camden East. I know that flying field and its clubhouse. When my son was about ten years old and we were living in Camden East, we visited the KRCM site several times. He had developed an interest in radio-controlled cars and planes and he spent hours wandering the aisles at Leading Edge Hobbies, a Kingston purveyor of "kits," as the RC models are called.

My son eventually lost his enthusiasm for the hobby. But some boys grow to become men who, like Alberto Domenech, retain their passion. The kits can be extraordinarily expensive—a radio-controlled jet airplane may cost $20,000—but you can also buy a simple used kit for about $100. A Canadian kid with a paper route and a piggy bank could afford it. But in Cuba, where the average monthly wage is $20, a radio-controlled model is beyond the reach of most families.

Back in February, Alberto Domenech wondered if the folks at KRCM and at Leading Edge Hobbies might be willing to part with some of their used equipment. The owners of Leading Edge (also members of KRCM) dispatched about seventy kilograms of material—five kits, fifteen radios, four planes and many boxes of miscellaneous parts—to the Club Aeromodelismo in San Nicolas, a town sixty kilometres south of Havana on Cuba's south coast.

A great pile of unused equipment had gathered in · the store over the course of its fourteen-year existence before it was boxed and sent to Cuba. It occurred to me that my son's own remote-control plane might have been in that shipment. He had assembled a plane eleven years before but rarely flew it, then left it at Leading Edge on consignment and then (I'm ashamed to report) we forgot all about it.

Alberto showed me pictures of club members in San Nicolas unloading the treasure trove of donated material. You could see the joy in their faces. It was a way for him to tell the story, to make it real. The distance between Kingston and San Nicolas, between Canada and Cuba, seemed to shrink in the telling.

This month, Alberto Domenech is hoping that a few kind Kingstonians will help him achieve another altruistic dream: to put six used computers into the hands of young hobbyists in Cuba.

"This is not about toys," Domenech told me. "It's about building imaginations." With the right software, a computer can act as a simulator, offering the user at least the virtual experience of controlling a plane in the air. Along the way, says Domenech, lessons are learned in design and electronics.

In June, four Cubans from the San Nicolas flying club will come to Kingston, the cost of their airfares being shared by the Cuban club, the Kingston club and Alberto Domenech himself. One highlight of the stay will be a Father's Day Fun Fly on June 15 at KRCM's home base. Domenech hopes for another memorable moment with the presentation of computers and printers to the four Cubans.

A local computer store I call, Altair Electronics, is both receptive to the idea and optimistic that they can gather at least some computers before mid-June. The hobby store will likely be called upon once again to donate some equipment.

"I get huge satisfaction from this," Domenech says. He is thrilled by the way that members of the Kingston Radio Control Modellers have opened up their hearts—and their homes—to his countrymen. I will be very surprised if those Cubans go home without the kind of cargo that Alberto Domenech has in mind.

FOUR MONTHS into my project, and I understand better the impulse to form a foundation, as John Geddes did. The foundation allows him to tell the stories of those he has encountered in Africa, and it allows his friends (the ones he "beat up") a window into a world most of them will never see. These friends can donate to the foundation, knowing and trusting that the funds are not going to oil a huge NGO bureaucracy or to line a dictator's pockets but directly to people in desperate need.

One of the books I read along my way is *Six Months in Sudan,* by James Maskalyk. The Toronto doctor spent half a year in the border town of Abyei in 2007, and his diaries make for painful but compulsive reading. What he comes to understand is the value of story, the importance of bearing witness. Dr. Maskalyk's goal is to "erase the distance" between Sudan and Canada because, as he says, "it's not about trying to reconcile two different worlds, it's about understanding that it's one."

This is the revelation that dawns on me as I end the fourth month in my twelve-month odyssey. Connecting with other realities is possible—if not by going to other places then by making contact with people who have been on the ground. I haven't been to Tanzania, but John Geddes has and what he described had an impact on me. I haven't been to the DRC either, but Justine Bihamba's testimony took me there, just as *Six Months in Sudan* took me to Abyei. We need reliable witnesses, we need stories, we need knowledge—especially where there's distance. But there's *always* distance, isn't there? Vinnie's is close by, yet it's light years away for too many of us.

The more people who know about what's going on in Abyei, says James Maskalyk, the better. "Perhaps," he writes, "what [urban activist] Jane Jacobs said of city streets is true of dusty border towns; it is the number of eyes on them that makes them safe."

·   ·   ·

[THE TOBIN TAX]

ALMOST FORTY years ago, James Tobin, an economist and Nobel Prize laureate at Yale University, came up with an idea to put some brakes on foreign exchange trafficking. His idea, since modified, was to put a tax of 0.1 to 0.25 per cent—ten to twenty-five cents per hundred dollars—on currency trades. (You should know that speculators trade more than $1.8 trillion a day across borders.)

Since then, social justice advocates including the World Council of Churches, the American Federation of Labor, Rainforest Action Network and the North-South Institute in Ottawa have warmed to the tax as a tool for dealing with global poverty. If it were ever implemented, the tax could create, in buoyant economic times, an annual nest egg estimated at between $150 billion and $300 billion. The United Nations' estimate of funding required for universal access to basic social services is $200 billion a year.

The major hurdle lies in getting all countries to agree to such a plan. Several governments around the world, including Canada's, back the proposal, but it's a mighty task mustering worldwide political will. Collecting the tax and delivering the money to where it's needed most, without corruption, constitute the other great challenges. Nonetheless, the Tobin Tax, perhaps because it appears so simple—I'm tempted to say ingeniously simple—has never faded from view.

PLACE
of Hope

MAY 3. On a hot Sunday morning in San José, Costa Rica, we sit in a small park dotted with palm trees opposite the Iglesia La Dolorosa, the Church of the Suffering. With us, under the shade of a flimsy canopy, Arturo relates his own suffering.

We are a foursome in white plastic chairs: Ulrike, Claire (a psychologist who acts as our interpreter), Arturo and me— "Lorenzo." Arturo has paid his one hundred colones (twenty cents Canadian) and so he is entitled to several helpings of the beans and rice, bread, salad and orange *refrescos* on offer this morning. This weekly outdoor soup kitchen is called *carpa*, the Spanish word for tent.

The streets and back alleys of San José are home to an esti- mated three thousand poor people. Some forty have come to Carpa San Vincente to eat this morning. The rest of us are here to serve food and to listen.

Arturo, like his alcohol-addicted brethren, literally lives on the street. He lies there in the shade by day, eats and begs there, sleeps there at night. It's hard to tell where his own black skin ends and the acquired grime begins. Something I learned from keeping company with Toronto street folk is how quickly they start to wear the sidewalk's dirt.

There's a reek coming off Arturo and his rags, and a small glacial spill of pale green snot protrudes from his left nostril. His eyes are heavy, and his mouth is permanently open, as if closing it requires a strength he does not possess. There are great gaps in what passes for his dentition, yet the teeth are surprisingly white, and his curly black hair looks like it would respond nicely to a good shampoo. I think he was handsome once.

Arturo speaks of his recently broken ribs and the beating that induced them, but not, as far as I can tell, as a complaint. His words come as more of a report, as of weather or news. "Last night it rained... Last night we burned newspapers in the street by the park to stay warm... Last night I was set upon just feet from where I sit." By way of introduction—there is no hint of *braggadocio,* confession more like it—he also tells us that he once stabbed five people and spent fifteen years in jail. This, in brief, is his life.

Arturo talks, we listen. He can, he says, play basketball, chess and soccer. He was a welder by trade and is a Sagittarian, born December 8, 1966. "There were fireworks," he tells us, "on the day I was born." He adds a curious detail: "My mother had cat's eyes."

His wife's name was Ana Isabel, and Arturo is proud to say, "I buried her well. Thank God we had no children. No one knows what I have inside or what I have suffered." Claire stops translating here and chides herself aloud for knowing Arturo a long time yet not being aware of this critical piece of information about the death of his wife. When I look over at Ulrike, the tears are welling up in her eyes. She ducks away soon after, and when I find her later, sitting in a back pew in Iglesia La Dolorosa, she tells me that she was just as much moved by Claire's compassion as by Arturo's testimony.

Carpa is the brainchild of Orlando Navarro, who brought Ulrike and me to this park in the early morning by car. We have put ourselves at his service and that of his agency, called Humanitas, one of twenty-three organizations in Mexico and Central America that are helped financially by Horizons of Friendship. Horizons wants me to see how their money ($25,000 annually) is being used by Humanitas.

Orlando is sixty years old but looks far younger, with thick curly black hair only lightly tinged with grey, a full black moustache and a ready smile. There's a photo at his office of him shaking hands with former U.S. president Bill Clinton at an AIDS conference. He keeps his blocky body trim with long morning jogs, and he exudes calm, even when the cellphone won't leave him alone. (His ten-year-old son chose the Superman theme as his ring tone.) A priest for twenty-five years, Orlando lost faith in the church but never his faith in God or in his own methods for dealing with addiction. He believes with all his heart that people who are poor, destitute, marginalized and alcohol- and drug-addicted must be heard. If they are to be rescued, Orlando believes, they need to talk and they need someone to listen to their stories.

The usual contact between people such as Arturo and San José's fast-moving pedestrians is the same as on any city street in the world: a curt exchange at best, he with his hand out, they skirting or most often ignoring him altogether. Arturo exists in the way that a fire hydrant or telephone pole exists. He rarely exchanges words with anyone but those who face the same hurdles he does in surviving from one day to the next.

Orlando's idea—and it struck me first as simplistic and only later as profound—is to sit down with these people, connect with them and take the time to learn their histories. Return week after week after week and come to know them. Only when there is shared confidence and trust is the subject of addiction broached. In this scenario, the addict comes to the right conclusions by himself. I need help, I have to stop or I will die an early death.

I later put Orlando's theory to a friend of mine, Ross Laird, a fine writer, a deep thinker and a registered clinical counsellor who works among addicts in Vancouver's notorious Downtown Eastside. "Psychology," he tells me, "is 150 years old. Compassion is thousands of years old. But there are two universal things about the healing process when it comes to addiction. One, it cannot be done alone. I have never met anyone who healed alone. And two, the healing process is a mystery. It's why so many approaches in the addictions field have a spiritual base. Alcoholics Anonymous, for example, refers to a higher power."

I take Ross to say that we should all just slow down a little and talk to each other more, including to people on the street who desperately need such contact. "Once you make a present and open your heart to them," he says, "you become part of their world. Of course, it's hard to face. There's guilt. There's 'What do I do?' You can get stuck in all kinds of ways." Yet his advice is the same as June Callwood's and Orlando Navarro's: don't just toss a coin into a beggar's cap and walk on. Stop and make contact.

UNDER THE watchful gaze of the white angel statues on either side of the dome of Iglesia La Dolorosa, the dozen or so helpers at Carpa this morning—volunteers from the church, a street priest, a psychologist, some fresh troops from the HIV/AIDS shelter that is another of Orlando's creations, and two Canadians—have all been given the same mission. Engage these men and women. Treat them with humanity. Shake their foul hands.

Sit with them and spend leisurely time with them. Honour them by your company, give them your respect and leave no one out.

Before we leave him to chat with someone else, I ask Arturo if he would write his name on my pad of paper. The A in Arturo he writes as a mountain. The middle name starts with a D and has the elegance of a musical note. The Q in his last name he draws with a flourish below the line, where it ends in the shape of a sharp fish hook.

If Arturo's is a hard case, Johnny's is even harder. He can't make it to the tent thirty feet away, so food and drink are brought to him. He's on the ground in the shade, propped against a wall on one elbow. His hair is thickly matted, one arm is encased in a bloodstained cast (the result of a bike accident), and his leg, he tells us, is throbbing after he was run over by a car and beaten by people who mistook him for someone else. They also, for good measure, stole his crutches.

"God was with me," he declares, "or I would not be here." Around his neck is a grey metal cross and on the back these words in Spanish: "Christ is counting on you." He is twenty-seven years old and his hollowed face reminds me of the actor Johnny Depp. His drink of choice is paint thinner, and he has covered himself with a vile and tattered blanket that is redolent of urine and sweat. One running shoe is visible, its sole peeling away from the main so his toes are in plain view. I give Johnny some Tylenol for his pain. He kisses the little red vial before dropping it into his shirt pocket.

We sometimes complain in Canada that the social safety net has holes in it. Here there is no net, just a seemingly bottomless abyss. There are no shelters, no showers, no sanctuaries to go to. Sometimes the men and women who gather here wash themselves in the fountain. Near Johnny, by the curb, are the blackened remains of last night's fire. He and his friends burned newspapers to ward off the chill, much to the chagrin of people who live in the apartments overlooking the street. Who wants beggars on their doorstep?

Pablo Richards, the street priest who translated Johnny's words for me (and who later drove him to hospital to tend to his injuries), is part of a roundtable meeting in the church loft after we dismantle the Carpa tents.

"My parish is the street," Father Richards tells me. "I am a priest, despite everything." Church and state, he says, have done nothing for Johnny and his woebegone tribe. While the Carpa served the poor, I could hear singing coming from the mass taking place inside the church. The sturdy all-white church with its heavy arched doors was going about its business while we went about ours. The church stored the tent, let Carpa use its chairs and allowed us to meet there afterwards to wash our hands with plenty of soap and hot water.

This is what we do with the poor here and everywhere. We wash our hands of them.

FOR THE first two weeks of May, Ulrike and I are billeted in Desamparados, a suburb south of downtown San José. We are staying with Doña Esilda, as we call her. Esilda is her first name, but Spanish courtesy insists that a woman of seventy-eight not be called by her first name alone. *Doña* literally means "Mistress," and we soon embrace its use.

Doña Esilda is the mother-in-law of Patricia Rebolledo, the executive director of Horizons of Friendship, the Canadian NGO for whom Ulrike and I have volunteered for more than twenty years. Patricia was born in Santiago, Chile, in 1953. Her parents were both prominent in the theatre and she remembers growing up in a house that was often filled with poets and musicians, artists and writers. In 1973, the right-wing dictator

Augusto Pinochet took power in a coup d'état. One of Patricia's brothers, a student activist at the university, went into hiding; the military imprisoned and tortured another brother.

Under Pinochet and martial law, reading or even possessing the wrong kind of book was very risky. "I had many books on social justice and on the plight of the poor, political books, and I tried to burn them," says Patricia. "However, pieces of the books would fly up the chimney when I was burning them and neighbours would rush over to the house to tell me to stop. You could still read some of the printing on the paper and even that could get me imprisoned or killed." Patricia loves books, but fearful that the police would raid her house any day, she put these incendiary tomes in the bathtub and used bleach to erase the words and destroy their covers. She and her family eventually fled to Costa Rica, where she earned a degree in international relations with a specialty in human rights. From there, she made her way to Canada where she has dedicated her life to the poorest of the poor.

Every spring, Patricia comes to Kingston and speaks at the Horizons of Friendship—Writers & Friends fundraiser. The money raised is matched by the Canadian International Development Agency. I feel a powerful connection with Patricia, with Horizons and with the work they do in Central America and Mexico. My ties to that part of the world go back almost twenty-five years when a friend got me interested in Guatemala and its tortured past and present, and in the genocide that was unfolding there at the time. He formed a group called Friends of Guatemala, which aimed to raise funds and awareness. It was a short hop to becoming involved with Horizons of Friendship, which got its start in 1973.

What I like about Horizons is its scale. The staff is small (a half dozen or so individuals operating on an annual budget of about $1.5 million) but the commitment runs deep. In the past thirty-five years, some $74 million has gone to its grassroots partners for health clinics in remote mountainous areas, solar co-ops, micro-credit enterprises and groups that support the promotion of human rights. I never doubt that the money is wisely and usefully deployed.

And I like the fact that Horizons has an eye on the poor at home as well as on the dispossessed of Meso-America. On the first floor of its offices in Cobourg, Ontario, is a thrift shop that gathers and distributes to the poor of that region all manner of second-hand clothing, kitchenware, books and toys. Local women's shelters, the St. Vincent de Paul Society and the Salvation Army are issued these goods without charge. The turnover is remarkably brisk and all the loonies and toonies add up: fully 10 per cent of the Horizons operating budget derives from thrift shop sales.

Patricia's annual address at Writers & Friends is always unvarnished: inevitably, an earthquake has struck somewhere in Central America and the need is greater than ever. Yet there's a fierce joy about this woman and an abiding respect for the dispossessed she champions. Patricia, who is short enough that she must step to the side of the lectern to be seen, speaks gritty truths and spares us none of her outrage, but her warmth and cheer are quite infectious.

She and her colleagues at Horizons have paved the way for our trip to Costa Rica. By phone and e-mail, they have set up the contacts and arranged for a bunk in Doña Esilda's neat little blue-stucco house.

There are few street names in Costa Rica. Houses are typically identified in relation to a prominent nearby site. Were you to mail a letter to Doña Esilda, it would read, in part: 100 sur, 75 este, estacion de bomberos, Barrio La Fortuna, San José,

Costa Rica. That is to say, her house lies 100 metres south and 75 metres east of the fire station in the barrio of La Fortuna. You would summon a cab to her house by giving the same details over the phone.

The windows, doors and often the grounds of just about every house, public building and commercial enterprise in Costa Rica wear an armour of bright and ornate grillwork (*rejas* in Spanish), meant as protection against burglary. Doña Esilda's house is no exception. One tall gate spans the width of the house and permits entry into a small courtyard, another gate bars the entryway, and then there is the door. When we leave her house to walk the neighbourhood, as we often do, we need three keys to get back in.

APRIL 28. Orlando's HIV/AIDS shelter is called Hogar de la Esperanza, Place of Hope. Less than four thousand square metres in size, it sits on land next to the National Seminary of Costa Rica. Indeed, the land was parcelled off from the seminary. High, soft-yellow walls of concrete and stucco define both the seminary and the shelter, which we access through heavy steel, wine-coloured doors.

On our arrival on a Monday morning late in April, my first and immediate impression is of sanctuary. The shelter comprises a series of one-storey modular buildings clustered on a high bluff overlooking dense vegetation and a narrow river valley. The nearest houses opposite the bluff seem a long way away. In a city so noisy and densely packed as San José, this setting must be a relief to those who have taken refuge here. I can hear birdsong and the sound of rushing water, antidotes to the ceaseless whine of scooters and the grinding gears of trucks and buses. Most days, laundry flaps in the breezes that almost always cool the place. When it rains, the idyll is tarnished a little by the smell of sewage wafting up from the river. Still, over the course of the next two weeks, this place will begin to feel like home.

When we first arrive, we are stared at. But the stares soon give way to *holas* (hellos) as we become fixtures at the shelter. Orlando takes us around our first day, leading us into the dormitories, the office, the meeting room where residents gather once or twice weekly as a group and try to resolve their differences with the help of Orlando and his staff members.

Of the twenty-eight men, women and one child here, only three do not carry the AIDS virus. Another ten or so infected people drop around every day to shower and do laundry and get a meal, then return to their abodes outside these walls. People in the shelter sometimes have their own rooms, but many sleep two and four to a room.

One day, while playing soccer with two-year-old Carlos, I catch sight of something in the room of Samantha, one of the resident transvestites. She walks with difficulty and I was told that her legs were ruined by the injections she once took to create breasts. What I see in her room are three orange feather boas. Souvenirs, I'm guessing, of her time on the stage.

When Patricia Rebolledo first broached the possibility of me working inside an AIDS shelter with transvestites and male hookers, I wasn't sure I had the constitution for it. I imagined having to tend to terminally ill people, bathing them, changing their diapers, holding their hands as they took their last breath. Mother Teresa did that. I am no Mother Teresa.

Had I come here in the early days of Hogar de la Esperanza, in 1993 say, before retroviral drugs, before advances in understanding the role of nutrition in HIV/AIDS, I would indeed have encountered the near dead. But now it is different and my fears soon drop away.

On that first day, as we tour the grounds with Orlando, I meet Mario, a beaming little man with a perfectly brilliant smile. He welcomes me into his shared room, and the first thing he shows me is his nursing diploma, hard won over the course of many years.

"I was into drugs," he tells me in English, a language that Orlando is always after him to use. "I was into crack, living on the street for three years. Two years and ten months ago I came here. I could not walk. I weighed less than fifty pounds. I came here to die. Then I started to believe in myself and I accepted help."

Mario's recovery has been miraculous. Mario works at Hogar de la Esperanza as a nurse, he attends seminars and conferences on AIDS in other parts of Central America, and he has become a kind of ambassador for Hogar and its mission. Living proof that one can descend into hell and make it back alive.

In our time at Hogar, nothing is hidden from us. Everything is laid bare.

APRIL 29. At our first roundtable meeting at Hogar with Orlando and all the residents, we go around in a circle and everyone introduces himself or herself. Before my time comes, I feel my hard-plastic chair go soft and yielding. It yields some more, then explodes beneath me and I land on the floor, hard, on my bottom.

Shock in the room turns to relief that I am unhurt, then laughter when I rise from my heap, flex my biceps and loudly blame the chair's destruction on my manliness and all the tortillas I have been eating. The ice is broken.

THIS IS the shape of help at Hogar. Clients meet each week with Helen, a staff psychologist; Yadira, a sociologist who happens to be Orlando's wife; or Orlando himself. These sessions last an hour or two and are part of a systematic approach that Orlando calls "ECO squared": E for education and ethics, CO for completeness and community.

The interviews are meant to measure any advances or declines in the residents' (Orlando prefers they be called "beneficiaries") mental and physical health. Each person who comes here must sign a contract and abide by the basic rules: no drugs, no weapons, no violence, no stealing, no staying out past curfew at 10 p.m. One transvestite here, the irrepressible Marylene, has been banished four times only to be welcomed back. But she goes AWOL again and Orlando finally has had enough. She will no longer be welcome as a resident, only as a day visitor.

Helen loves the work and the people ("No book could have taught me what I have learned here"), but she admits, "It's hard. You work with a lot of human suffering." Certain people she cannot abide; rapists, for example. Helen passes those individuals on to others.

She describes the isolation of her patients. Ask them to list their sources of support and some will write "no one." Many of them crave physical contact: a hug, a handshake or any acknowledgement that they are still human and worthy of respect.

ORLANDO THINKS there is value in the residents of Hogar de la Esperanza telling their life stories and in me hearing them. He wants me to meet "the people," as he often calls them. Shades of Thelma at Vinnie's back home.

I begin my one-on-one interviews with the residents of Hogar right away. For these sessions, during the big-circle meetings or whenever I need help with Spanish, Yanci is my translator. She is good, very good. Quick of mind, faithful to the words, able to find the English turn of phrase that perfectly matches the Spanish.

Yanci was born in Costa Rica forty years ago but left with her mother for New York when she was four. As a young adult, she got hooked on crack cocaine and soon lost the cleaning agency she had started. She was working as a cab driver on Long Island and carrying three kilos of coke when a high-speed cop-car chase ultimately landed her in prison for four years. It was there that she learned of her HIV-positive status. This, I gather, was the hardest of all her hard knocks: to be given such shattering news while alone in a jail cell.

Yanci walks with a slight roundhouse limp, a legacy of childhood polio. She has a broad smile and a habit of running her palm over one nostril—the one she used to fill with white powder. When she tells me how much she loves it at Hogar, and how she would never do anything to jeopardize her place here, how she has a job at a call centre lined up and the first thing she will do with her paycheque will be to buy meat for everyone (she is weary of the steady diet of rice and beans), I suspect that she is talking to convince herself more than me. These are the words she believes she should be saying and that I should be hearing.

Yanci has been a resident at Hogar for only six days; prior to that she was a hooker for two years. I like her New York humour and accent and the fact that she can laugh at herself. She complains that the transvestites at Hogar "have better tits than me."

"My home," she tells me, "is my sanctuary. Owners of the two-bit, roach hotel rooms where I sometimes stayed in New York—they loved me. I would get high and want to wax the floors, wash the curtains, clean the windows."

MANY DAYS have the same shape. Ulrike and I hop on the bus at Desamparados around 8 a.m. and five kilometres later hop off at the big park where kids fly kites on the weekend. We cross the park, then walk up the hill, past the ad hoc dump at the intersection, press on to the seminary with its line of tall pines along one wall, and down the hill to Hogar. I seek out Yanci and find her puffing on a menthol cigarette, her hair still wet from the shower. Residents are sometimes lounging on sofas near the kitchen and office, and Yanci hauls them in one at a time. Not everyone is keen to be interviewed, but two-thirds do talk to me. No one ever says, "That's too personal. Next question." They are all forthright.

We meet in a high-ceilinged room opposite the office, me in a hardback office chair, my subject in the fanciest chair in the place, a high-backed rocker with graceful arms and a cane backing. In one corner of the room stands a rather sorry book-shelf, which residents sometimes pick over. On the other two walls are Christ on his cross gazing downwards and a gilded framed painting of a chubby child angel staring skywards.

No story is ever the same, yet there are recurring themes. Effeminate boys tossed out on the streets by their disapproving fathers. Parents who abuse in every way imaginable. Impoverished households with a dozen mouths to feed and no way to do it until it occurs to someone that a boy's body can be sold for pleasure. Sex, often rough sex, at the age of six or seven. Descent into alcohol or drugs or both, prostitution, sexually transmitted diseases, and finally, the day they are told they have the HIV virus or full-blown AIDS (in Spanish, it's *sindrome de inmunodeficiencia adquirida,* or SIDA). Many attempt suicide or suffer street violence, rampant against transvestites in machismo societies like Costa Rica's. They endure injections to grow breasts, with terrible side effects later. My Norman Rockwell childhood—a bungalow in the Toronto suburb of Scarborough, a loving and supportive family, a backyard skating rink, meat-and-potato meals—seems a universe removed from the folks of Hogar.

Xavier, now thirty-four, was sexually abused by his stepfather when he was just nine. At seventeen, he was kicked out. That same year, he met a fifty-two-year-old woman who took him to her home in British Columbia with promises of getting him an education. And maybe she was sincere, but she also wanted kinky sex. Back in Costa Rica, he got a job at Manuel Antonio, a tourist beach on the country's west coast, bringing food and drinks to patrons around the pool. He learned how to give massages and it wasn't long before he was offering full-service sex. "I would earn $90 a day. Not bad for a Tico boy," says Xavier. But there were costs: syphilis, tuberculosis, surgery to repair his torn rectum.

At Hogar, he is brooding over what he calls his "hard mission." The father of two young girls, he is not looking forward to telling his wife that he carries the virus. His wife and daughters are at risk and will have to be tested. Orlando will go with him for this duty, but Xavier has to say the words. It is either that or leave Hogar, and Orlando will do the awful deed himself.

There are many such moments of high drama in the two weeks we are there. One day it is Kyra. We have hardly entered the compound that morning when her storm erupts, and Orlando—when he understands the sketch of it—invites us into the interview room so that we, with Yanci interpreting, can hear the story revealed for ourselves.

Kyra has had her teeth knocked out by drug dealers. She has seventeen different wounds on her body from knives and bullets. (The only time she teared up was when she bared her arms and legs to show this doubting Thomas the scars.) Kyra also has an eighteen-month-old baby named Deborah, and yesterday she went to the children's hospital in San José where she was told—in a waiting room, in front of a dozen or so other patients—that Deborah was HIV-positive and that it was her fault. Kyra believes this breach of confidentiality was

129

perpetrated by a doctor, but when Orlando makes inquiries— his niece is a doctor at the same hospital—he learns that a male nurse was the likely culprit.

Kyra is calm as she relates the story, but she concedes that she was hysterical when it all unfolded last night.

"It hurt me so much," she tells Orlando.

Orlando is calm and sympathetic but he takes nothing at face value. He tells Kyra that such a flagrant violation of doctor-patient confidentiality is not only a breach of medical ethics but of the law. He wonders aloud if it happened quite as Kyra remembers it. At the same time, he makes two calls: one to his niece and the other to a lawyer. Both call back at once, so he must juggle two cellphones.

Yanci tells me that a mother has a fifty-fifty chance of passing on the virus to her child, that often the baby will initially test positive but be clear at eighteen months. That is precisely what happens in this case. Kyra's storm passes.

RETIRED HOOKERS and men with breasts are not the only ones who come to Hogar. Every Wednesday a particular group of women arrive, sometimes thirty at a time. These are women who have contracted the virus through their husbands and who come for mutual support, a meal and whatever financial or other help Hogar can muster to pay a utility bill or buy some groceries. I am reminded, again, of Vinnie's.

I ask Rosa, a woman with a kind round face, "What's the hardest thing about living with AIDS?"

"Discrimination," she says. Rosa cleans houses to make a living and last week she was spotted entering a building run by a foundation that helps women with AIDS feed their children. The woman who saw her tattled to Rosa's employer, and Rosa lost her job.

ULRIKE AND I return every afternoon to Doña Esilda and her ample home-cooked meals. *"Comen, comen* (eat, eat)," she urges. The fare at Doña Esilda's is always made from scratch. Beans and rice are constants at almost every meal, even breakfast, but she has myriad ways of dressing them up, and she serves her meals with home-made juices *(guanábana, tamarindo)* and her soup *(olla de carne),* a Costa Rican specialty. Doña Esilda tells her favourite fruit vendor that he has to give her the best because she has Canadian visitors and she wants to make a good impression. Over dinner, we relate the stories of the men and women of Hogar, and the impact on all of us is the same. We ask the same question: how can we help?

Ivan, Doña Esilda's son, a former architect who turned to ferrying tourists when his other work dried up, mentions Hogar to his girlfriend, who promptly shows up with a plastic bag full of jeans and T-shirts and other clothing. One day Ulrike and I take enough juice to the shelter for thirty people. Another day we visit Doña Esilda's fruit dealer and come away with bags of melon and papaya, pineapple and banana and strawberries, which those on duty in the kitchen at Hogar immediately use to make *refrescos.* I buy colouring books and crayons for little Carlos, then a piggy bank fashioned from a coconut. Unfortunately the little brown pig with the big eyes frightens him and he flees from it.

What we receive in return are lessons in the resilience of the human spirit. Take Michelangelo, for instance. He had sex with a man at the age of seven and was on the street not long after, selling his body to survive. A transvestite since the age of twelve, he was addicted to crack cocaine for sixteen years. Now forty-nine, he works in a restaurant kitchen. Some residents at Hogar have jobs, and the aim is for everyone to be self-sufficient.

"I want to get ahead," Michelangelo tells me. "I want to learn how to sew." He is a small man with delicate features. I am taken aback by his dignity, by how much there is left after the street has had its way with him.

"Will you design women's clothes?" I ask him.

His face brightens.

"Yes! I have a flare for design."

"Do you miss," I ask him, "anything of your other life?"

"I miss putting on the dress," he replies. "I miss transforming myself." This other transformation—leaving the street and all its temptations, kicking the drugs—is harder, he concedes.

My last interview question is always the same. Will you let me take your photograph? Almost always, the answer is positive. They are delighted. The errant Marylene is more than willing but wants to dress up for the photo. On the day we chat, she is wearing her hair in blonde ringlets, a lime tank top that calls attention to her breasts and a black-and-white necklace. We arrange to meet again on Friday. Marylene says something during our talk that stays with me.

"Is the life of a transvestite inherently tragic?" I ask her. "Can that life ever be one of happiness?"

"Nobody is full of happiness," she says. "Not everybody is full of disgrace."

Marylene calls herself one of the first transvestites to walk the streets of Costa Rica and she wants to write a book about her life. She does not lack for confidence, and reads from a finely crafted letter that she hopes will kickstart a lawsuit against the police for jailing her at the age of seventeen. The rapes she suffered in jail, she argues, derailed her life. "I could have been a psychiatrist," she tells me in all seriousness. "I could have been an astronaut."

The following Friday, Marylene disappears once more and I never see her again. At Hogar, there are those who seek rescue and there are those who resist it.

LUIS-MARTIN, THIRTY-EIGHT, has landed here along a different trajectory. The former lab worker contracted an eye disease two years ago that left him blind, and a hospital employee told him about Hogar. Smart, well-educated (he studied law for a time), he is one of the few here without HIV or AIDS.

I ask him if the rich of the world have an obligation to share with the poor. *"Si, claro,"* he replies. "Yes, there is an obligation," he says. "Before the laws of God."

Martin seems proud, almost prickly. He hates to ask for anything.

"Si tengo, tengo. Si no, no (If I have, I have. If not, that's fine too.)," he says. But he will not beg.

"This place," he says, "is a bridge to help me over to the other side. That's how I see it."

MAY 1. We perform a variety of assignments at Hogar de la Esperanza. One day, Ulrike makes colour copies of the Humanitas logo (a blue stylized figure in the act of leaping) and takes them home to Ivan who uses a manual machine to stamp out buttons, which we then wear in the Labour Day parade in downtown San José. It's a colourful and, in places, a literally gay parade. Speakers on car rooftops blast out songs and speeches while patriots carry blue, white and red helium balloons or wave the Costa Rican flag—blue bars top and bottom, white bars in between and a red central bar with the nation's coat of arms. Some of the banners are half a street wide, and though the causes being championed are serious and political, there's elation in the air.

Along with Yanci, Marlon, Peru, Kyra and Mario, we join the parade as it passes. We tuck in behind the Communists, then walk with the teachers' union before finally finding a natural niche with the gay pride contingent. One long white banner with red lettering reads *Luchemos contra el Capitalismo, el Machismo y la Homolesbophobia.* (Let's fight against capitalism, machismo and homophobia.)

Other days we serve in the Carpa soup-kitchen programs, putting up tents, taking down tents and talking to those who come to be fed. Ulrike cuts up vegetables in the kitchen at Hogar, I paint the grilles of its heavy metal doors, she teaches English classes, I continue to interview the residents, we both attend the circle meetings and we both polish the document that Orlando plans to present (in Spanish and English) at the XVII International Conference on AIDS slated for Mexico City from August 3 to 8. The occasion will mark the first time that an international AIDS conference is held in Latin America.

DURING CIRCLE meetings at Hogar, whether to discuss the role of nutrition in combatting the disease or to iron out the clashes that inevitably arise from a thirty-strong community of vigorous personalities unaccustomed to living cooperatively, the one constant is Carlos, also called Carlitos or Charlie. In the big room with its floor-to-ceiling murals of birds and turtles and fish, the men and women of Hogar air their dirty linen, declare their allegiances and take their stabs at governance, while little Carlos kicks his soccer balls at their feet or heads.

Carlos and his several plastic soccer balls have the run of the place. I never hear him cry the whole time I am there and I almost never see him without a ball. As children do, he takes some of the edge off this place. Everyone speaks to him, offers him treats if they have them and wants to pick him up.

Carlos doesn't go to just anyone, and I make it my mission to befriend him.

Carlos Senior works as a security guard in a coffee plantation hours from the city and comes to Hogar occasionally to visit his wife, Mirna, and their son. Mirna was abandoned by her family even before she discovered that her husband had brought home the virus.

She and her son have lived for a year at Hogar, where she serves as the de facto office administrator and holder of the keys. Smart and capable, she is a natural office manager and hopes one day to find such work after Hogar. Mirna knows what else the future holds: "I'm HIV-positive," she tells me. "The disease is in a window period. It will appear later on."

Hogar will miss Mirna when she goes, but they will miss Carlos even more. "They love him," she says. "A little person softens the place. He brings a lot of peace to a lot of people."

"What have you learned here?" I ask her.

"Tolerance," she replies.

"And what role do the landscape and the quiet play in the healing process?"

"A place like this," she says, "we can meditate here. Or return to the places you have been and imagine where you might go."

I HAVE my favourites in this little community of lost and found souls: Carlos, whom I cherish; Mirna, for her innate good sense; Kyra, for her spirit; Orlando, of course, for his bold plans and unceasing compassion; and Michelangelo, for his quiet dignity.

I like Yanci as well, but I wish she had an off button. She is like an all-news radio station, one where the news is all about her and the news is always good. Maybe she believes that if she gives voice to her dreams they will come true. I have paid for new glasses for her ($12 at a discount optometrist who caters to the poor), payment, I tell her, for all her translation work. Orlando has coached me on the idea that it's better for everyone at Hogar to understand that the glasses were not bestowed, but earned. This is a way of cutting off at the pass the obvious question, the one that dogs all charity: why her and not me?

Yanci told me she needed glasses for her new job at the call-in centre. Later, when I learn that Yanci is AWOL and has not been seen in days, I wonder if I have been duped.

Hogar, the Place of Hope, is also the place where the waters are constantly being tested. "They are always," says Orlando, "trying to manipulate me." Clients go into the office at Hogar and plead for money, for bus fare so they can see their families, for cigarettes or toiletries. There is a crack house between Hogar and the Humanitas office minutes away, and there are many residents at Hogar who dare not pass it, so great are its temptations.

Some of the tensions that swirl at Hogar derive from fear of theft: laundry gone missing on a line or a brush left on a bed that mysteriously disappears. Most of the men and women of Hogar are penniless addicts whose possessions are few and all the more valued. The temptation to steal, then sell an item to pay for a hit, must be enormous.

MAY 5. Another round chamber meeting at Hogar, this one to iron out specific issues. Who let in Lucretia (a transvestite in her sixties)? Should Laura (another older transvestite who has been visiting during the day) be allowed to stay? Should Marylene be forgiven (again) for flouting the rules? Orlando lets everyone speak, but I see a resolve in him. He may seem the softie but he's not.

Later he will tell them that those few who receive a pension from the government should share it with the others by buying fruit. "Think collectively," he tells them.

TODAY'S INTERVIEW is with Jonathan. In the rocking chair of the interview room, he sits staring at the key on a string around his neck, as so many here carry their keys. There are ten keys on my loonie-sized metal key chain: two to my house in the city (front door, back door), three for my cabin in the country (north door, south door, tool shed), the car, the truck, the lock on my bike, my mother-in-law's house in Toronto and a mystery key I am loath to toss. The number of keys is a measure of my possessions and privileges. Jonathan, like almost everyone at Hogar, has just the key to the cupboard in his room. His one key is the symbol of his penury. Some people here, like Xavier, can't even muster the money to buy a lock and therefore have no key.

Jonathan once worked as a boy messenger in a pharmacy. He left home at the age of seventeen, a victim of his own good looks.

"I was cute," he says. "I got corrupted. I became a high-end male prostitute. I got into life modelling at the university. I worked in TV, commercials for milk, a paint company, clothing. On the side, I was a hooker. I was the best." Here he pauses. "The best idiot, actually."

I find it so hard to reconcile this tale with the man wearing the mischievous grin whom I see walking purposefully about the grounds of Hogar. The others mosey; Jonathan strides. When I ask him if he has thoughts on how better to run Hogar, he says what I have been thinking: "Put everybody to work. I think if your mind is busy, you have no chance to think stupid things. I always work: cut the grass, study, paint, make repairs, clean Orlando's office." He can pass the crack house with no thought of stopping.

Jonathan lived here six years ago for a year, before the new drugs arrived. He remembers how terribly sick everyone was, how he bathed them because they were too weak to do it themselves. He's been here six months this time, and his plan is to continue living here and find work in a restaurant.

I ask Jonathan about his experience—the prostitution, the drugs, eight months in jail (after a prank went wrong) where he continued to ply his trade in exchange for food and drugs—and its scars. He admits that there are scars, that he has no family (he was one of seven children) to support him and that he feels alone a lot, and that sometimes he has no strength. However, he also says he tries to stay positive and he feels grateful to be alive after believing at first that AIDS was a death sentence.

When I ask to take his photo, he declines and gets teary-eyed. Later, I tell him how sorry I am for upsetting him with questions. Every time after that, he is bright and impish with me. When I ask to paint the wrought-iron door to the meeting room, he sets up the pails and brushes, finds cardboard to protect the floor and appraises my work approvingly when he passes me.

It takes me two days to finish the job. After day one, I try to explain to him in my broken Spanish that I will touch up any missed spots next day. *"Pero..."* I begin. But...

"No pero," he says with a smile. No buts.

On the day we leave, he gives Ulrike and me a token, a small sculpture the size of a grapefruit of quarter-inch metal tubing and ball bearings forming two figurines on a bench, the male with his arm around the female (though it could be a tall man and his short male partner, or a tall woman and her smaller female partner). If you push the bench, it swings. It's a simple, charming memento.

"It's you and Lorenzo," he tells Ulrike when he presents it to her.

I remember the day he accompanied us back to Desamparados. We got off at the fruit stand by the church, but Jonathan insisted on walking us all the way home. No need, we pleaded.

But he said he had spotted some unsavoury characters at the corner. "How do you know they're unsavoury?" I teased him. "Do they have marks on their foreheads?"

He just pointed to his eye, as if he knew things I did not. Indeed he does.

MAY 6. Another *carpa,* this one in the town of San Isidro, which lies over the mountains and some one hundred kilometres southeast of San José. We have fun today. Ulrike and I speak first with two alcoholic men named Oscar and Victor, two *buenos amigos* (good friends). Oscar is elephant-eared and intense, young and thick-bodied, with hands twice the size of mine. He works in construction and is immensely strong, so naturally I challenge him to an arm wrestle.

Our little bit of theatre causes a stir, lightens the mood. Everyone turns to watch and smile as Oscar mows the gringo down. After that, he puts out his knuckles to meet mine, as buenos amigos do.

I learn on the long and winding three-hour trip to San Isidro that Orlando owns and trains horses and has broken many bones riding unschooled mounts. He understands full well that forcing a young horse to do something never works well. Better to use gentle persuasion so that the horse is offered choices. No doubt such thinking has guided Orlando's work with addicts.

MAY 8. Our last day at Hogar. I feel a great sadness as Ulrike and I walk to the bus. So many of these people have let us into their lives.

Jimmy, for example, the black cook from Puerto Limón, has shown us his room, the mirror at the head of his bed, the dozen stuffed toys dangling from the ceiling, the fridge, one fan and one chair, two phones (one red landline phone plus a cell upright in its stand), the whole place impeccably neat. Jimmy has HIV but, to his doctor's astonishment, no symptoms.

He credits botanical knowledge gained from his mother. He drinks teas made of fever grass and other concoctions rich in garlic and onions. Others at Hogar gag at the thought of drinking the stuff, but Jimmy looks the picture of health.

I am touched that he has invited us into his room, and that Jonathan has shown Ulrike his room. In prison, there is a taboo about cells: you are not to look in another man's room unless you have his permission, and you never enter that room without an invitation. Many of the men and women of Hogar take great pride in their rooms. It is sometimes all they have, and I understand that an honour has been bestowed.

BEANS AND rice and corn are all critical to the Costa Rican diet, but their prices soar while we are there. These crops were once produced in sufficient abundance to meet the country's needs, but the globalized economy has changed all that. Farmers here cannot compete with cheap black beans imported from China, cheap red beans brought in from Nicaragua and cheap corn coming from the United States. Many farmers have turned instead to export crops like bananas and coffee. Importing staples is fine as long as fuel prices are stable.

But the rising cost of gasoline and the mad rush all over the world to grow corn for ethanol production means that running farm machinery to grow crops and then transporting them to market have become much more expensive. When the price of rice, beans and corn doubles, the poor are hit the hardest.

"There will be great discontent," one economist dryly predicts in the May 2 *Tico Times*.

Costa Rica is a tourist destination, and a favourite of Canadians, to bring this a little closer to home. A million visitors a year come to this country to see its million-year-old rain-forests, but sex tourism is also on the rise. Paul Theroux, in his malcontent travel book, *The Old Patagonian Express,* talks about meeting men in Costa Rica on alcohol- and sex-fuelled vacations. That was in the late 1970s. Such behaviour is much more prevalent now, and I'm betting that rising food prices will only drive up the desperation levels.

One morning at breakfast, Doña Esilda's son Ivan announces that a high school friend of his has been shot and killed while trying to stop thieves from taking his car. This occurs in the same barrio where Hogar is located. We were warned before coming never to wear flashy jewellery, to keep our money in money belts, to avoid any displays of wealth. "You can be killed for your cellphone," warns Doña Esilda, who gets her TV news from a Fox News—like channel that offers a steady diet of murders and gruesome car accidents. I have never felt unsafe here, but I have to believe that the general feeling of insecurity will only grow.

IN A world where the gap between the grossly rich and the grossly poor widens by the minute, contempt must flow between them like a law of physics. How could it be otherwise? A rich man can't be thinking of the poor starving and dying outside his walls, for it would get in the way of sleep. The poor man likewise gives no thought to the rich man, only to loathe him for his appetites and excesses. Each might be contemptible to the other, certainly as long as there is no contact between them.

What Orlando and others who share his compassionate view are saying is just this: let there be human contact. The rest will follow from that.

What I take from my time in San José are names, faces, stories. I keep a picture on my desk of Carlos and I think of him often. He looks like a tiny cowboy, with his white shirt, blue jeans and blue-jean jacket, and his hands at his hips as if he were ready to draw. *"Para que me recuerden siempre y no me olviden* (So that you will remember me [Carlos] and never forget me.)," Mirna has written on the back. I cannot and I will not. I have Jonathan's little swing figurines on my bedroom window and I smile at the thought of him every time I raise the blinds.

Their gift to me is the pleasure of their company, and I feel beholden to them. Something has passed between us.

This brief time spent in service to a community of people far removed from our own took both Ulrike and me out of our comfort zones. One time over lunch, when it was just Orlando, Ulrike and one of the residents, talk turned to facing up to one's demons.

"Tell her what you did," Orlando bluntly ordered him. What he confessed to was molesting children, and I felt a momentary revulsion when Ulrike later told me the story. He had himself no doubt been molested, and I had many reasons to admire him for the way he had recovered from his past. The cloud lifted.

The world of HIV/AIDS, transvestites and sex-trade workers was one I had only previously considered at a safe remove. Once up close, I took hope in the discovery that whatever assumptions I brought with me quickly crumbled and fell away. In face-to-face contact I found our common humanity.

. . .

[**MICRO-CREDIT, MACRO-EFFECT**]

SOMETIMES, POOR people simply need a step up. The Grameen Bank of Bangladesh was established in 1976 when a Bangladeshi economics professor named Muhammad Yunus came up with the idea of micro-credits—small, collateral-free loans to some of the poorest people in the world. The bank has so far loaned $6 billion to seven million Bangladeshi villagers, 95 per cent of them women. Yunus, the so-called "banker to the poor," is proud of the program's 99 per cent loan recovery rate. (The idea of micro-credit loans took a beating late in 2010, however, as for-profit banks saw their ability to recover small loans deteriorating. Indian banks were accused of lending to poor villagers at exorbitant interest rates and without heed to their ability to repay.)

Percy Barnevik, a Swedish-born entrepreneur living in London, is another who thinks that poverty can be managed out of existence by miniscule loans. He told *The Guardian* in January 2008 that much international aid is "naive and useless," and that many NGOs are "fluffy, unfocused and inefficient."

Of his own charity, Hand in Hand International (HHI), Barnevik says, "I don't want [it] to be the best NGO. I want it to be the best company." HHI operates in the southern Indian state of Tamil Nadu, where it is on course to create 1.3 million jobs within five years. The approach is simple: offer micro-credit loans to groups of fifteen to twenty women so they can launch enterprises such as bakeries and garment factories. HHI never loans to men, who, Barnevik says, are likely to drink or gamble the money away.

Barnevik is no flake. The sixty-eight-year-old Swede regularly tops polls as Europe's most respected chief executive. So people listen when he says that extreme poverty in the world could be eliminated if just 7 per cent of global aid were reallocated and spent his way.

TIME
Inside

KINGSTON IS sometimes called the Limestone City, a quaint-sounding moniker. And at first glance the city *is* quaint, with its stately cut-stone buildings lending an attractive historical veneer. The commanding view of the city and lake from the heights of Fort Henry, a nineteenth-century British fortress built entirely of stone, is one of my favourites. But many of those handsome grey stones were cut by convicts in the nineteenth and early twentieth centuries. Rifle-toting guards on horseback would have overseen their hard labour in the quarry at Portsmouth Harbour, close by Kingston Penitentiary.

As Merilyn Simonds puts it in *The Convict Lover,* a portrait of prison life in those times, "a hundred blows with an eight-pound sledge would sink the bit one inch... Commercial quarries used steam-driven hammer-drills that punctured the rock in a fraction of the time. But at Kingston Penitentiary, time was not money. The harder the labour, the better."

The Kingston region is home to nine prisons that house 2,611 inmates. Correctional Service of Canada is a major employer in the area and a significant contributor to the local economy. The prison community—the officials, the guards, the social service workers and the families of inmates who have moved here— functions in our midst yet seems to exist in a world of its own, across another divide in the community.

JUNE 4. I spend the morning at the utilitarian John Howard Society (JHS) building on Montreal Street in north-end Kingston. There I meet staff members Derek, Jenny, Cynthia, Gayla and Emmett, and arrange lunch with Lisa Finateri, the executive director.

John Howard, I learn, was an eighteenth-century Englishman whose pioneering studies of conditions in English and European prisons launched a prison reform movement. The John Howard Society dates back to the time of Confederation in Canada and continues to have a presence all across the country. Its mission is "effective, just, and humane responses to crime and its causes." Society personnel work with people who have faced criminal charges, advocate for changes in the criminal justice process and educate the public about that process and prison conditions.

The staff I meet seem committed and compassionate individuals with a pretty good sense of humour. Hearing about their work and the obstacles they face, I marvel at their perseverance and that of some of the prisoners and ex-prisoners they try to help. My friends at Hogar de la Esperanza come to mind: the worst life has to offer will irreparably scar some, while others survive and emerge with even greater dignity. One Kingston man in his mid-seventies will later tell me that prison was the best thing that ever happened to him. He wished he had been incarcerated sooner, for it brought to a halt his old life and patterns as a petty thief.

There's a mystery in this I will try to fathom in the days ahead. But something happens that first day, and it almost derails my mission.

THE STORY requires a preamble. I have to admit that volunteering in a prison setting was not an experience I looked forward to. Until this stint with the John Howard Society of Kingston (JHSK), I had been inside only one prison, Millhaven Institution, east of the city. Some twenty years ago, I was cajoled into volunteering inside the prison by a John Howard Society staffer who happened then to be married to a friend's sister. The task seemed innocent enough and certainly worthy: go talk to the lads behind bars every Monday evening, play a little cards and socialize.

"The men have no idea of civil conversation," I was told. "Teach them. Just be yourself."

I did it for about four months, but aspects of those visits have stayed with me. I remember the metal detectors, the coolness of the guards, the barbed wire, how our small cadre of volunteers was hushed—overwhelmed really—into silence as we made our way in.

I remember a river of men walking the other way, tall iron bars between us. We met in a high-ceilinged room that was too vast for our numbers and made the whole venture seem more pitiful than it was. Maybe a dozen inmates came; it was nobody's cup of tea. But I learned a few things. I learned that "goof" was the nastiest of insults and might be forgiven of an outsider but could get you killed behind those walls. I learned some of prison's basic rules: never stare, never pry.

Of course I did pry. Approaching forty years of age then, I had been a journalist for almost two decades. I think I was intimidated by prison, and the refuge of the awestruck has always been to let the other one talk. Most people are only too happy to talk—about themselves, their cars, their jobs, their children. When in doubt, pose a question.

I do not smoke cigarettes, but I would bring a pack to these gatherings, small tokens to pass out while we played euchre. I observed and I absorbed.

Although I almost never write poetry, there have been a few times in my life when it seemed that putting pen to paper was both urgent and necessary. I drafted a poem that drew on my evenings at Millhaven, kept it and only discovered it recently when I was cleaning out my desk on one of those days when tidying seemed more attractive than writing. It was produced on my old dot-matrix printer, and the two pages of the poem were still connected, the perforation intact. "Bobby" is the title, written in pencil at the top.

My wife, our banter over hard-boiled eggs
one version
of how things are.
I am learning about others.

Bobby, his arm thigh-sized,
blue with tattoos.
A black hole where a tooth was.
My job is to be unafraid
and with Bobby I am
absolutely unafraid.
No wounded bear was ever kinder;
It's the skinny guy with the stare I fear.

Bobby's wife at P4W
must pay for conjugal visits.

Here's how it is,
Bobby tells me over cards,
for this, too, is banter.
They probe her body,
spread her like an oyster
Fist every orifice
seeking drugs.
Make the bitch eat
some humble pie.

I'm beginning to fathom
and like
this man.
Only when he says *fuck you*
does he have any power.
It's not a lot to ask,
a little power in a man's life.

"Suffering and hurt," Bobby
told the parole board.
"My life has been suffering and hurt."

P4W refers to the notorious Prison for Women, another gothic stone pile that was finally closed in 2000. Queen's University has since bought the building to house its archives. The "skinny guy" was an inmate whom I crossed one night by asking about racism inside the joint. He boiled over, and while I never felt physically at risk (Bobby would have saved me), emotionally I had been levelled—as if he had hit me in the belly with his fist.

"I warned you once before not to ask me questions like that," he hissed, and I'm sure my face went beet red. How could I have been so stupid? If I were to commit such a blunder again, what would he do? I felt a rush of fear and dread, and on the way home, a line uttered by Julius Caesar in Shakespeare's play came to mind: "Let me have men about me that are fat ... Yond Cassius has a lean and hungry look; He thinks too much: such men are dangerous."

That was my last night at Millhaven.

TWENTY YEARS later, I'm dining with Lisa Finateri at a down-town bistro. It has been a productive morning marked by engrossing chats with John Howard staff and now a tasty lunch. Then Lisa begins to describe some of the harassment she has endured at the hands of Corrections staff. She's been accused of playing footsies with convicts, of flirting with them, of hav-ing sex with them. She's been denied entry to the prisons, had her vehicle searched while being interrogated, had her house searched by the ROPE squad (police officers with the Repeat Offender Program Enforcement unit). Male staff at John How-ard, she says, are spared these indignities. We finish our meal, I drive her back to the office and I proceed home.

Coming in the front door, I greet Ulrike and tell her, "This is going to be hard."

We have a brief afternoon nap, as is our custom, but I can neither close my eyes nor relax. I am not at all prone to the black dogs of depression, but I feel a wave of despair now, along with a fear that it will not soon leave.

This brief peek into the maw has rattled me. All I can think to do is this: mow the lawn, cut the heads off dandeli-ons, impose some order in the garden, get the body moving. In another time, I would have gone for a good long run. Blow the dark spirit out, expunge it like sweat.

Four hours later I feel more my old self. I can only guess at what had brought this on, but I think that it was this: the cool hatred implicit in Lisa's treatment. She thought of suing the Correctional Service of Canada or filing a human rights complaint, but she believed it would only make a bad situation worse, and the men inside would suffer all the more for it.

JUNE 10. On the phone with Paul Gervan, discussing details of that benefit concert to help pay the legal fees of a group trying to stop a uranium mine from despoiling the watershed north of Kingston.

Paul and his wife, Ev, are my heroes. One might call them "retired" but the word hardly describes their life of volunteer and humanitarian work. Proof that the oak does not fall far from the tree, their daughter, Asha, has worked all over the world with Médicins sans Frontières.

The Gervans are colleagues on Horizons fundraisers, and they're active in the Canadian Cuban Friendship Society, where they raise funds to send medical supplies and aid to Cuba. Paul has been a force in the anti-nuclear movement for more than four decades. Yet they manage to combine this activism with a keen sense of fun.

Some years ago, Paul served on the citizens' committee at Joyceville Institution, another of the prisons in this area. His advice to me? "Don't look for truth inside a prison." He and his fellow committee members would listen to the complaints of the convict committee and then hear from the administration. He believed the cons were conning and the staff were prevaricating.

A friend of mine once had a partner who did serious time, and she visited him often in prison. She was aghast at how "guarded" the prisons are: "They're very secretive," she says. "Which just tells me they have a lot to hide."

JUNE 12. Day one inside. At Bath Institution, rolls of razor wire crown high parallel fences that stretch north and south, a wide grassy moat between them. Black heavy-metal doors slide open, then close automatically behind us as the next one clicks open. We are, of course, under surveillance and someone somewhere has decided that we are free, as it were, to enter.

Lisa had left her purse in the back seat of her green Jetta, wallet visible.

"Don't you want to put that in the trunk?" I asked her.

"Nah," she replied. "Security cameras everywhere."

Today is the annual "pre-release fair" at this medium-security prison west of Kingston. Imagine an old gymnasium, the nets a little worse for wear, and several dozen tables arranged for the forty or so organizations that have come to set up their displays and lay down their brochures and stacks of calling cards. Each organization is here to offer some sort of help to any inmate about to make the jarring transition from inside to outside. I feel like a Tupperware salesman at a trade convention. My task is to direct inmates who come to the John Howard Society booth seeking assistance.

Some have lost their ID or are trying to recover it from police or prison limbo, waiting for a cop or guard to answer a con's phone call. Some offenders have just given up and need help to get new documents—a health card, a birth certificate, a passport. They may want a hand writing a resumé or need coaching for a job interview, but their first and most pressing requirement upon release is finding a place to live.

There are a hundred or so halfway houses scattered across the country. Incredibly, the only one in Kingston closed recently when neighbourhood families objected to the presence of men found guilty of molesting children. I confess I wince when Lisa tells me that at least 60 per cent of the inmates in Bath Institution are sex offenders. At the same time, I applaud organizations like the John Howard Society that exist to help ease the transition from prison to street—regardless of the crime.

One of my assignments while with the Society is to write copy for a new six-page newsletter that will explain to the local community what the John Howard Society does. After huddling a few days ago with Lisa and Ian Malcolm, who chairs the JHSK Board of Directors, we agreed that the newsletter would also include interviews with some former inmates to make the case that it is possible to serve time and still succeed in later life. What to call the quarterly newsletter was not decided. But as I help man the JHSK booth at Bath, I think of these inmates one day walking out the door. The newsletter's name, perhaps, should capture that moment, that exhilaration, but also the trepidation they must feel. How about *The Wild Blue Yonder?*

The Salvation Army is here at the pre-release fair, as are Volunteer Kingston and Kagita Mikam, which offers training to Aboriginal offenders. So too is Lifeline Inreach, which offers one-on-one counselling by lifers to lifers. (A "lifer" is an individual serving a life sentence and eligible for parole after ten or up to twenty-five years.) The prisoners walk round and round the gym floor, picking up brochures, chatting with halfway house personnel. Many, it seems to me, have simply come to ogle the young females staffing the booths.

Jenny, a half-time institutional services worker with the Society, tells me that it costs taxpayers on average $81,000 a year to house a male inmate in a federal prison, $169,000 to house a female. You would think that agencies such as John Howard and Lifeline—key contributors to an offender's successful transition from the jail to the outside—would be welcome inside. Surely the guards, who live in the community, would embrace these agencies for their vital work.

"Many of the guards," says Jenny, "are hostile to people like us. They think the convicts are scum, unworthy of help."

One prisoner, a lifer, tells me that he's very worried by what he's hearing about the Harper government's plans to make a life sentence just that—a sentence with no chance of parole.

"How would it change prisons?" I ask him.

"There'd be a lot of blood," he replies. "Lifers would have nothing to lose."

John Leeman, a Lifeline counsellor, served a life sentence and has spent the past eighteen years on parole and offering help to offenders and ex-offenders inside and outside prisons in the Kingston area. He and the four other counsellors at Lifeline provide the kind of guidance that no one else can: their own bittersweet experience, and hope. "I made it. So can you," is their counsel. Pity, then, that there are only five of them offering guidance to some 1,100 lifers, dangerous offenders with indeterminate sentences, and men with long fixed sentences. Like the John Howard Society, these counsellors are stretched painfully thin. Funding is always an issue. All the more so when the mood in Ottawa is to lock 'em up and throw away the key.

JUNE 13. Lisa and the others all say the same thing: going inside leaves you drained and fatigued. These places, they warn, will suck the life right out of you.

Today we have a double whammy, with two pre-release fairs. The morning will be spent in the almost leisurely confines of Frontenac Institution and the afternoon in the more severe Collins Bay Institution, known as The Bay or Disneyland (for its tall red turrets). The two prisons are adjacent to each other, and just minutes from downtown.

Frontenac is a minimum security jail and, at 325 hectares, may well be the largest urban farm in Canada. There are no fences, no razor wire. More than a hundred inmates wake every morning before 4:30 to attend the cows and chickens raised here; some work the fields and vegetable gardens that help keep the institution's food costs down. Frontenac has an atmosphere different from any other prison I have so far visited, and I am led to believe by talking to inmates that working with animals and with living things is the best sort of rehabilitation. There is ample evidence in the scientific literature to buttress that argument.

Andrew McCann, who teaches a course on sustainable agriculture at St. Lawrence College in Kingston, remarks on the peaceful environment of the Frontenac farm. Farming can soften the blows of incarceration; it lets confined men breathe again and connects them with primal elements: the soil and seasonal round, the birth and death of creatures that offer milk, meat and eggs. Prisoners work with local farmers, one of whom told McCann that he understands why Frontenac's unique chemistry works on even hardened convicts. "These cows are all mothers."

(The federal government would announce plans in 2009 to close down all six prison farm operations in Canada and, in the case of Kingston's Frontenac and Pittsburgh Institutions, replace them with super prisons—an American invention that many criminologists say is disastrous. Mega prisons may offer some savings, but they also become virtual universities where the worst of the worst teach others to become like them. Eventually, the vast majority of prisoners get out. Will some emerge with a newfound sense of compassion, or seething with rage?)

Frontenac is typically the last stop for an inmate who has progressed from maximum- to medium-security institutions. One inmate I speak to is an ordained minister. Volunteers are warned before going into a prison not to ask about the circumstances that led to incarceration, but I did wonder what a man of the cloth had done to earn time inside. I never did find out, nor did I want to. In the book of prison etiquette, discretion is rule one.

I SPEND three days at pre-release fairs in five Kingston area prisons—Collins Bay, Frontenac, Joyceville, Pittsburgh and Bath—and gain a new understanding of "prison time." Collins Bay is by far the worst. Maybe it is that airless gym, or the guards walking in pairs and looking straight through us, inmates and agency workers and volunteers alike. No smile, no acknowledgement, just the hard forward stare. I have heard that female guards have to earn the respect of male guards by displays of toughness, and while I will encounter female staff who seem kind, I also encounter the other type in Collins Bay.

The warden who welcomes us before proceedings begin seems appreciative enough, but a reference to "our inmates" sounds uncomfortably proprietary. Could he not have acknowledged them in some other way? Referred to their aspirations upon release? Or simply offered thanks on behalf of "all of us here"?

Barb Hill, who is retiring after thirty years with the John Howard Society of Ontario, just shakes her head when I talk to her later about the warden's choice of words. "There is no attempt made," she says, "to acknowledge that these men are human beings. Maybe that's the contract. Maybe that's what you have to do to work inside a prison. You have to shut down, pretend the inmates are not human."

I too make my rounds of the booths and get to know some of the people staffing the other tables. A woman who works for Kagita Mikam tells me that a lifer complained to her, "Jail isn't what it used to be." A prisoner I spoke with at Joyceville had said much the same. As did Connor McCollum, who works for PASAN (Prisoners' HIV/AIDS Support Action Network). Prison, they all agreed, has changed.

Said my lifer contact: "I'm a career criminal. I've been stealing since I was eight years old. It used to be that jail was for common criminals who knew the rules and the culture. No more. Now it's young crack heads who commit crimes to pay for their addiction, and they end up in jail. They don't know the rules. There are no rules now, and it makes it stressful for everyone—guards and inmates."

Connor told me that prisons are much more punitive than in the past, and he related a story that shocked me on several counts. He said that inmates who are junkies will make their own crude needles, using them over and over again—not a wise practice, of course. In an attempt to sterilize the needles, the convicts will use bleach, which the guards are obliged to supply. But, says Connor, the guards sometimes dilute the bleach with water. Why? Is it because pure bleach could be tossed as a weapon? Or is it so inmates will become infected with hepatitis and HIV/AIDS? This is the level of malice that exists in our prisons.

Connor also told me that only small amounts of drugs get past the intense security at the prison gate. The newest drug detection device at Joyceville is an ion machine, a blue chamber that resembles the beam-me-up apparatus on the starship *Enterprise*. The device issues jets of air all at once, freeing up the ions around the person standing inside, which means the ions can then be tested for the slightest drug residue. After I had been gone over by the machine (it made a compressor sound, like so many tongues clacking), a guard took a swab from my leather watchband.

The whole process was so slow and the line-up so long that some agency staff, who had driven to Kingston from London and Hamilton and points beyond for the fair, simply walked away. The chances of a visitor carrying drugs into prisons would seem to be slim. How, then, do the drugs get inside? Not every prison has state-of-the-art drug-detection devices, so visitors do sometimes smuggle in drugs. Packets can be tossed over the walls, and prisoners returning after day passes are also conduits. But another route, I am told, is through the staff.

Even though guards have been caught selling drugs inside Canadian institutions, staff are not asked to enter ion chambers or bend over to have their cavities explored or be subjected to search by sniffer dogs. The union is far too strong for that. Yet guards are sometimes set upon by prisoners, who may be especially violent and dangerous when they're high on drugs, contraband that guards themselves may have brought inside. It is a bizarre world I have entered.

IT IS not my world, though. I am just passing through, unlike a number of those I meet inside who have returned again and again. A study undertaken by the RCMP in the mid-1990s found that up to 44 per cent of incarcerated males are convicted of another crime within two years of their release from prison. Why that is so is the subject of much debate and speculation, but the questions that gnaw at me are these: if 56 per cent go on to lead normal lives—sometimes after horrific experiences in prison—how did they manage it? Who helped them? What do they know that re-offenders don't? And why is the story of those who left prison with their humanity intact, or somehow recovered, so seldom told?

Lisa Finateri directs me to four men who have done serious time in prison. One is retired, one works with an employment service, one runs a publishing enterprise from his home and one works with the developmentally challenged. The men range in age from their twenties to their seventies, each is bright, and each has a different take on prison life and the keys to successful reintegration. But on two points they all agree: first, a small act of kindness inside a prison has enormous power and resonance and is never forgotten; and second, change will only happen if an individual prisoner has the will to change and someone who believes in him.

Gil was the oldest former inmate on my list. Most of Gil's friends have no idea he spent five years in Kingston Penitentiary. A thoughtful, soft-spoken man with a heavily lined face, he got out nine years ago and now leads a quiet life walking, biking and reading.

Sometimes, through the John Howard Society, he gives talks in Kingston high schools. The question the students all want answered is, What's it like inside? "I tell them exactly what it's like," Gil says. "I tell them about the rapes, especially of the young. I tell them that going in with a Mr. Tough Guy attitude doesn't cut it in prison because there's always someone tougher."

Several months before Gil got out, he heard about the local John Howard Society through the prison chaplain. Jack Wilson, JHSK's longest-serving staffer with sixteen years of experience, met Gil at the doors of Kingston Pen on the day of his release. Jack helped Gil find a place to live, open a bank account and buy used furniture. Later he visited Gil when consecutive heart attacks put him in hospital. "Jack has helped me in so many ways," says Gil. "Without his help, I would have been lost."

Some of the former inmates I talk to have little good to say about prison, but not Gil. "One thing I learned in prison," he says, "is empathy." A psychologist put Gil and others through a program that taught them to consider the victims of their crimes, the habits that lead to crime and "how to break the cycle," as Gil puts it.

We sit in a Princess Street café while Gil dismantles his Styrofoam coffee cup by degrees and stares out to the street as he delivers some hard truths about prison. "Some offenders have a conscience, some don't," he says. "A lot of guys go to these programs and pull the wool over the eyes of the psychologists and laugh like hell behind their backs." But some guys do change. The challenge is to decide who is genuine and who is not.

The second man I talk to, a man I will call Jerome, did twenty-two years in prison before being released nine years ago. He credits two people with helping him achieve his remarkable turnaround: an unusual psychologist named Louisa Gembora (she's also a race car driver and one of the judges on the reality TV show *Canada's Worst Driver*) and a prison guard who discreetly took a shine to him.

Dr. Gembora urged Jerome to write down four ambitions and challenged him to achieve them. He had always wanted an education (his schooling had ended in grade 7). He had always wanted to be a musician. He had always wanted to excel in sports. And he had always wanted to work with mentally handicapped people.

"I achieved them all," says Jerome. He got a degree from Queen's, mastered the guitar, learned to play and coach several sports and now works with mentally challenged adults. "I love my job," he says. "I feel like a rock star. They start screaming when they see me coming." He helps his clients with every aspect of their lives, from cooking and laundry to day trips and bathing. Jerome got the job, in part, because he had participated for many years at the Collins Bay Olympiad for challenged people held every July. An agency took a chance on him and now they are glad they did.

The other agent for change in Jerome's life inside was a guard. He would escort Jerome to hospital when that was necessary, and afterwards the guard would park the bus behind the hospital and they would share a meal of Kentucky Fried Chicken. "Totally unheard of," says Jerome, who has little good to say about guards otherwise. "Getting my education was such a struggle inside. Anything of benefit, they make it hard. Corrections Canada don't want to correct you. They'd be out of a job."

But when Jerome was released from prison, this guard did something that, if known, might have landed him in serious trouble with his colleagues. He gave Jerome his telephone number and said, "If you ever need anything, call me." The two men had an understanding, one that I sense is rare in jail.

When the guard died, Jerome thought about going to his funeral but he knew his presence would have antagonized some there. "It's still us versus them," as Jerome puts it. But later, he went to the gravesite and poured a beer on the ground. The guard apparently had a fondness for ale.

When I update her on Jerome's life, Dr. Gembora says, "I am not surprised he's doing so well. There were certain inmates I expected more of. They had the ability to engage in psychological insight. Past behaviour is not a predictor of future behaviour. Some inmates want to create a new future and are willing to pay what it takes. Maybe they need someone who believes they can do it. A volunteer in a prison can have that same impact."

Dr. Gembora recalls doing a psychological assessment on a prisoner who was a hit man most of his life. "I remember his cold, dead eyes; he was a blue-eyed killer. The next time I met him was eight years later and he had come into the halfway house at Portsmouth for counselling. He was married, had a young child and was working in a garage in Gananoque. I was blown away. That man had once scared me, but something had moved him. Anything is possible and we may not know what that is. A small act of kindness can ignite the soul."

I meet the third ex-offender, Thomas, at his home in the north end. The phone is ringing when I walk in (he operates a home-based publishing business with several others) and he seems harried. "Another day in paradise," he says, as he motions me in and deals with two phone calls before plunking himself down on the couch. But then he says this: "I could be flat broke and I'd be happy. I am so grateful to be where I am."

Thomas, who served nine years in prison, has an astonishing memory. He can provide precise dates for every event in his life and he peppers his story with them. His is a tale with twists and turns and setbacks and yet, there he sits, beaming. "I've been clean for twenty-eight months and one week. I'm very proud of myself and I'm very proud of what I've accomplished."

Thomas's drug of choice on the street was cocaine; inside, it was marijuana. There was no violence in his history. He simply stole to pay for his drug habit. A substance abuse program in prison did him no good. "It didn't stop my addiction to pot," he says. "I sometimes went to the group meetings high."

A couple of things saved him. Thomas had the good fortune to be assigned a parole officer who saw something in him and who recommended him for the minimum-security institution at Frontenac, where he worked in the apple orchards of Adolphustown on escorted day passes.

Then a friend enticed him to join a Narcotics Anonymous program run out of the Correctional Staff College on Union Street. "Come on," the pal cajoled him. "Free coffee, pretty girls." It was six meetings before Thomas said a word, after which someone handed him a pamphlet called "Staying Clean on the Outside." The next day, back in his cell, he read the pamphlet and started to cry.

"Why?" I ask him.

"Because I had had enough."

Later, Thomas read a book published by Narcotics Anonymous and in it a story called "Alien" that also left him weeping. "'Alien,'" he said, "was about me. It was about drug use and disconnection. Prison is an incredibly lonely, very disturbed environment. There's no trust, it's cold and dark and hostile. Whoever has drugs has power. I never met anybody I liked. So I turned inwards—to drugs."

After his release, Thomas pitched and rolled from one awful job to the next: telemarketer, door-to-door salesman for a phone company (a job at which he excelled), coffeeshop baker, telephone surveyor. His real break came when Lisa Finateri hired him as a receptionist for six months. "John Howard," says Thomas, "has been kicked in the teeth by so many people they've tried to help. But they continue to help."

Not everyone is sympathetic to ex-offenders or those who assist them. I'm told that the United Way regularly receives cheques from individuals who include instructions that the funds are to be given to any agency except the John Howard Society.

Last on my list is Ryan, a very smart, very eloquent young man. He now works with an employment counselling service and is three-quarters of the way into a commerce degree at Queen's. Lisa Finateri remembers this about him when he was inside: "He was the only prisoner I ever interviewed who was shackled, even after I objected." Ryan had caused a fuss, to put it mildly, and the guards had responded. He was a long time shaking his reputation.

Ryan did ten hard years after the usual downward spiral: family problems, alcohol, drugs, bad company and crime. His defining moment came in 2003 when he was twenty-two years old. "I got lost in the system," he says. "I lost myself. There is a very small amount of rehabilitation in prison. There are programs, but the staff is inadequately trained. Sometimes they are guards as well, so they have that prison-guard mentality. So I escaped into drugs and alcohol." But one day he said to himself, "There has to be more to life than this."

Ryan had several advantages to draw on. One was that even in grade 7, when he dropped out of school, he could read at a grade 12 level. Ryan decided to pursue his high school diploma, then he got accepted into Queen's. But staff inside never believed him when he insisted he was bent on change. He would order books and they would sit on a unit manager's desk for three and four weeks. "The system," says Ryan, "fought me tooth and nail."

He has come to certain conclusions about what's required for a convict to change, for the leopard to perform that magic trick of changing his spots. "What inmates need," says Ryan, "is someone to believe in them."

"Don't judge," he pleads. "Don't write people off. Make room for those who want to change. The proof is in the pudding. If a guy is going to school, talk to his teacher. Is the student enthusiastic? Don't automatically assume he's lying. Let him prove himself."

As I leave him, Ryan asks me if I have read *Crime and Punishment* by the nineteenth-century Russian novelist Fyodor Dostoevsky. Of course, it's a masterpiece, one of my favourites. Ryan's too.

IN THE several weeks that I spend with John Howard Society personnel, with prisoners and former prisoners, I gather strong impressions. The first of these is that guards and convicts walk a kind of tightrope. A convict who spends too much time talking to a guard risks being labelled a snitch, whereupon the shanks come out. A guard who shows ordinary sympathy to a convict risks the ire of other guards who may have little or no sympathy. But when a guard, say, escorts a prisoner outside the institution (to hospital, for example), those rules sometimes go out the window.

The other is that what the released prisoner needs first and foremost is a friend. This person cannot be from his old circle, and must be reliable and trustworthy and have his best interests at heart. For several of the men I have interviewed, the man waiting for them when the prison door closed behind them was Jack Wilson, an "intake worker" with the John Howard Society.

"There's no easy explanation of what I do," Wilson says. "What I do, no one else does."

His office in the Society's Montreal Street facility looks like a collection depot for a yard sale. There are blankets and bedding stacked on shelves, a small collection of ball caps, an assortment of glasses, mugs and kitchen utensils. You never know when a fellow is going to need help setting up his first apartment.

But Wilson's real value to the man entering the community after a long period in jail is not the stuff in his office but the stuff in his head. "I know the system as well as anyone," Wilson says. "I know what an ex-offender's rights are. And I'm pretty good at what I do."

Jack Wilson sees more than a thousand clients a year. He laments that JHSK no longer has the high profile it used to have in prisons and he wishes it had the budget to hire more institutional/intake workers like him. "It all comes down to funding," he says. The Society once employed one worker to serve each prison in the Kingston area; now one part-time worker must cover all nine.

Jack Wilson has some empathy for guards and he concedes that a few prisoners are simply rotten and beyond rehabilitation. But it's wrong, he says, to make sweeping generalizations about men in prison.

"If you tie up a dog in the backyard and leave him, what have you got?"

"An angry dog," I reply.

"A *very* angry dog," he says.

For a convict to change—or so my modest survey suggests—he needs someone to have faith in him, and he needs to be rewarded for positive behaviour. It's a tenet from the world of horses, one I know something about. The wise trainer will tell every rider: "Reward every effort, no matter how small."

JULY 3. My prison volunteer stint meant for June has spilled over into July. Today, I am working with Krista, JHSK's volunteer coordinator, and Lisa Finateri on the six-page newsletter (in the end, sedately titled *Community Connections*). Krista, the crackerjack, soon has a draft ready for me. It looks good. I will go in later with Ulrike, a former magazine art director, with suggestions for improving the design.

JULY 19. Every year for thirty-two years, Collins Bay Institution hosts an Olympiad for developmentally challenged adults.

"It's extraordinary," one volunteer tells me. "The Olympiad humanizes two dehumanized populations—challenged adults and federal inmates."

The idea is quite simple. Each athlete is paired with a prisoner, a so-called god-brother, who is responsible for getting that athlete to each competition site on the grounds, for keeping him or her hydrated in the hot treeless yard, and for offering encouragement and tips. As a volunteer with the Society, I somehow find myself as the starter, armed with a megaphone, for the fifty-metre and one-hundred-metre dashes. My job is to shout each runner's name to the timers down the lane, to announce the "class" (A, B or C, according to the sprinter's level of coordination) and, of course, to start each race.

The athletes have come from Toronto, Ottawa and southeastern Ontario. Some have Down's syndrome, some are autistic, some deaf, and all are challenged. They come in all shapes and sizes but I am struck by their almost universal pre-race cool and ready humour.

One athlete, just seconds before his heat, leans over to the runner in the next lane and says, "I'm gonna smoke you." And all the nearby god-brothers—the ones with the blue tattoos and the brown Corrections Canada T-shirts—roar their approval. "That's it," one says. "Intimidate the opposition."

Another runner, when asked his name, says "Michael," then adds impishly, "The Vicious." So I shout into my megaphone, "Michael ... The Vicious."

Some runners shuffle, some waddle, some are possessed of astonishing speed. But every single runner gets the same shouts of encouragement from the inmates, athletes and volunteers lined up along the length of the four-lane track. There are high-fives exuberantly delivered, there are ribbons worn with pride, and smiles all around.

I shake the hand of Madelaine, an athlete from Ottawa who has been coming to the Olympiad, with only a few misses, for thirty-one years. Across her chest are half a dozen red and blue ribbons. "I never think about losing," she says with a grin.

I also enjoy a memorable lunch in the company of John Ross Matheson, a judge for twenty-five years and a regular at these games. Judge Matheson has been dubbed the Father of the Canadian Flag for the critical role he played in the adoption of the maple leaf flag forty-four years ago. Almost ninety-one, and in a wheelchair with a small Canadian flag atop a pole at the back, this man who helped create the Order of Canada has the revolutionary idea of initiating a new order. Named after the mythological bird that would be consumed by fire then rise again from the ashes, the Order of the Phoenix would recognize individuals who have turned their lives around after serving hard time.

We live in a society, the judge tells me, that favours the rich, the gifted, the lucky. "What about the losers?"

No losers at the Olympiad. Not a one.

MY GOING into the prisons as a volunteer got off to a rocky start, and I can't say that the demons disinterred then were entirely laid to rest by the end. I don't think I would ever get used to the sniffer dogs or the crackling tension that seemed so palpable and pervasive in a place like Collins Bay.

And yet I remember sitting on the stage of its gym, my legs over the side, and talking to a young black man who told me he had once played varsity football at the University of Toronto. I didn't ask about his circumstances, but he offered them nonetheless. Being in the wrong place at the wrong time when a drug deal went sour explained why he was inside. This was his version of events, of course, but he had no reason to lie to me and nothing to gain. Later in the day our paths crossed again, under the sun this time. We talked about hockey and literature, then he went his way and I went mine.

What I take from my time inside is that as bad as prisons are, and as bad as some of its denizens are, it is possible to endure years and decades of such places and come out the other side with one's humanity intact. Think of Nelson Mandela and his twenty-seven years in prison.

I had the sense that what convicts crave is what street people in San José and Kingston and Toronto crave and are almost consistently denied: a little respect. The scary skinny guy at Millhaven is very real, as real as a ticking time bomb. But so are Jerome and Ryan and Thomas and Gil—survivors all. I left with a little more hope than when I went in, not because I became convinced that prison time "corrects" offenders but because I saw reminders that the human spirit has resilience.

"People who do bad things," says Lisa Finateri, "are still people, and no person should be defined by his or her worst act."

·   ·   ·

[**MOTHER ANTONIA**]

THERE IS volunteering in prisons, and then there is Mary Clarke. Now in her early eighties, she has lived for more than thirty years inside a Mexican prison near Tijuana, working to alleviate the suffering of prisoners. This twice-divorced mother of seven sold all her possessions, sewed up a nun's habit (the kind nuns used to wear), called herself Mother Antonia and took up residence in a jail cell. She literally reinvented herself as a nun, with a very specific calling.

"Charity is not a thing you do," she told Mary Jordan and Kevin Sullivan, two Pulitzer Prize–winning journalists who wrote a book about her (*The Prison Angel,* published in 2005). "It's love. It's who you become."

Mary Clarke raised her children in Beverly Hills, California— the signature address of the beautiful people—but was always ambitious in her charitable work. She used to send clothes, medicine and supplies to developing countries by convincing ship captains to transport the stuff for free. But as she explained to her biographers, "I had always been an outsider to suffering all my life. I had been on the outside helping people on the inside, whether it was Africa or Bolivia or anywhere else."

Few of us hear the call as this woman did, but the notion of *inside* and *outside* is a useful one. Maybe that's the lesson. We have to literally get inside to make a difference and to receive the benefit. Meaningful, hands-on engagement over time in a cause you believe in comes with rewards. Ask Mary Clarke/ Mother Antonia. "I have not been depressed one day," she says. "Perhaps sad, but *never* depressed."

OFF
to Summer Camp

JULY 4. The first thing I do is count the animals. Dare to Dream, the therapeutic riding program run out of Charmaine Green's modest thirty-five-hectare farm northeast of Belleville in southeastern Ontario, is a Noah's Ark of rescued, stray, adopted and sometimes wayward creatures. Many, it seems, have found their way here by instinct.

Take Wilbur the Pig, for instance. When just a piglet, he escaped the farm next door and would neither be caught nor enticed back home. He stayed in Charmaine's woods for a month, living on who knows what and managing to stay clear of the coyotes, then befriended the horses in her paddock. By this time, the neighbour had cut his losses. Wilbur—today a formidable three-hundred-kilo boar but quite tame—lives with one of Charmaine's horses in what she calls "the bad boy field."

Wilbur shares the field with a stud named Prince. Like Wilbur, the stallion is an escape artist, given to crawling under fences in order to visit the mares. Wilbur has his own little bunk behind the paddock's run-in.

It is not unusual, says Charmaine, to see both Wilbur and Prince "lying down together sharing a moment in the sun, though I'm not sure Prince is keen on Wilbur constantly walking away from the bale with hay in his mouth to bed down his nest. And when the hay is low, Prince just starts eating Wilbur's bed."

I look on as Charmaine strokes Wilbur's back over the fence and the tall white hairs on his wide pink back fly this way and that while he grunts in delight. Then Charmaine hoses him down to cool him off on this hot bright day and lets the hose run long enough in the dirt to make the mud he uses as all-purpose sunscreen and bug repellent. Wilbur's own little wallow.

"Will he ever be bacon?" I ask.

"Oh no," she replies, mildly indignant. You don't eat pets.

The first creature I encountered when I knocked on Charmaine's front door that morning was a tawny rabbit in a cage on the porch. Welcomed in by her eighteen-year-old daughter, Victoria, I noticed, on my right, a leopard gecko in a heated aquarium and, next to it, a white dove in a cage. A chinchilla occupied a crate by the couch. There were three dogs inside the house, Lucky, Duchess and MC (for Mixed Chocolate—he was born Easter morning), and four more outside, several cats (the number shifts from day to day), fourteen horses and six ducks. Two raccoons, I was told, had only recently vacated.

Charmaine's house reminds me very much of Maria Meyering's house. Maria, her husband, Willy, and their daughter, Tiny, ran Wilmarny Farm (a name that paid small homage to each of their names), just south of the village of Camden East. I learned to ride at Wilmarny in my late thirties. Both Charmaine and Maria value horses and tack more than homes and gardens. With women such as these (and it must be said, the horse-mad are far more likely to be female than male), bits and bridles invariably make inroads into the house. On Charmaine's wrought-iron banister by the stairs hang various saddles and halters, lead ropes and saddle pads. Visitors are invited to keep their shoes on.

Charmaine has long, thick strawberry blonde hair which she usually keeps in a braid. Her smile is not the muted, tight-lipped variety but more the kind you see on toothpaste commercials, testimony to her upbeat manner. I have the sense that it would take a lot to rattle her. Some of her horses, like some of her clients, have tested and defeated others. "I am told," she says, "that I have a lot of patience."

She grew up in Mississauga, just west of Toronto, and parlayed her love for animals into equine studies at Humber College. She earned her Level 1 coaching certificate and competed in dressage and show jumping on the Trillium circuit (a series of competitions sanctioned by the Ontario Equestrian Federation) before taking a job as a groom and hot walker at Woodbine Racetrack in 1987. It was there she met the man who would become her husband, Shawn Green.

"Shawn," she explains, "rode pigs on his father's farm and he discovered he had a gift for riding. He fulfilled his dream. He became an exercise rider and pony boy at the track. But he broke his back several times riding, then he had a horse flip over on him. Then he broke his neck and back on the stairs here." Today, Shawn has regained some of his ability to walk but he suffers from chronic pain.

Charmaine and her fifteen-year-old son, Christopher, and daughter Victoria run the farm on York Road with Shawn's help. Like many in this rural area, Charmaine pays the bills in a variety of ways: she gives riding lessons, trains, sells and boards horses, works in a store part-time and does a little commissioned art on the side. Shawn is a First Nations man and the farm is set in the Tyendinaga Mohawk Territory, where there is a market for Charmaine's art: nature scenes, horse paintings, totemic creatures painted on warrior shields, and even— by special request—wolves painted on a man's prosthetic leg.

"That is so gross," Victoria declares when the plastic foot plus lower leg is brought out from a back room.

"This man loves wolves," says Charmaine, "so that's what he got."

IN 2004, Green's Dream Stable, as she calls her horse farm, took on a new clientele when the Dare to Dream Therapeutic Riding Program came into being.

"It was a result," says Charmaine, "of Shawn getting hurt and the emotional, physical and financial stress that was inflicted on the family. I saw how limited our systems are and how many people fall through the cracks due to technicalities and end up not getting help. I began the Dare to Dream program to give other people an outlet from life's stress."

Horses had always been an integral part of her life, but when Shawn got hurt, again, and the system failed them, yet again, she says, "I turned to my horses to help me through this troubled time of my life and my family's life."

To her regular list of able-bodied student riders, Charmaine now added riders seven and up who are deaf or blind, autistic or learning disabled, or coping with an array of physical or mental challenges. Whatever hand we've been dealt doesn't change the fact that it feels good to be up on a horse. Yes, you may ask, but isn't riding a horse dangerous, and surely doubly so for someone not in full command of his or her faculties?

This is the extraordinary thing. Not all horses make allowances for disabled riders, but many do. I remember interviewing a young equestrian with cerebral palsy. When she was in the saddle, the gelding was invariably kind and soft and did precisely as he was told. But when her instructor got on him, his inner bucking-bronco self was revealed.

Therapeutic riding, or hippotherapy as some call it (*hippos* being the Greek word for horse) dates from ancient times when soldiers wounded in war would be put on the back of a horse as therapy. The motion of a walking horse soothes and stimulates a wide variety of muscles in the rider; the view isn't bad either. According to CanTRA, the Canadian Therapeutic Riding Association, the modern version of therapeutic riding was launched in 1952, when a Danish rider with a history of polio won a silver medal in dressage at the Helsinki Olympic Games. Therapists working with disabled people began to seriously ponder the benefits—both physical and psychological—of putting the handicapped on horses.

The North American Riding for the Handicapped Association now lists almost eight hundred therapeutic riding centres in the U.S. and Canada serving more than 42,000 riders, but countless more small or unaffiliated programs, like Charmaine's, do the same work. Dare to Dream operates under the umbrella of CanTRA, a provisional arrangement until Charmaine earns her certification as an instuctor formally trained to work with disabled riders. For now, she relies on instinct and common sense, gaining expertise as she goes.

A talent for picking and training the right horses for the delicate task of teaching these special riders came to her naturally. Depending on the type of handicap, an able-bodied volunteer may be needed to help out, and that person's selection too is carefully considered. High school students fulfilling their obligation to perform community service eagerly sign up, as do college students studying sociology or specialized health care. Young people who have had a brush with the law and need hours of community work to fulfill their terms of release are also candidates.

Dare to Dream is non-profit, which means that Charmaine keeps separate ledgers for that part of her income. She also relies heavily on other help to keep the program viable. Canadian Saddlery, for example, donates helmets and paddock boots on a regular basis.

Many would argue that the traditional horse business—giving lessons to able-bodied riders, and raising, training and boarding horses—is also a non-profit enterprise by definition. "Horse poor" is a familiar expression that hints at the way horses can swallow dollars. Vet bills, farrier bills, the cost of grain and hay, the amount of time required to teach a horse manners, to train and maintain that horse, the expense of bridles and bits, saddles and boots, stall bedding, fencing and indoor arenas—there are many ways to lose your shirt in the horse business. And because Charmaine lives in the Mohawk Territory, where incomes are typically low, she keeps her rates low. Summer camp for one child is $200 a week; riding lessons are $35 an hour, $25 for half an hour. These are bargain prices.

JULY 11. For two weeks in July, I'll be a farmhand at Charmaine's day camp. The average age of these students is twelve, and I've written four books for readers that age so I will suggest that during a quiet time at the end of the day I might read to them.

In essence, my job is to do what I can to make Charmaine's various tasks a little easier. On day one, I remove the hinges from a fence post that broke off at ground level when a horse— probably trying to avoid another horse higher up in the herd hierarchy—sideswiped it. I ride a nineteen-year-old Thoroughbred called Jake who needs some light exercise. I lead a horse called Mr. Romance while Kay rides him and Charmaine instructs. The idea is that the rider has control of the horse through the reins, but my lead rope offers extra insurance should the horse spook or bolt.

Kay is a sixty-year-old woman who suffered severe brain damage in a car accident and now walks gingerly with a cane, but who nonetheless wants to learn how to ride a horse. Dressed in blue jeans and a long-sleeved white shirt, she tends to look down more than up, but there's nothing downcast about her spirit. After a winter off, she is keen to get back in the saddle.

Kay is the most polite rider I have ever encountered, and when I tell her so as we make our circuit over the sand-and-wood-chips ring, counter clockwise and then clockwise, she smiles broadly. Instructed to steer Mr. Romance, a flea-bitten Polish-Arabian grey, around orange cones, she first formally asks him to go forwards. Instructed to rise into a posting trot, Kay again asks the horse and thanks him when he complies. It is the same with the halt. At the dismount (onto an elevated ramp built especially for riders with mobility problems), she thanks Mr. Romance for standing so still and gives him a hug. She cannot stop smiling.

Some of Charmaine's students have behavioural problems, like the blind boy who used to habitually explode in anger at loud noises—until he could be persuaded over time to accept them peaceably. The same patience that guides her work with horses is usefully applied to her Dare to Dream students.

"I remember," says Charmaine, "when a deaf woman took her first lesson here. Afterwards, she went right to the van and I thought, 'Did she have a bad time?' Two or three lessons later, when she started trotting, there was this huge change in her facial expression." She had discovered what Kay has discovered—that there's nothing quite like being on the back of a horse.

JULY 14. I am, once more, a kid at summer camp, though "horse camp" is more accurate. Work on and around horses occupies the morning, starting at 9 a.m. Then lunch, crafts in the afternoon, then more horse stuff (lessons on parts of the horse's body, the colours of horses, basic horse care, and the names of all the equipment used in riding). At 4 p.m., we call it a day.

The camp will have more attendees next week, but this week there are only four: a local boy named Maverick; a girl called Willow who is visiting her grandparents; her cousin, Allen; and Cale, a fourteen-year-old autistic boy who is keen to ride. In fact, he rode all winter at the farm, braving cold and snow. "At first," says Charmaine, "his mother had to bribe him to come. Now he's the first one ready to go. In the beginning, his parents wouldn't allow him any control of the horse, and now he's doing a posting trot. I can't believe the difference."

I stand by Cale several times during the day as he pats a horse, and each time this non-verbal child issues a kind of guttural cry of glee. The pleasure is mutual. The horse, that handsome bay called Prince, is glad of the attention: Cale is unfailingly gentle, even when running his hands over the horse's eyes. And the boy seems utterly thrilled to be communicating with this powerful animal through touch.

I have read about autistic people, Temple Grandin, for one. I know Oliver Sacks's *New Yorker* essay about her and have read one of her own books, *Animals in Translation*. I know about the "squeeze machine" she invented that desensitized her to human touch and allowed her to function, more or less normally, at Colorado State University, where she teaches animal science. I know too that she invented "the stairway to heaven"—a radical adjustment to abattoirs that makes the killing of cattle at slaughter somewhat more humane.

Autistic people often see things that we do not, and what Temple Grandin observed was that cattle going to their maker were alarmed, even terrified, by the lowing of other cattle and the smell of blood. In those days, the ramps were long lines that led—well, we know and cattle know where those lines lead. Grandin's gift was to make the route to the sweet hereafter a circular one. Cattle take comfort in circling, so Grandin suggested to the abattoir managers that if they allowed the animals to circle as they moved towards their inevitable fate, they would be more relaxed, less stressed, and their meat would be more tender. Reading about the butchering of animals in factory abattoirs is very unsettling; Temple Grandin has raised the ethical bar, at least a little.

What Cale offers me is a reminder of the pure joy that comes from stroking a creature. He loves cats, loves dogs too. His sign for dog, two quick pats of the hand on the hip, is one he gives often. I know from experience that brushing or petting a horse relaxes us, makes us feel good to be alive.

At Dare to Dream, there is no barn, no stalls. The horses are turned out twenty-four hours a day, with shelters in the field offering shade in summer and protection from the wind in winter. This arrangement is ideal for horses, and it also means that the entire herd is in plain view. I'm one of those people who believe that seeing horses graze, watching them play with each other and groom each other is a deep source of contentment. At Charmaine's camp, during the lunch break, there are always one or two of us leaning on the fence stroking a horse's head or plying him with handfuls of tall grass from our side of the fence. The interaction with the farm's horses, dogs and cats was near constant; even the ducks and chickens had our attention.

It struck me too that my stint volunteering in prisons, where I heard about farm work as a form of therapy for inmates, had led naturally to my work at this family farm. In both cases, people on the fringe were benefitting from the company of animals.

CALE WALKS stiffly and unsteadily, his feet wide apart. He understands everything he is told, and when asked if he wants to ride, he smiles and nods eagerly, an unmistakable "Oh yeah!" I learn that Cale loves Mr. Bean, the bagpipes and computer games, that he has a formidable memory and that he hopes one day to ride Wilbur the Pig.

Cale's helper, an educational assistant named Ron who has known Cale since he was in kindergarten, jokes that his charge should run for political office. People with autism engage in repeated behaviours, crave predictability in their lives and balk at change. Cale's ritual is the handshake, which he offers while gritting his teeth and thrusting out his jaw, what Ron calls his "tough guy routine." Cale this day shakes my hand about forty times—when he gets distracted, when the day grows long, when he feels he needs the comfort of a familiar gesture. I imagine him to be saying, "Welcome to my world."

JULY 15. The days at Dare to Dream are falling into a pattern. Eleven-year-old Maverick, who is fearless on a horse and a bit of a rascal, calls out to me the second I pull in the driveway and asks to borrow my riding helmet. It offers a better fit than any of Charmaine's. I help the riders tack up the horses—Dusty, the black Newfoundland pony; Mr. Romance and Dewey, the Polish-Arabian greys; and Jake, the old bay Thoroughbred. Then it's mounting and, later, once more cleaning horses' hooves. Poop needs scooping as the lessons unfold.

Charmaine issues encouraging instruction while Christopher and Victoria and I guide the horses by their bridles when they go into trots. I might swat nasty biting flies for the benefit of the horse and offer my own two cents to the riders. All those years of lessons have taught me about the need for heels to sink into stirrups, about quiet placement of the hands, about when to insist with a horse and when to leave him be.

There's an art to being a volunteer here. Most important, I think, is to anticipate. Charmaine seems to glide through her duties, but she does have four riders, four horses and three volunteers to keep in mind. At one point in the day, I open the four-string, 1.5-metre-high electrical fence separating the riding ring from the lawn in front of the house. This will allow the horses some time to graze the fresh grass, a reward for their work under saddle. I then give a horse on a lead shank to a young rider to hold, forgetting that the rider doesn't know about the need to keep the rope clear of the horse's feet. Charmaine—without ever raising her voice—is striding to the house, but she tells the student as she passes to lift the rope and why.

YESTERDAY I helped Shawn fix fences. Charmaine's husband is a tawny-brown, sinewy, jockey-sized man who drags his right foot as if a twenty-kilogram weight were attached to it. The fractures in his back and neck mean that he has no feeling in his hands, and when I helped him drive a bolt-hinge into a fence post I suggested that using a wrench might be easier on his fingers.

"Last year," he replied, "I was cutting wood with Christopher and he had to tell me that the axe had gone into my leg. I didn't feel it." So he turned that bolt with his hands, centimetre by painless centimetre. Despite its sharp point and thread, the bolt refused at first to bite into the wood and so Shawn and

I took turns, one turning the wrench to drive the bolt, the other hammering the bolt from the side. Our joke was that maybe I should be the one to wield the hammer. I could hit him and he would feel nothing.

After an hour of struggle under a merciless sun, after two broken drill bits, we finally had two hinges embedded solidly in the wood and lifted the gate into place. It felt good to see the gate swing freely and whisper quiet, as it should.

JULY 17. Hot, muggy weather settles over the farm. Old Jake, who is allergic to dust, begins to heave at his belly and struggle for air. His flaring nostrils tell the tale. His rider, Willow, is quite content to run the hose over him (and me, after her aim wanders), to squeegee him dry and then to hold his lead rope as he snacks on Charmaine's lawn. She scouts for horseflies on one side of Jake, while I do the same on the other. When she grows bored of all this swatting, Willow excuses herself and goes to sit down with Nanna, the border collie.

Heaven, for Willow, is lying on the grass in the company of dogs and cats. One young dog, a yellow Lab called Whiskey, folds into her and collapses into a boneless heap at her touch. Cale likewise reaches out to the cats and the dogs, though he becomes anxious when they get too close to his face. At lunch, the kids and I gather at a picnic table under the oak.

Often, once his sizeable lunch has been dispatched, Cale will turn to me for another handshake. One day, I grab the other hand too and slowly begin to rock our linked hands back and forth while singing "Row, Row, Row Your Boat." A look of surprise and joy comes over his face. Then I quite suddenly turn the melody frenetic and my hands start to pump his as if I am maniacally sawing a log, and he laughs heartily at this game. It becomes a new and regular ritual between us.

Cale is not much for crafts in the afternoon (I'm with him on that), nor for games to teach the parts of the horse's body or the basics of the bridle and saddle. What matters is real contact with a horse, the perspective from up there, feeling the wind on your face when the trot picks up, communicating and controlling a creature that weighs ten times what you do but that is, more often than not, agreeable to your wishes and commands.

JULY 21. It's not all a bed of roses. In week 2 we are joined by Allen's cousins from Connecticut, Haley and Zoey, and a boy called Nate. The girls are the daughters of school teachers and they come every summer to see their grandmother who lives not far from the stable. They are thrilled to ride, content to brush and sponge and feed the horses assigned to them. Horse campers to the bone.

Nate, though, sometimes displays frustrations. He's nine years old, but owing to a rare disorder, has the mental capacity of a five-year-old. Watchful and independent, he's not keen to be the only rider here with a minder. That would be me.

Every day he rides Dusty, the Newfoundland pony who has been many times around the paddock. I'm the pony's "emergency brake," as Charmaine puts it. Nate has the reins, but I have the lead rope. When the pony goes into a trot, I run alongside and Dusty makes little biting tries at my hand. In the horse world, ponies are the brats, the imps, the troublemakers.

A friend of mine in Florida is a trick-horse trainer, and she used to take her travelling circus to schools and fairs. Horses and miniature horses worked together in her show, but one time during a performance a miniature horse—a stallion— slipped under his bigger counterpart and bit him in his privates. In equines, courage and size have nothing to do with each other, and ponies are notoriously Napoleonic and prone to mischief. Thus the precautions with Dusty and Nate.

"I can do it by myself," Nate insists. He tests our patience, but we get through the lesson by old methods. Encourage, divert, encourage some more. What works with horses works with humans.

"What's Dusty's bit called?" I ask Nate, who keeps calling it a "mackawhore." I tease him, tell him that "hackamore" is the password, and that if he forgets it he will have to spend the night in the ring where he and the others ride each morning. Nate doesn't mind being teased. He learns that word and retains it, a small victory. He can even spell it, and is proud of that. We work from there.

By lunch time, all the edge has gone from him. Nate is playing with the pups, filling their water pails, topping up the horse troughs, getting soaked, having a ball.

CHARMAINE'S FARRIER needs a hand trimming the horses. Of trimming, I know nothing except what I have gleaned by watching my various farriers over the past decade. It can be a risky business. My job is to hold the horse's head, keep him calm, talk to him. The farrier has the hard part.

Hold the foot upside-down. Trim the foot with a sharp hoof knife. Use a heavy metal rasp to file the bottom, then file the top and sides. What works with Nate works with Story, their gorgeous Arab-Morgan-Paint. When his head comes up and he goes a little wide-eyed, I tell him what a good boy he is, stroke his muzzle, try to take some of his weight when he starts to lean. Sometimes the farrier punctuates a hoof trim by falling to the ground, he's that exhausted. The other day when it was hotter and he was trimming Jake's feet, the sweat came off him like rain from a leaky eavestrough.

The farrier and I will do another horse tomorrow and another the day following. Before I leave, Charmaine thanks me as she always does, then compliments me on my work with Nate.

"He can be a handful," I acknowledge.

Charmaine sets an admirable example. She fully understands Nate's circumstances yet she still asks that he become a better rider. She expects him not to cross his reins over the horse's neck, to keep his heels down, to sit the trot. And Nate, in his black hockey helmet and brush cut, gradually backs off from his insistence that he knows everything, that he needs no help.

JULY 23. It's a long drive, forty-five minutes on Highway 401, from my place to Charmaine's. There is time to think, to make connections, maybe to draw some conclusions. As I drive east, I ponder two quite disparate items I have read in the past twenty-four hours.

One is a piece by Elizabeth Kolbert in the July 21 *New Yorker,* the issue remembered for its controversial cover depicting then presidential candidate Barack Obama and his wife, Michelle, in the garb of Muslim terrorists. Kolbert's piece is about how the lawn came to be, how it got its start in England early in the eighteenth century, took root in the United States in the mid-nineteenth century and how it eventually gave rise to a $40-billion-a-year industry in the U.S.

According to Kolbert, it all started with a book published in 1841 by Andrew Jackson Downing, of Newburgh, New York, who inherited a nursery from his father. He had notions of the Beautiful and the Perfect, and an expanse of "grass mown into a softness like velvet." Downing's book went through eight editions and sixteen printings and made him famous. One of the men he influenced and encouraged was Frederick Law Olmsted, who would design Central Park with expansive lawns. In 1851, President Millard Fillmore invited Downing to landscape the grounds around the Capitol. The lawn took hold and flourished.

Pretty well everyone in North America would eventually sign on to the same ideal, and a lawn has become both a symbol and a statement. I am a good neighbour, a good citizen, I am reliable; and if I'm not reliable, the weed laws will make sure I think twice about such an insult to the community. We are starting to rethink the environmental costs of lawns, but it will be a long time before lawns disappear entirely, if they ever do.

If we can all sign on to lawnness, might we all sign on to philanthropy? Is there some way that we could signal to our neighbours the particular values and causes we embrace? Many of us have pet charities; surely those charities could be captured in logos imprinted on a flag. The Tibetan word for prayer flag is *lung ta,* and it means "wind horse." The small bright flags, set on vertical or horizontal lines, are meant as blessings, to bring good luck, to cheer the human heart. What if every house were to fly such flags, on the porch, on the front door, and what if those flags were to become topics of ordinary conversation, like the weather or this summer's dandelion crop? What if we tended to others the way we tend to lawns?

JULY 25. Last day at Dare to Dream. I have become fond of the horses at this riding camp. Jake, with his huge bouncy trot and soft eyes. Dewey, who avoids trouble at all costs. Mr. Romance, with his lively walk. Dusty, with a look of resignation that seems at odds with his eagerness when asked to trot and that ever-present promise of naughtiness.

The kids have been a joy to work with. Zoey and Willow are animal-mad girls who have no greater desires than to have a dog or a cat in their laps. Hayley is one of those children—smart, agreeable, quick to smile—whom teachers love to have in their classrooms. Allan is all boy: when I showed him a photograph in one of my books about hockey (me in a team photo), he expressed disappointment that I wasn't the captain or at least an alternate captain. He is kind and patient with everyone, including Nate.

But I can see that life is a struggle for Nate. Fearful of wind and lightning, smart enough to know his limitations and to be angered by them, prone to foul moods, it seems to me that his moments of real joy are rare. This morning offered one such: the riders played knights on horseback, snagging plastic rings on their plastic swords and then dropping them into a net. Nate felt the confidence that comes with accomplishment and a new skill mastered.

Still, there were times in the past week when he almost drained my patience, when his grumpiness just wore me out. I admired his independent streak, but it would have been reckless to give in to his demands that I let go of the lead rope. There was a pattern to our play and a pattern to our battles: he would demand sole control, I would explain that he had control through the reins; he would fold his arms and pout, I would try to cajole him into good humour. He would be happy one minute, sulking the next. I would be gritting my teeth.

This too is part of the deal in volunteering. If you open your heart, leave your nerve endings exposed, you will almost certainly end up taking on someone else's pain. In July there was a lot of lightning. Some nights I would stay at our cabin, only half an hour from Charmaine's farm, and admire the light show illuminating the sky to the southeast, over the lake. And then I thought of Nate in kinder terms. Dusty, our dog, has the same trembling fear of lightning, and there is nothing we can do to calm or reassure her. We just have to wait for the storm to pass.

Charmaine seems to possess a great well of patience and understanding, deeper than mine. With Nate, she simply presents her guidance, offers correction, but never expresses frustration or anger. He receives no more than the others, and she seems to know that this is precisely what Nate wants and needs. To be treated like all the rest.

I BUY everyone pizza from the restaurant nearby and I receive in return a thank-you card signed by all the summer campers and a Belgian chocolate almond bar the size and heft of a book.

Two weeks here have involved some sacrifice on my part: I saw my own horse less, the days often felt long, the ninety-minute commute seemed arduous for someone who normally works out of a home office. But there have been indelible rewards too, not least the satisfaction of working with a smaller, less-well-known enterprise where the impact of one volunteer can be significant.

I am leaving with genuine appreciation of what it takes to operate a riding camp. Youngsters can be casual around horses, walking behind them despite repeated warnings always to let the horses know they are there by talk or touch. Children will run, even after all the Pony Club safety lessons are read to them and the danger of spooking a horse with sudden movement is explained. Kids will let reins or the lead shank drop from the horse's neck to the ground, with the risk of the leather snapping or the horse tripping, then turn away, diverted by something or someone. They will leave a closed gate open, when the rule on all horse farms (almost always) is to leave a gate precisely as you found it. Charmaine's daunting task is to keep her charges motivated, to save them and the horses from harm, to fill the days with memorable riding and stimulating crafts.

On the last day the riders are all given blank white T-shirts and paints to create mementos of their time at the camp, and I still have that image in my head: half a dozen spattered and boldly coloured T-shirts hanging on branches to dry in the hot wind.

By the end of every day, and certainly by the end of two weeks of horse camp, I am both exhausted and exhilarated.

. . .

[NEWMAN'S OWN]

A HOMEMADE salad dressing concocted as a lark one drunken Christmas Eve by actor Paul Newman and a friend has, decades later, morphed into a multinational charitable enterprise, with more than $260 million to date going to the actor's favourite causes, including eight Hole in the Wall Gang summer camps for children with life-threatening illnesses in the U.S., Britain and France.

The first vat of Newman's Own salad dressing was so large that Newman had to use a canoe paddle to stir it, and the plan was to fill old wine bottles with the stuff, cork it and leave it on the doorsteps of neighbours in Westport, Connecticut. One recipient was Martha Stewart, a local caterer who was just then emerging as America's self-appointed homemaker extraordinaire. It was Stewart who convinced Newman to take a bottle to a local supermarket run by Stew Leonard, who ordered "a freight-load."

Newman's Own is now a conglomerate, selling salad dressings, pasta and steak sauces, salsa, popcorn, ice cream and lemonade. Newman's daughter, Nell, manages the organic division, which sells, among other things, chocolate, olive oil, coffee and pet food.

Newman's collaborator that Christmas Eve was the celebrated author, A.E. Hotchner, who published a biography of Ernest Hemingway (*Papa Hemingway*) in 1966. Newman and Hotchner sketched their sometimes hilarious philanthropic adventure in a book called *Shameless Exploitation in Pursuit of the Common Good* (2003).

The original Hole in the Wall Gang camp is in Ashford, Connecticut. The name comes from the movie *Butch Cassidy and the Sundance Kid* (1969), starring Newman and Robert Redford. The Hole-in-the-Wall Pass in Johnson County, Wyoming, served as a base of operations for several outlaw gangs from the late 1860s to the early twentieth century. The canyon was the perfect hideout: remote, easily defended and with a lofty view that gave ample notice of approaching posses. The pass was a refuge, just as Newman's summer camp is a refuge.

Paul Newman, who died of cancer on September 26, 2008, never took acting or the food business too seriously. He was that rare Hollywood actor who adored his wife, actress Joanne Woodward (he once said, famously, "I have steak at home. Why should I go out for hamburger?"), and loathed his own fame. Politically liberal, he noted that being on Richard Nixon's enemies list was the single-greatest honour ever bestowed on him. He was also a world-class car racer and a fine cook.

"I'm like a good cheese," he told *The Guardian* in 2005. "I'm just mouldy enough to be interesting." As for his charitable impulse, he said he was confounded by the stinginess of some people. "I don't think there's anything exceptional or noble in being philanthropic," he said in 2002. "It's the other attitude that confuses me."

DAVID
Versus Goliath

AUGUST 18. The death of Carl Brand in 1956 is recorded in Richard Haskill's diary, a handwritten, large-bound volume that kept a daily record of weather and chores, of cattle bought and sold, the state of crops, all the minutiae of a farmer's life.

One of the oldest bloodlines in the area, the Haskills came from the Boston area to Port Britain, near Port Hope in southeastern Ontario, in 1793 and worked an eighty-hectare farm near the village of Welcome starting in 1796. Richard Haskill's son, Sanford, and Sanford's wife, Helen, still have thirty-two hectares of the original homestead, including an enviable four hundred metres of frontage on Lake Ontario.

A powerful bond linked the Haskills and the Brands, whose tenure here is almost as old as the Haskills' Sanford Haskill, now sixty-three, has a full head of white hair, the bearing of a former athlete (he once played elite hockey) and a penchant for straight talk. He tells me the story as we sit at the kitchen table of his handsome brick house on Haskill Road, and I hold in my hands his father's diary. Carl Brand's death—the terrible manner of it, especially—hangs in the air.

"They were God to me, the Brands," says Sanford, whose fate it was as a boy of thirteen to come across the body. Sanford's father recorded the event dispassionately in his diary: "Carl Brand was very despondent over the pipeline going through the road allowance on his property and committed suicide." There is no mention of the knife he used to accomplish the deed, a knife that Sanford still possesses. "That pipe will be built over my dead body," Carl Brand had apparently told his neighbours. He was right about that.

We can never really know what drives someone to take his own life, and I have no idea what other circumstances may have propelled him to do what he did. We know only that uranium has been processed in the Port Hope area since the 1940s, that the company doing it (formerly called Eldorado, owned and operated by the federal government from 1942 to 1988, and now called Cameco) began dumping radioactive waste at a site in Welcome, and that contaminated leachate from the site fouled nearby creeks and killed Carl Brand's cows. After consulting a lawyer, he was compensated for the loss, but how do you compensate someone when the blow is suffered at some far deeper level and feels irreparable, even ruinous?

Over on Brand Road, just a minute away, is a perfect little board-and-batten house, plunked, it seems, in the middle of a soybean field. Lynne Prower and her husband, Tony, have lived in this house since 1984. An American friend of Lynne's had bought the eighty-hectare piece before her life took another direction, and the friend—a rich and kind-hearted woman— gave Lynne carte blanche to live in the house and to do with the property as she pleased.

In the sunroom that Lynne and Tony built onto the house, Lynne shows me her file on the same issue that irks Sanford Haskill: the ongoing saga of radioactive waste.

"I don't own this house," says Lynne, "and I don't own this land. I'm a steward. I'm acting in defence of this place. I am," and here she pauses for effect and points a finger at me, "a volunteer." She strikes me as bright and single-minded, with lots of gumption and no end of questions.

I have come to visit Lynne Prower and Sanford Haskill with Mark Mattson, president of Lake Ontario Waterkeeper (LOW), an environmental organization marked for August on my volunteering calendar. Joanna Bull, a young law student articling with LOW for a year, accompanies Mark. What has brought us all together is the same thing that apparently led to Carl Brand's death some fifty-three years ago: the despoliation of land and water.

Lynne Prower had a grand plan to erect wind turbines on the land as a means of paying her ever-rising taxes, but, as she puts it, "I've had to put wind aside. I've been sidetracked by water."

Without nature's intervention, Lynne would not be on this mission. Ontario got whacked with snow last winter, and great sheets of ice formed down by the lakeshore where Lynne and Tony invite their visitors to swim in the summer. This spring, when the ice receded and melted, they discovered a black pipe spewing water—and who knows what else—on the shoreline. The entire Port Hope area is more or less a hot zone, with many buildings and even schools built over radioactive waste. Lynne knows the history.

The ice had severed a pipe that had been taking treated radioactive waste from about three kilometres away and dumping it into the lake some three metres out. Now the pipe protruded from the rock and sand on shore, like some giant worm periscoping up for a look-see.

Lynne took photographs of the pipe when it was spewing liquid and she sent water samples to an independent laboratory in nearby Peterborough. The tests showed that water from the pipe was high in uranium, arsenic and radium 226. But "high" is a relative term. The uranium and arsenic levels were five and eleven times higher, respectively, than the interim guidelines set by the province. (Mark Mattson suspects that the record wet summer may, in fact, have diluted the levels of contaminants and that a dry summer would have produced a dramatically higher reading.) However, those measured levels are within standards set by the Canadian Nuclear Safety Commission, the federal agency that oversees nuclear matters.

Joanna Bull explained all this to me beforehand back at LOW's Toronto office and she asked the obvious question. "Surely, when you have two standards, you apply the lower standard?" Apparently not.

Lynne alerted her neighbour, Sanford Haskill, who promptly called his friend, Mark Mattson, who has been working with LOW on the radioactive waste issue around Port Hope for almost two decades. He is a former criminal lawyer and, at forty-six, still young enough to possess an exuberant energy while experienced enough to have gathered some savvy. Mark's advice was that Sanford and Lynne should launch a citizens' complaint (formally called an Application for Investigation) under Ontario's Environmental Bill of Rights (EBR) legislation, and he has invited me along to see how the process works and to meet the principals.

There is tension in the Port Hope area between those like Lynne and Sanford, who give no credence to company or government assurances about radioactive waste, and others who worry about property values declining. Those in the latter camp complain that local environmental concerns are overblown and they wish that Lynne and Sanford and their kind would just shut up. That's not likely.

"It's the first chance we've had," Sanford told me, "to kick these buggers in the stones. A ninety-five-year-old man called me the other day. He used to swim down there [where the pipe now protrudes] and he told me that he phoned the vice-president of Cameco's fuel division and told him to get the hell out of town."

The photograph of the broken pipe, the lab results and a signed and witnessed affidavit—a legal document that Joanna Bull has prepared—will be sent to the Ministry of the Environment. Delivering such a package is not like making a phone call to complain about pollution. Callers can be brushed off, and the complainant may have a devil of a time finding the right person to talk to. This affidavit, however, insists on a formal response and triggers both a process and a timeline that must, by law, be followed.

There is always the chance, Mark tells Lynne over strong coffee, that the Ministry of the Environment and Cameco may decide that the best thing to do is reconnect the pipe, rebury it and run it a mile farther into the lake. Mark views that as likely.

"The bigger issue here," he tells her, "is to try to get the province to start protecting the people of Ontario and not leave this to the federal regulators, who have acknowledged that they are there to facilitate the industry and who own and basically created the industry. We want Ontario to protect Ontarians and not leave it to the federal government."

He warns Lynne that the other side will do all it can to trivialize her complaint and to make her look foolish. "There's a playbook," he says. "There are a lot of tricks played to minimize the problem." The same issue of the Port Hope newspaper that carried a story in which a Cameco spokesman downplayed the broken pipe carried another story (and photo) about the company's $250,000 donation to the local conservation authority. When I worked on a small daily newspaper in British Columbia in the late 1970s, we called it "the handshake shot" or "the cheque shot": lots of smiling faces, clasped hands and, front and centre, a cheque the size of a compact car.

The war being waged where the land slopes gently to the lake is an old one. It's money, power and influence versus an outraged citizen, or two.

As I take notes and record the conversation, then watch Lynne sign the EBR document, I realize my good fortune. Mark Mattson is giving me access to the inner workings of Lake Ontario Waterkeeper. I am a volunteer, in service to an outfit I believe in, and I have no doubt that my skills are both valued and appreciated. But I marvel at all that I am receiving in return: insight into a hot and tangled issue, stories like those of Carl Brand, characters like Sanford Haskill.

A TEN-MINUTE walk from my house takes me to the shores of Lake Ontario, one of the aptly named Great Lakes. Within their six thousand kilometres of shoreline lies 95 per cent of North America's fresh water—enough to cover the entire continent to a depth of 1.5 metres. Some forty million people live in the Great Lakes Basin, and that's where the problem begins.

Residues from factories and farms, from pesticides, sewage and various other contaminants have led to bizarre events, like the Cuyahoga River (it flows north past Cleveland into Lake Erie) catching fire several times in the 1960s. *Time* magazine described it as a river that "oozes rather than flows" and in which a person "does not drown but decays."

The river's health, like that of the Great Lakes in general, has improved since those days. But now there's the new threat of global warming, which may cause temperatures around the Great Lakes to hit highs of 48°C in the summer. The resulting evaporation could lower lake levels by as much as 1.5 metres. This may in turn require the dredging of shipping canals, which will stir old toxic sludge from lake and river bottoms, releasing contaminants into the air and returning pollution levels to those of the 1960s. The health of the lakes is more fragile than ever.

That's why I wanted to spend one of my months with an environmental charity that concerns itself with the lakes. The one I've chosen, Lake Ontario Waterkeeper, was formed in 2001 and trains individuals and volunteer groups to document and publicize sources of pollution. Waterkeeper also educates the public about Lake Ontario and the Great Lakes Basin and conducts research in the watershed.

Some environmental groups are registered charities or non-profit organizations capable of issuing tax receipts. There is a perception among some of these groups that unless they are guarded in their criticisms of government policy on the environment, they risk backlash. Greenpeace, for example, was delisted several years ago and now says, in effect, "We give no tax receipts, and we give no quarter either." Revenue Canada grants charitable status to environmental groups on the grounds that such organizations both educate and benefit the public, but under what some call "the 10 per cent rule," any outfit that devotes more than 10 per cent of its resources to political activity may see that status revoked.

One could argue that the seeds for LOW and its like were sown back in 1969, when a Democratic senator from Wisconsin, Gaylord Nelson, predicted that a grassroots movement would spring up to protest continued assaults on the environment. He helped organize the first Earth Day in 1970 and saw his dedication to conservation and environmental protection spread around the world. In 1969, a newly formed group called Pollution Probe held a mock funeral in Toronto for the badly polluted Don River. That same year, the most famous of the Cuyahoga River's many fires drew international attention: the numbing image of a grey-brown, fishless river on fire seemed to strike a chord, and the Environmental Protection Agency was born in the U.S. a year later.

Lake Ontario Waterkeeper is a licensed member of the New York–based Waterkeeper Alliance, led by Robert F. Kennedy, Jr. Each local Waterkeeper chapter is akin to an environmental neighbourhood watch program. Waterkeepers patrol in boats looking for environmental threats, they address water pollution concerns raised by others in the community, and they deploy legal and democratic processes designed to protect water quality. LOW also maintains a comprehensive website, and when I wrote as a journalist about environmental matters close to home, I came to rely on it as a credible media resource.

At any one time, LOW may have twenty volunteers on board, many of them law students doing internships. Waterkeeper lists almost four hundred donors, many of them professionals such as doctors and lawyers. Supporters are less inclined to volunteer their time, believing instead that the best way to help is by backing Waterkeeper financially. As Mark Mattson puts it, "Our donors know that we work hard, that we know our stuff, and they trust us to do the job well." In a way, LOW swims against the tide. Unlike many charities that clamour for volunteers, Waterkeeper tends to embrace volunteers with expertise in the law—which is why legal interns land so frequently on LOW's shores.

However, when good-hearted souls call wanting to help, there is no shortage of office work for them. There is always filing and photocopying, the admittedly tedious but essential work of a non-profit agency.

LOW differs from traditional charities in other ways too. At an institution like Vinnie's, the beneficiary is a small group of people. LOW aims to benefit something more nebulous—Ontario's waterways. "We're trying," Mark Mattson told me, "to protect the environment for the community, as a public good. Not to be owned or privatized. Once it's private, the signs and fences go up. I look at the big charities trying to end cancer or child slavery. It feels like you can't stop these scourges. Whereas if Toronto wanted to clean up its lakefront, that's doable. At Waterkeeper, we work on stuff that can be done and that we think *will* be done."

AUGUST 8. My first day with Lake Ontario Waterkeeper. I had noted their Bay Street address in Toronto and immediately assumed they had swank digs. Maybe, I thought, LOW believes you have to live among the suits to do battle with the suits.

Then I spot the door to their building. Bay Street is the financial heartland of the country, but the door to 600 Bay is battered and scuffed, and Chinatown is just around the corner at Dundas Street. The stairway, with several bicycles locked to its ground-floor railings, bears a thick layer of dust, and the elevator is a hundred years old, according to its operator. Sliding glass door outside, metal accordion door inside, the kind seen in vintage French movies.

Lake Ontario Waterkeeper's fourth-floor office is ample and bright and desperate for a paint job. The organization moved into the space in May and decorating fell prey to the demands of ongoing work. Mark is away on holidays, and when I peek into his office I see a finger width of daylight through the

window casement and cracked pane of glass. Bullfrog Power—
Ontario's certified green supplier—brings electricity to the
office, but until that window is fixed, some of that politically correct energy is going right out Mark's window. (For the
record, when I returned to the office a week later, a brand new
casement and window had been installed.)

In the main office, with workstations arrayed around its
periphery, a tall bank of west-facing windows lets in a formidable amount of light. The view is of asphalt and pebble roofs,
the aluminum housings of heating and cooling vents, and one
lone tree.

Rest assured, LOW's $800,000 annual budget is not being
spent on lavish offices. I am given the grand tour and meet
Julia Hambleton, the office administrator, LOW vice-president
Krystyn Tully, and the two legal interns, Joanna Bull and Anne
Sabourin. They are all, to a woman, upbeat and knowledgeable.

In the LOW office, the phone will ring with all manner of
environmental woe being reported by distraught individuals
from across Ontario, and LOW staff must decide if and how to
proceed. Guidelines have been laid down to make those decisions. If other environmental groups are on the case, LOW is
less inclined to wade in. But if the caller has been unable to
muster help from anyone, LOW may respond. I liked the last
line in LOW's guidelines to staff: "What are the Outrageous
Factors? Can you sleep at night if you don't act?"

I had known Mark Mattson, the president of LOW, at least
indirectly for several years. I had heard him speak at several
public meetings on environmental issues, and I had interviewed him and quoted him. I liked his candour, his eloquence,
his straight-ahead approach. Plus we had in common an old
adversary.

NOT EVERYONE has a file on Lafarge, the multinational cement company. I do, and much to my dismay, it keeps getting thicker.

My file dates back to 1995 when I helped form a community group to fight a massive quarry that Lafarge wanted to blast north of my home in Camden East. This was a true David versus Goliath battle, pitting many of Camden East's 250 souls against a powerful corporation that operates in several dozen countries around the world. We fought them hard for three years, organized public meetings, launched a newsletter, raised funds for lawyers and expert witnesses, then took Lafarge to the Ontario Municipal Board (OMB), the quasi-judicial body that decides such squabbles. But the OMB gave the cement company all it asked for, and more.

Faced with the prospect of gravel trucks lumbering through the village from dawn till dusk, my family and I sold the century-old riverfront home we cherished, left the place we had called home for seventeen years and moved into the city of Kingston forty kilometres away. I was devastated—not that we lost, but that we lost so utterly.

Cut to the fall of 2004, when word came that the same Lafarge operation that had sent me packing from my village was about to play havoc with the air and water in my city. The cement plant, located in the village of Bath just upwind of Kingston, floated a plan to save on the cost of fuel in its kiln by burning used tires and used oil, municipal waste, animal bones and non-recyclable plastic. I had two thoughts. One, everything that goes up must come down, so that both my air and my water were imperilled by this nutty idea. Two, is there no escaping these turkeys?

Over the next four years, I went to more meetings, did research on tire-burning, wrote long features for local newspapers and observed as dozens of environmental groups, including

Lake Ontario Waterkeeper, citizens' alliances, individuals and a high-profile rock musician, took on the cement plant. (Gord Downie and the Tragically Hip have a farm they use as studio space literally in the shadow of the plant's smokestack.)

Those opposed to the plan never bought the company's assurances that burning tires (and those other unmentionables, some of which Lafarge eventually dropped from their wish list) was safe. It made no sense. I sat in a packed township chambers office one evening in the summer of 2006 and saw people roll their eyes and smirk when a Lafarge engineer insisted that burning tires would actually improve air quality. "A win-win situation," as he called it.

There have been some celebrated tire fires in North America in recent decades (Winchester in Virginia and Hagersville in Ontario come to mind), fires that burned for many months and consumed millions of tires. The image of billowing black smoke rising skywards is not easily forgotten, and we have grown wary of the smoke's noxious contents. Lafarge wanted to burn a million or more tires a year in its thirty-four-year-old kiln. The company claimed it would save $3 million or $4 million annually on its fuel bill by burning tires, but one environmental coalition estimated that the figure was closer to $20 million.

All through the summer of 2006, I received several e-mails a day from a retired university professor who seemed to be spending most of his time delving into the subject of TDFs ("tire-derived fuel," or "alternative fuel," in cement company parlance). A local family doctor sent a letter to the provincial Ministry of the Environment objecting to tire-burning on twenty-eight different counts. A small army of residents, scientists, lawyers, environmentalists, poets, artists and others had joined organizations that sprang up to try to defeat the plan. It's impossible to calculate how many hours they spent attending meetings, preparing briefs, writing press releases and lobbying politicians. They had become, like it or not, activists.

Then just days before Christmas in 2006, Ontario's Ministry of the Environment gave Lafarge permission to burn tires in a test trial. Those of us opposed to the licence thought the timing was a nasty and cynical piece of work. The announcement gave us just fifteen days to articulate our appeal arguments. The government message was also extremely confusing. On that same day, the province banned tires as cement kiln fuel elsewhere in Ontario but had apparently decided to permit an experiment at the Lafarge plant, effectively turning the citizens of Bath and Kingston into unwitting guinea pigs.

There then followed a flurry of moves and countermoves: various appeals, a ruling by an environmental tribunal that burning tires "could result in significant harm to the environment," an appeal by Lafarge to that ruling and, finally, a high court ruling that upheld the tribunal's finding.

I have no idea what Lafarge paid in lawyers' and consultants' fees over four years to advance their scheme to burn tires, but half a million dollars seems a reasonable guess. I do know that Lake Ontario Waterkeeper alone spent about $170,000 battling against it (a conservative figure since many of its lawyers and experts worked pro bono). But in the summer of 2008, the cement company began to issue statements suggesting that their resolve to pursue the plan was weakening and, by degrees, they threw in the towel.

I ASKED Mark Mattson to make sense of Lafarge's capitulation. He agreed that public agitation in Bath and Kingston helped win the day. "But that alone," he said, "would not have stopped Lafarge. Two words explain the victory: due process. We beat them by forcing them to prove their evidence and by bringing our own. What stopped Lafarge was that they could not prove that tire-burning was safe."

The last thing the cement company wanted, Mark told me, was a public hearing that would take an in-depth look at what comes out of those stacks when tires are burned as fuel. Truths revealed in such a hearing might have jeopardized Lafarge's use of tires in other provinces and other countries. Intense legal and scientific scrutiny at a hearing would also have revealed precisely what the stacks emit now—information that may never be known. On that score, there was disappointment that a public hearing seemed unlikely.

Krystyn Tully looked back on the four-year battle and made a point echoed by Katie Tucker, the articling student who worked alongside Mark Mattson through 2007 and 2008. In cases like this one, both women observed, seemingly innocuous documents proved their value. Documents such as the province's Environmental Bill of Rights (EBR, passed in 1993), and its Statements of Environmental Values and other guiding principles figured in the Lafarge decision. The province's EBR, in particular, says Tully, "gave us the right to appeal, as well as other environmental protections." These protections include the Environmental Commissioner's Office, a watchdog of environmental decision-makers, and the new Environmental Registry, which forces business to serve notice of plans that might harm the environment. All these pieces of paper, all this bureaucracy, helped bring down a dim plan to burn tires in an old kiln.

The lesson for Tully? "Common law has to be respected. Lafarge said no. The court said yes."

"What did you learn?" I asked Katie Tucker of her year fighting a cement company. "I learned how government works," she said. "To see industry and the Ministry of the Environment sticking so close together... Government is supposed to represent our interests. They're on our dime. It wasn't just us versus Lafarge. It was us versus the Ministry of the Environment."

Mark Mattson is fond of analogies. He likens the coziness between industry and government to a cop catching a drunk driver, taking him home and letting him off with a warning. "After all," the cop says, "no one was hurt." We don't do that with drunk drivers, Mattson says. Why do we do it with polluters?

"The new model," he explains, and he sees it everywhere in North America, "puts the corporation in charge of regulation. Neo-con thinking has government removing 'barriers' and 'red tape,' and letting business and communities fight it out. In Ontario, the Ministry of the Environment is less a regulator and more a 'facilitator.' Government sees industry as a client."

Mattson lamented the fact that the province of Ontario has had no environmental hearings since the early 1990s. What we get instead are "assessments," which he says can be proponent driven. "Hearings," however, mean public participation, transparency, independency and unbiased decision-makers. Assessments, says Mattson, "continue to make it look like we are fulfilling the public review mandate." He thinks the role of regulatory agencies needs to be reviewed, but until that happens he has this advice for those fighting cement companies wanting to burn tires: if you can, get them into judicial hearings where proponents must prove their case about safety, benefits and impacts, and promises are turned into terms and conditions.

"We're at a low point," Mark says. "I hope we have turned a corner with the Lafarge case. The lesson of this case is that due process is a powerful tool. Due process frightened away one of the biggest corporations in the world. All we had was the truth. The company blinked."

LIKE MANY other charities and non-profits, LOW relies on donations from individuals and a few foundations. And musicians. It makes no sense, but fighting the good fight invariably pulls in artists and musicians, most of them badly paid in the first place. "Help our cause," is the plea. "Sing and paint for free." Typically they do.

Julia Hambleton, a musician herself (she plays the clarinet and studied music performance at university), says, "There's this huge crossover between our work at Lake Ontario Waterkeeper and musicians. They really understand what we do."

Take Sarah Harmer, for instance. On August 9, she sang at a music festival on Wolfe Island sponsored, in part, by Lake Ontario Waterkeeper. Earlier in the summer, on June 14, she sang in Kingston as part of the fundraiser to help those trying to stop uranium mining north of the city. In 2002, she accepted our invitation to appear at that year's fundraiser for Horizons of Friendship—for free, of course. I continue to marvel at artists who give so generously.

For people like Julia Hambleton and Krystyn Tully, for Mark Mattson and interns like Katie Tucker, Anne Sabourin and Joanna Bull, the work they do is fuelled by a personal commitment and passion.

"I was attracted to the work," says Julia when I ask her why she got involved with Lake Ontario Waterkeeper. "I felt stress about the environment. Being in the office and doing the work is grounding somehow."

When I approached Mark about volunteering for Waterkeeper, he knew exactly how to deploy me. For *Waterkeeper* magazine, a thick and slick full-colour publication that comes out of Waterkeeper headquarters in Irvington, New York, I will chronicle the Lafarge case from my vantage. I will listen to LOW's radio show, come on as a guest and (as a former CBC producer) offer suggestions for improving the program. And I will head out with the crew of the Waterkeeper's boat and see first-hand the work that Waterkeeper does.

AUGUST 21. In a perfect world, every person in the province would be informed, every person would be a steward (one among many) of a local body of water, be it pond, river or lake.

Every week, Mark and Krystyn troop down the hall to an Internet radio station and tell listeners at three campuses, Queen's University, Trent and Guelph, what LOW has been up to. It's a half-hour radio program in which the two environmentalists take turns at the mike. They have a digital tape recorder, which they take on trips, so the broadcast often includes snippets from their travels, from public meetings, wherever life at the barricades has taken them.

On this day, I am a guest on that show and we talk about volunteering. I tell them that a sea change is occurring in the world of volunteering, that people are no longer willing to lick stamps and stuff envelopes or just write a cheque. They seek deep involvement and they want to use their skills and put them at the service of the agency they have selected to help.

Krsytyn jokes on the air that while stamps always need licking, and volunteers are always welcome, what LOW staff would really love is for someone to make a loaf of banana bread and bring it into the office.

AUGUST 29. There's something about viewing my city from the water that changes my thinking. When I look out on the lake from shore, I am in the city's shoes. But out on the water, I am more inclined to view things from the lake's perspective and to see Lake Ontario as a living organism. Though I live just minutes from the lake, I have not been on the water off Kingston—aside from trips on ferries to Wolfe Island—since I was a boy fishing with my cousin.

The LOW patrol boat, a cream-coloured six-metre "limestone," is parked at Mark Mattson's family's waterfront place on Wolfe Island. The boat is called the *Angus Bruce* and is named after a man who, in his eighties, proved to be an invaluable resource for Mattson during dump proceedings at nearby Storrington Township. The *Angus Bruce* was purchased with money LOW received after successfully prosecuting the city of Hamilton for polluting Lake Ontario.

I HAVE arranged to meet Mark and the boat at the Kingston ferry docks. It's a grim day, with a fine spray riding an in-your-face wind and virtually no other boats on the water. I begin to think that weather has cancelled the rendezvous, when the *Angus Bruce* swings into view.

What Mark wants me to see is the city's waste-treatment facilities. Off we go, the fibreglass hull pounding the waves and rearranging my backbone with every hard thump. We head east and stop finally in the waters off the Ravensview Water Pollution Control Plant.

At $115 million, this is the largest capital project ever undertaken by the city of Kingston, Mark says. The K-Rock Centre, as the arena cum entertainment centre here is now called, has occupied the front pages of Kingston newspapers for years, but if Kingstonians want to know where many of their tax dollars are being spent, they should flush their toilets and think about where the contents are headed.

Chris Mattson, Mark's uncle, is along this day as first mate and he opens a side flap so I can stick my head out into the rain and take photographs for LOW's website. I pitch and roll, trying to snap pictures without falling in the water. Anne Sabourin, the law student volunteer who has spent the summer in LOW's office, compiled an exhaustive forty-four-page report on the treatment of waste water in Toronto, Hamilton and Kingston. LOW will eventually post the report, called *What Goes into Your Lake,* on its website along with the photos I take.

After Ravensview, we travel west to the downtown shore-line. That whole shore takes on new meaning as I scan the map that forms part of the report and that Mark is using to guide my photography.

I am taking shots of what Utilities Kingston crews call "combined sewer outfall tanks," or CSO tanks. It says a great deal that no city in Canada allows new combined sewer systems (storm water and sewer water running along a single pipe) to be built—for the obvious reason that they only work tidily in winter or dry times in spring, summer and fall. Heavy rains can muck up everything. But these combined sewer systems, the LOW report says, exist in seventy older cities across Canada, including mine.

The CSO tanks are meant to hold combined sewer outflow until it can be treated. But the tanks have a limited capacity, and when monitors show that the tanks are close to being full, the tanks are automatically bypassed and untreated sewage goes directly into Lake Ontario. It's either that or the waste backs up into basements. But what kind of a choice is that?

Something Mark Mattson said keeps coming back to me.

"Where would Toronto get its water if that lake were tainted in some irreversible way?" I recoiled at those words. I don't choose to dwell on that possibility—the notion that even continued practices, never mind some terrible chemical or nuclear accident—could permanently render the water unfit for human use. Only 1 per cent of the water in Lake Ontario is renewed by rainfall every year and the same holds true for all the Great Lakes. The rest is a one-time deposit from glaciers that melted ten thousand years ago. This means that Lake Ontario is essentially a vast well from which millions of people draw water for personal and other uses.

"We would never put toxins in our well," Mattson says. "Yet we put sewage and toxins into the lake, one of the most precious freshwater resources in the world."

Mark wonders if Toronto might build a pipeline to Georgian Bay, an impossible thought, and not unlike the Grand Canal project. The latter is a whacky scheme to build a dyke across James Bay, let natural riverflow gradually convert the salt water into fresh water, then build a billion-dollar pipeline to the parched southwest of the United States. Water really is the new oil.

As we cruise along the downtown shoreline, Mark points out all the cso holding tanks, many of them named after nearby streets. There are seven shown on the map—the Clarence Inline cso Tank, the William, the Earl, the Gore, the Lower Union, the West, the Okill—each with its own pipe running out into the lake.

Jim Keech, the president and chief executive officer of Utilities Kingston, later tells me that cso tanks, some the size of underground parking lots, "offer the biggest bang for the buck" in dealing with overflow. I ask him if he is worried about climate change and the possibility of massive amounts of rain to come.

"Yes," he says. "The industry is worried. We're looking at storm-of-the-decade and storm-of-the-century data, and we're starting to wonder, are the data right? It may be that we'll need even bigger pipes and different systems in the future." As Kingston upgrades its infrastructure, Keech does foresee a day when there will be no CSO problem—but not in his lifetime.

This much is certain. The most recent data from the utility (as of August 22, 2008) show that 490,799 cubic metres of combined sewer outflow have gone out into the lake so far in 2008, all from thirty-one "events" or times of heavy rainfall. That's compared with 85,431 cubic metres for all of 2007, which featured a dry summer.

Mark Mattson has seen figures from sewer-main companies suggesting that it would take $8 billion to $10 billion to eliminate combined sewer overflows from every municipality on Lake Ontario, "about half the price of a nuclear power station." He thinks the money would be well spent.

What Goes into Your Lake makes for sobering reading. It notes, for example, that *E. coli* counts in raw sewage may exceed the provincial water-quality objective by a factor of 1,000 and that the highest concentration of substances in CSOs occurs during "the first flush," when a heavy rainfall has just begun. Things like grease, motor oil, excrement, paint thinner, antifreeze and countless unknown substances go into the CSO cocktail.

Mark Mattson commends the city of Kingston for its upgrades to the Ravensview plant. "Good for them," he says, "but Ravensview has nothing to do with CSOs. I give all cities on the Great Lakes a failing grade. We have long used the lakes to dilute our waste. Toronto still puts billions of cubic litres of raw waste into the lake every year."

In Kingston, Mattson says, local government has to stop the bulldozing of marshes and wetlands that help with filtration. Grass and trees and green space all absorb rainwater. Individual homeowners can use rain barrels to limit water from rooftops draining into sewers, while aiming down spouts at lawns and gardens.

Ecojustice Canada, a non-profit environmental law organization formerly known as the Sierra Legal Defence Fund, released its second National Sewage Report Card on August 18, 2008, and it noted that more than one trillion litres of treated or partially treated sewage is dumped into the nation's lakes, rivers and oceans every year. The poets at Ecojustice declare that this volume of waste would cover the length of the Trans-Canada Highway to a depth of six storeys or, my favourite, fill the main chamber of the House of Commons every three and a half minutes for one year.

. . .

[QUEEN FOR A DAY]

THE MODEL of charity that has governed North America for centuries, simply put, goes like this: let the rich amass their wealth, unfettered by taxes as much as possible, and let us hope they "give back" before dying. *The Globe and Mail* even has a Saturday column called "Giving Back" that celebrates this notion. I have mixed feelings about such cheerleading, for while it usefully raises the profile of people in need, it also puts donors on pedestals.

I am likewise conflicted about a website whose name says it all: www.wishuponahero.com. This virtual charity brokerage house was conceived by a New Jersey man named Dave Girgenti after the September 11, 2001 attacks. He observed thousands of people posting pictures of missing loved ones at the site of the devastation in New York and all over the city. There had to be a better way, he thought, to connect people in distress with people who can help.

By the fall of 2007, he had created an online platform "for people to help people," as the website proclaims. The last time I looked, more than 60,000 wishes had been granted. Maybe you've inherited a few thousand dollars and want to help someone in need. Maybe you're a single mother with no money to replace the washing machine that just broke down. This website links the two.

I like the way technology can bring them together. What I don't like is any arrangement that gives all the power and glory to the giver, the "hero" in this case. That single mother is forced to plead her case. That donor, should one come forward, gets to choose. I guess it's true that beggars can't be choosers: in this context, you're either one or the other.

I am reminded of that dreadful game show from the 1950s called *Queen for a Day*. Four women would come onto the stage before a live audience and describe their always dire circumstances. They were terminally ill, maybe, with six children under ten at home, and yes, the washing machine had broken down. Each woman was given several minutes to state her case, and when all had finished an "applause meter" allowed the audience to clap for each and decide who would be crowned queen for a day. The lucky winner was given a ceremonial robe, a tiara, a brand-new washing machine and a great deal more. The three other women went home with nothing to show for their tears.

DUSTY
Makes Her Rounds

SEPTEMBER 15. A tiny man with an S-shaped torso, a clenched fist and a fixed open mouth stares up at the kind of revolving musical toy that used to hang above our son's crib when he was an infant. The man looks delighted by the tiny airplanes as they circle not a foot from his head.

This room at the Ongwanada Resource Centre in Kingston is further brightened by dozens of gleaming mobiles that hang from the ceiling and by splashes of colour on the walls. I see lava lamps, faux aquariums, photo galleries, massive landscape posters, huge boxes of toys and brightly coloured balls—all meant to stimulate the senses.

Every client here is in a wheelchair or a rolling cot, or curled up in one of several elevated blue mattresses which, were they called beds, could sleep four. Dusty and I are making our rounds to meet the participants in three day-programs that Ongwanada offers to people who are profoundly challenged in mind and body. Not one of them uses language, though all communicate in their way.

Dusty has been my companion since my wife and I got her as a ten-week-old pup from the Napanee Humane Society shelter. Still handsome despite her venerable age (she is twelve as I write this), she is equal parts husky, terrier and border collie. Her colouring is bright yellow, the colour of wheat in the sun, with white highlights that owe something to those husky bloodlines. In size and conformation, she is coyote-like, and when we walk her off-leash and she trots up behind people on the sidewalk, those not accustomed to dogs are sometimes given a start.

"It's just a wolf," I tell them.

However, in the park she is liable to provoke admiration from the dog crowd. "Beautiful dog," many have told us.

In one area of the resource centre, a gathering place for clients who are able to leave their wheelchairs and move about on the floor, a blond-haired man who is in the habit of clapping does so. That gets Dusty's notice. For her, two quick claps is a call to attention, and she wheels around to see who has issued the command. Another fellow has made a game of tossing a toy through the door every time someone opens it. His aim is quite good.

Nicole Arthur, supervisor of the day program, is taking me on a tour and educating me on everything from the awareness levels of clients to which ones might be likely to grab Dusty's fur—not out of malevolence but unfettered eagerness.

I'm trying not to be wide-eyed, but it's difficult to ignore a tongue permanently rolled and protruding, or a head lolling, or the bent postures of men and women who have not been issued the standard body form: some are prone to compulsive behaviour, mouth gymnastics, groaning or hand movements like those of a maestro leading an orchestra.

Dusty was given a Timbit (the round centre of the donut, for those who have never ventured inside a Tim Hortons coffeeshop) back in the first room, and she continues to nose the floor seeking more of the same. But she, too, is trying to get her bearings here. She's used to friendly pats and cooing, and she received lots of that out in the hall where not one of the staff failed to greet her. They knew why she was here. The clients to whom she is repeatedly directed are different. They're hanging back and will need coaxing.

ONGWANADA IS an Ojibwa word that means "our home." Funded by the Ontario government, this non-profit charitable organization for people with developmental disabilities oversees thirty homes in the Kingston region, each one shared by four to six clients. The Ongwanada Resource Centre offers a variety of day programs and support services to some six hundred boys, girls, men and women who come to the facility with disabilities that range from mild to major. The facility, though quite modern in its architecture and suffused with light, traces its history back to 1948 when the name Ongwanada adorned a tuberculosis sanatorium and then a chronic care hospital on the same site. The grounds were always well kept and it was said that wedding parties would stop there to have photos taken.

By the 1970s, parents of children with physical and intellectual challenges began pushing for something better. Custodial nursing care gradually gave way to developmental programming, a whole new language was introduced and, with it, a radical shift in approach. These children were not "patients" in need of ongoing medical care but "individuals" capable of living, with support, of course, in the community.

Up to one hundred volunteers now work alongside Ongwanada's four hundred–plus staff, performing clerical or canteen work, helping out during therapeutic swims in the pool, assisting on day trips, and walking with clients in the centre's gardens. "Some have family members or friends with a disability," says Paula Smith, the volunteer services coordinator, "but only about 10 per cent. And we get a handful of students who need volunteer hours for their diplomas. But most of our volunteers come because they want to give back to the community." Dog therapy is another service that volunteers can offer, and it is the one that Dusty and I have signed up for.

PET THERAPY is a very old idea, though that phrase dates back only to 1969, when it was coined by an American child psychiatrist named Boris Levinson. We are, it seems, hard-wired to pay attention to animals. Primitive humans had to learn the habits and migration patterns of birds and animals or risk starvation. As John Berger, the British-born novelist and art critic, points out in his essay "Why We Look at Animals," the first subject matter of human art was wild animals and the first paint surely derived, in part, from animal blood.

I have seen the caves at Lascaux in southern France and been mesmerized by the ochre and black paintings of bison, deer and horses. What I was seeing was not the real thing (human breath and high humidity have proven harmful to prehistoric art) but an absolutely precise replica created right next to the genuine article. Still, for a mere copy, the effect is spellbinding. Eighteen thousand years have passed since those drawings were made, and some things have not changed. We humans still delight in animals.

Sigmund Freud mentioned the therapeutic value of companion animals in psychotherapy. He noticed that patients, and young patients especially, were more inclined to be open about painful subjects when his dog Chow Chow was in the room. The patients could clearly see that the dog, ever attentive, was unaffected by anything they said, and Freud wondered if this gave them a sense of security and acceptance.

Since then, science has documented the medical benefits of animal companions. Heart patients, Alzheimer's sufferers, nursing home residents and troubled adolescents: all benefit from contact with animals. Watching fish in an aquarium, grooming a horse and patting a dog have been shown to lower blood pressure. Outcomes for someone who has suffered a heart attack are significantly better when there's a dog at home. A Texas physician, Larry Dossey, once observed in the medical journal *Alternative Therapies* that "the evidence favoring the health value of pets is so compelling that if pet therapy were a pill, we would not be able to manufacture it fast enough."

When my wife and I visited my father-in-law in his Toronto retirement home, or my father in his, we always brought Dusty. The impact she had on those residences was astonishing. The disengaged perked up, the confused found focus, and everyone was keen to pet her, compliment her, talk to her as if she understood every word. Dusty basked in all their attention.

Dusty's job at Ongwanada is at heart a simple one. Be a dog. Be her old agreeable self. Hope those nice people in wheelchairs drop lots of food on the floor.

SEPTEMBER 16. Stock markets around the globe are in turmoil because giant lending institutions in the U.S. are on the brink of collapse. The news is on every broadcast and dominates many of my conversations.

That's how we view the world, an erratic line on a graph. It goes up, it goes down. We're always measuring growth, or lamenting the lack of it. At Ongwanada, though, the turmoil does not intrude.

"Yes," Nicole agrees. "Here it's about quality of life. We try to stimulate our clients, mentally and physically. We give them physical therapy, we take them on day trips." One day the staff took them to a skating rink where, pushed about on the ice, they could feel the sensations of cold and wind and speed.

The assignment for both staff and volunteers is to make the person happy. Some of these clients can be rough: some engage in self-abusive behaviour (one wears a padded helmet), some prefer one staffer to another. And they have ways of letting you know very clearly what they want.

Dusty received her Timbit from Roger, a man in Classroom One. Dark-haired, lean and long-nosed, he's quite vocal and expressive. After we had visited the second and third class-rooms, we came back to the first and just hung out with Roger for a bit.

"That's the first time I've seen you smile all day," one staffer chided him. Unlike many clients here who are unable to make decisions about whether they want to come to the day program or not, Roger can make a choice in the morning. Dusty, the donut mooch, stops now and again at his chair, looks him in the eye, tries to coax him into proffering another treat. Roger cackles, smiles broadly, demonstrates his delight.

In the other classroom, another man occupies a corner bed. This is William's favourite spot, and he insists on claiming it each time he comes. He loves to sit, propped against a pil-low, and watch the room—sometimes out of the corner of his eye. William can seem remote and disinterested then suddenly appear thoughtful, as if he were taking notes for a book.

"Look," a volunteer points out, "William is very interested in Dusty."

A glance across this wide room might be the only sign. A brief awakening from a dozing slumber, a widening of the eyes. This constitutes a show of interest, and those who work here don't miss it.

Dusty, meanwhile, is earning her dog therapy credentials and soon wins full acceptance. Some of the staff are preparing a card for a retiring colleague, and they are going around to all the clients to have them leave their marks (a fingerprint) on the card. Dusty, too, signs the card—with an ink-stained paw.

OF ALL my volunteer experiences this year, Ongwanada asked the least of my time: two one-hour sessions twice a week for several weeks from mid-September to early October. But in no other endeavour was I more thoroughly screened and prepared.

I had to produce a letter from the vet attesting to Dusty's upstanding character ("a very gentle and sweet-natured dog," the vet wrote, and "a well-tempered girl who is affectionate with everyone she meets..."). Ongwanada wanted the note to confirm as well that all of Dusty's shots were in order (of course, they were) and that she carried no fleas (of course, she did not). And the volunteer coordinator, Paula Smith, wanted to meet Dusty before proceeding.

I had to provide a document to show that I had no police record; several organizations likewise wanted this, so that was no surprise. I needed to visit an Ongwanada nurse several times for tests to prove that I had not been exposed to tuberculosis and would not pass on the disease to clients or staff.

Finally, I had to attend a three-hour volunteer orientation program that was meant to introduce me to Ongwanada, its history, the nature of its clientele, what it means to have a developmental or intellectual disability, and what services are offered to the clients and family who use the resource centre. I received a primer on operating wheelchairs, watched a video on people with intellectual disabilities and took a tour of the entire facility.

SEPTEMBER 18. Another round. This time I coax Dusty to leap up onto the plastic mattress in William's corner, and one of the staff puts a Milk-Bone in his hand before Dusty gobbles it down.

"How much awareness is there?" I ask his helper (each staff member is responsible for looking after four clients).

"No one really knows," she replies.

It's fair to say, though, that if all the research on cognition levels in comatose patients and in animal awareness is any indication, there is far more going on than we can guess at.

"What we do know," says the nurse, "is that they know what they want." If William doesn't get his favourite corner, he will begin to rock. Some clients howl to convey their displeasure. In the other room, Roger makes a face as Dusty and I walk in the door, but we are not the problem. When he screws up his face, his helper takes him to be signalling, "I've got a headache." And within minutes of receiving a Tylenol, he is back to his old self and Dusty is once more his centre of attention.

The question I have for all of these staff members (90 per cent are women) is "What drew you to this work?" One nurse tells me she accepts only occasional shifts here; she's otherwise a nurse at local hospitals. It's hard, she explains, to receive so little response from her charges, to not know if what she is doing is ever making a difference. Physiotherapy is the single treatment that gives her unassailable feedback. Some clients will gravitate to positions that give them comfort, but that can lead to stiff muscles and cramping. In physio, this nurse can feel the client's muscles relaxing, conveying what these clients cannot say directly—"Thank you."

Another staffer, here for ten years, loves the work and is not at all discomfited by the apparent lack of response. "The clients let you know when they like something," she tells me. It could be a smile, a twinkle in the eye, a simple reaction. She places a large yellow ball on Ray's tray and he tosses it off. They are playing catch.

This woman has been caring for Ray in the day program for three years, and she knows him as well as anyone outside his own family. He is a strikingly handsome young man with penetrating blue eyes and an air of neatness about him. I am struck by how much these caretakers give. They tussle the hair of their charges, they hold their hands, they talk to them constantly, encourage their victories and soothe their hurts. This is unconditional love and affection, the kind that Dusty gives me. No strings attached.

Today, homemade pie is on offer, a choice of apple or lemon meringue. Dessert is served with cheeriness here, a warm camaraderie.

But one client is given to tossing his food from his tray onto the floor. Some don't like a particular item on the menu and they might decline by giving it the old heave-ho. The staff respond with neither reprimands nor resentment, but something more like smiling acceptance. This is just how it is. All they can offer are patience and kindness. That, and vigilance. Sores on the skin are a constant threat, so staff are always watching out for the people in their care.

Each client here has a team of health care professionals—social worker, physiotherapist, caregiver, dietitian and doctor—seeing to them. I wonder, what must it be like to be a person who is intellectually or physically impaired without all that backup?

IT IS only as I am nearing the end of our time at Ongwanada that I realize that two of the participants are brother and sister.

When that fact is pointed out, I immediately see the resemblance. What must it have been like for the parents when each child was born? Did they view it as tragic that this son, this daughter too, would never be able to say his or her own name? Did the second birth seem like lightning striking twice, the height of injustice? Or did they embrace these children as their own, to be loved for all their "imperfections?" Did that word, that thought, ever cross their lips?

I have only one child, who was born healthy and intact, and I never had to deal with such questions. But I do have a vivid memory of my mother, who was a pediatric nurse before she became a geriatric nurse, coming to visit us when Kurt was still only days old. Clare Scanlan sat on the couch with my son in her lap and, talking to us all the while, took off every stitch of his clothing and inspected him. Ran her hands over him, counting, as it were, his fingers and toes.

AS WE leave Ongwanada that day, Dusty—whose aged plumbing means that she squats down to pee for forty-five seconds at a time—does one of her marathon drops on the lawn close by the offices. I watch her, waiting. Not once, but twice, someone emerges from inside the Ongwanada building to remind me to pick up after my dog. I assure the first woman that Dusty is simply watering the lawn. The second woman isn't buying it, and indeed, when I examine the spot, I am mortified to discover that she has done something more serious, and get out my plastic bags.

"Our clients use this space," the woman explains to me.

They are rightly house-proud here.

SEPTEMBER 23. Slow start. The light is lowered in Classroom One, and every client is having a post-lunch, in-place snooze.

But as Dusty and I circulate, some clients perk up at the sound of us. That is especially the case in Classroom Three, where Harold, an autistic man, seems quite interested in my old pup. Harold is normally in a wheelchair, but in this setting he is given the freedom of the floor. He sits cross-legged, his arms and hands extended and waving, thumb and forefinger delicately touching, in the manner of an Indian dancer. He seems one minute to be looking directly at Dusty, then through her, as if she were invisible.

One of the staff comes by, takes his hand, and with it pats Dusty at her neck. I cannot say this with any certainty since Harold's normal presentation to the world is a smiling one, but he seems to pause in his rumination to luxuriate in the feel of her fur. I too enjoy the moment. Both Dusty and I are becoming more relaxed in the presence of these people who communicate in the most subtle ways.

OCTOBER 7. Our second-last visit to Ongwanada is perhaps the most rewarding. William, set up in his usual location on a wide corner bed with its clear views of the room, continues to monitor our movements. It takes little persuasion for Dusty to leap up onto the plastic mattress. She noses his hands, investigating this man and his environs. William never changes his demeanour. Chin on fist, he looks as thoughtful and contemplative as Rodin's statue *The Thinker*.

Another fellow, in a wheelchair nearby, seems intrigued by Dusty's blue leash and takes it in hand. "Are you taking her for a walk?" I ask him. I am now doing what the staff do: I talk to clients assuming that they understand.

One of the staff later tells another that she's taking a client out to the "sensory garden," and I'm happy to join them. The client is an attractive young woman carrying in her hand a flat ceramic toy, and she seems—if I interpret her sounds correctly—keen to be out in the sun, going to the garden and watching Dusty prance alongside her.

The garden is divided into four quadrants: smell, taste, sight, touch. In the summer, a fountain operates in the middle of this four-metre-square enclosure. Although nearing its seasonal end, the garden still has much to offer in early October. In smell, there are, among others, evening primrose, pink dianthus, lemon balm and garlic chives.

In taste, there are basil, thyme, peppermint, chives, oregano and purple sage.

In sight, there are ribbon grass, New Zealand flax and hostas.

Touch offers blue fescue grass, sedum, foxglove digitalis and black-eyed Susans.

The girl in the wheelchair takes it all in, as best she can and as only she can. How she does it, and to what extent, is a mystery.

OCTOBER 9. We're back in the garden again. I would like a photograph to document my time here, but it's a delicate matter to ask for models. None of the clients whom Dusty and I have been visiting are in a position to give their consent for photos, and only a few guardians have granted approval.

But today I've been given the green light. I am to photograph Dusty with a young woman in pigtails. A staffer wheels her out to the garden, and, like her predecessor two days beforehand, she closes her eyes and basks in the sun, enjoying the fresh air. She breaks into a smile. Now the staffer begins to pose her two subjects.

She has a dog of her own and is comfortable urging Dusty into a sitting position, first verbally then with her hand. Oops. If you believe the dictum that one dog year is the equivalent of seven human years, Dusty clocks in at eighty-four. She is astonishingly spry for her age, but her hind end is starting to fail. She will hesitate and gather herself before jumping up into the truck, and she groans just a little as she settles into a lie-down. So when the staffer pushes down on Dusty's back, Dusty responds with a low growl and a rapid turn of the head.

Great, I'm thinking. My dog has been her usual gentle self on all her rounds and has made a name for herself. Then, on the last day, disaster. But nothing comes of this brief wrinkle.

We had dodged trouble earlier, too, in the hall where we had gathered for apple treats. A man in a wheelchair—there's an intensity about him I'm wary of—was invited to pet Dusty. He had rubbed her head a few weeks back, but it had bordered on rough, so I had a grip on Dusty as he and his helper approached. Within a foot of her, the client suddenly lunged forwards and made a grab for her. But I was ready and peeled her back. A close call.

I realized then that neither Dusty nor I had ever fully relaxed or dropped our defences here. But then, my vigilance is the one that any dog owner must have around unfamiliar faces, especially children. Dusty is kind in her heart, her track record around humans is impeccable, and I know about her ability to light up a room. That said, I am responsible for her and all the while we were at Ongwanada I kept the leash and an eye on her.

THE ONE fellow I have wanted to photograph with Dusty is Roger, the man who always welcomes us with keen interest. He will break into a chuckle, his whole body shaking as he laughs, almost bouncing in his chair.

"Where's your shoe?" I ask him.

Roger doesn't much like wearing shoes, and he has managed to kick off one. I sit by him, urge Dusty close and give her a pat, and ask Roger if he would like to do the same. Today, for the first time, he looks to be pondering just such a move. He holds his hand over Dusty, circling inches above her. Then he pulls back, as if there were an electrical charge coming from her and he is wary of receiving a shock. Then out goes the hand again, a little lower this time.

"Go ahead," I urge him. "Pat her." A few more seconds and he does just that. Then he cackles loudly.

"Aren't you proud of yourself?" I hear one of the staff members say.

It was as if Roger knew this was our last day, but then, how could he? I only know that some defence has been penetrated, a breakthrough made, and Roger is pleased as punch. Dusty, too, seems to recognize the moment, and she looks to me for reward.

"All well and good," I take her to say. "Now how 'bout a donut?"

. . .

[IS IT GOOD TO BE GOOD?]

I KEPT on looking for evidence that the subject I was pursuing, human generosity, was being pursued by others too. And it was. *The White Tiger,* by Aravind Adiga, won the 2008 Booker Prize (plus $102,000) for its dark and comic portrayal of the great divide in India, between those who have made it and those below. The author notes wryly that in the past there were a thousand castes in India, but that now there are just two: "Men with Big Bellies, and Men with Small Bellies."

In Canada, meanwhile, one finalist for the 2008 Giller Prize was a very good novel called *Good to a Fault,* by Marina

Endicott. In the book, about a woman involved in a car crash becoming mother hen to the victims of the accident, the author asks some of the same questions I am asking: What does it mean to be good? When is sacrifice selfish? What do we owe this life, and what do we deserve?

A full-page ad in *The New Yorker* of May 21, 2007, was headlined, "Is It Good To Be Good?" Sponsored by the John Templeton Foundation ("Supporting Science, Investing in the Big Questions"), the ad noted that new research points to a strong link "between doing good and living a longer, healthier and happier life." Since 2002, the foundation has been funding research by fifty scientists at Harvard, Princeton and Yale, among other universities, on the nature of selfless love.

About a year later, *Globe and Mail* columnist Margaret Wente interviewed a conservative political scientist who has written a book called *Gross National Happiness*. The author is Arthur C. Brooks, a professor of business and government policy at Syracuse University's Maxwell School of Citizenship and Public Affairs. His findings from examining a big chunk of data and surveys? The happiest people appear to be those who volunteer or who give their money away. The author's advice: be philanthropic. Wente concluded: "Money really can buy happiness after all—but only if you give it away."

There is mounting evidence from science that good deeds are at least good medicine. "Helper's high" is much like the endorphin high that long-distance runners experience and that we all feel when we do something nice for someone else. I felt it after buying those kitchen items for Vinnie's, and after the fundraisers for Robert Lovelace and Horizons of Friendship. This rush can boost the immune system, speed up recovery from surgery and reduce insomnia. Using brain scans, scientists have discovered that we are programmed to help each other: compassion registers in the brain's pleasure zones.

In their book, *The Healing Power of Doing Good* (2001), authors Allan Luks and Peggy Payne define helper's high as exhilaration coupled with a burst of energy followed by a period of calm and serenity. For the book, Luks studied more than three thousand Americans involved in volunteering and found that subjects reported a buzz that lasted several weeks. After that, simply recalling the act of helping others brought back that sense of euphoria.

Generosity appears to be good for both body and soul. Ninety per cent of those whom Luks studied reported that volunteering helped counter stress and chronic pain while lowering blood pressure and cholesterol counts. In another study, at Harvard University, researchers showed 132 students a film about Mother Teresa's work among Calcutta's poor, then measured the levels in their saliva of immunoglobulin A, the body's first defence against the common cold virus. Simply witnessing kindness jacked up their levels.

Sometimes philanthropy has the same feel as extreme sport. Zell Kravinsky, for example, is an American math whiz and English professor in Philadelphia who amassed a $45-million real estate fortune expressly to give it away to charities involved in public health. Then, in 2003, he donated one of his kidneys to an African-American woman who was taking the bus every other day for dialysis treatments.

"I used to feel," Kravinsky says, "that I had to be good, truly good in my heart and spirit, in order to do good. But it's the other way around: if you do good, you become better. With each thing I've given away, I've been more certain of the need to give more away. And at the end of it, maybe I will be good."

Jenny Oad, a Toronto writer in her thirties, likewise donated one of her kidneys to a complete stranger. She told a *Globe and Mail* reporter about having to explain to a psychiatric nurse, a psychiatrist and a bioethicist how this donation would benefit her and how Toronto General Hospital could justify risking her life to help a stranger. The recipient was a fifty-two-year-old man named Mike Fogelman, on dialysis and with a long family history of renal failure. Oad called her decision "an impulse to help that I have never second-guessed... It felt like the right thing to do."

Toronto playwright Michael Healey donated part of his liver several years ago to another playwright, Tom Walmsley, a man he barely knew. Healey's play *Generous* (actually four two-act plays about characters intent on doing something for others), ran to warm reviews in 2006. "People's motives are always complicated," Healey says. "Altruistic acts are not different from any other act in life. You are doing it based on your own psychology, your view of the world."

SWEAT
Equity

SEPTEMBER 28. An American Customs official—
a beefy fellow with shaven pate and no discernible neck—has
just removed an orange pylon blocking my lane at the border
crossing, and the light is green. So I may proceed, right? Wrong.

"You in a hurry?" asks the sourpuss in the dark blue uniform.
My first sin, apparently, was not waiting for his signal. My sec-
ond is to inform him that my passenger, Tom Carpenter, and
I are driving to Syracuse in New York State, then flying on to
New Orleans to volunteer with Habitat for Humanity.

"Habitat... for... Humanity," he repeats in a disapproving
tone. As if I have said "Communist... Party... of America."

The man in blue has not heard of Habitat for Humanity,
but this organization is certainly familiar to us. In Kingston,
there's a Habitat depot for used construction material, and
I have both dropped off material and shopped there. Money
raised goes towards the building of more houses for those who
badly need them.

Habitat got its start in Americus, Georgia, in 1976, with a
simple idea: those needing shelter would work alongside vol-

unteers to construct their own homes. Former American president Jimmy Carter and his wife, Rosalynn, raised Habitat's profile considerably when they worked on a Habitat building project in 1984. The movement spread to Canada in 1985 and is now active in ninety countries. It has so far built 250,000 simple, decent and affordable houses for more than one million people.

The Customs official wants the trunk popped (from inside the car, not from outside), he wants to see a letter from Habitat to verify our claim and he wants to know what we do for a living, if we have airline tickets and if we've ever been arrested. Finally, his grumpiness spent, he waves us on.

Why was he so surly? Does he resent high-minded volunteers? Non-profit agencies that sound vaguely un-American? This early morning shift? Maybe he's embarrassed that Canadians are still helping in New Orleans' St. Bernard Parish and the Lower Ninth Ward three years after the disaster of Hurricane Katrina. The first help that arrived after the hurricane hit on August 25, 2005, was provided by the RCMP, and a lot of people in New Orleans remember that fact. It's more than symbolic—and a source of ongoing bitterness—that the instinct to rush down there and help was at first more powerfully felt outside the country than inside.

Our first night, in a French Quarter restaurant, Tom and I get to know the rest of our Habitat team: Alex and Allegheny, massage therapists from California; and Allegheny's mother, Rose, a statistician. Stu, a social welfare administrator from Florida, who is on his seventh Habitat tour of volunteer duty in New Orleans; Karen, a specialist in wireless microphone systems for the classroom, and Karla, in computers, both from Toronto; Francine, a lieutenant commander in the Canadian navy based in Kingston; David, a superior court judge from North Carolina, and his daughter, Laura, a lawyer; and Sandy, a biologist and researcher and our tireless team leader, on her fourth New Orleans trip, and also from Kingston.

We are all pleased to be here, though all stumped by the reason for it. Why, three years after Katrina, are volunteers still trooping down to New Orleans? Why has Washington virtually abandoned that city? "You want evidence of racism in George Bush's America?" says Laura. "That's it." Laura—who will keep us laughing all week with her hysterically funny imitation of vice-presidential hopeful Sarah Palin—wonders if dumping a load of toxic trash from N'awlins on the White House lawn would wake up her government.

A T-shirt spotted on Canal Street that night: "Drove my Chevy/to the levee/but the levee/was gone."

SEPTEMBER 29. Up and at 'em. We pile at dawn into a white Habitat van and head north, to St. Bernard Parish. Our destination is a facility that was once a middle school, then a courthouse, before serving in the immediate post-Katrina days as a morgue and animal shelter. Renamed Camp Hope, it is now a warehouse for Habitat's trucks and tools, with a dorm and a cafeteria. Some forty thousand volunteers, many of them from AmeriCorps (a kind of Peace Corps for youth bent on volunteering in the homeland), have bunked here since Katrina hit.

The job site, minutes away, is an unfinished house belonging to Miss Edna, an elderly white woman with Little Orphan Annie hair and a thick southern accent. "All ma volunteers that has ever worked on ma house," she tells us, getting misty-eyed as she speaks, "are ma *he*-roes. Ah always hug 'em." Each of us in turn hugs Miss Edna, and I experience something unexpected in her heartfelt embrace: it feels like a gift.

Miss Edna lost her husband not long after the hurricane wiped out her house; this new vinyl-clad bungalow stands on the footprint of the old one. She is doubly grateful that we have come all this way to work on her place, and that Alex is massaging the tortured back muscle that kept her awake last night.

There is only one skilled construction person on this job site, and that's Tom: "Super Tom," as we come to call him. Tom is a wordsmith and an erstwhile colleague of mine, but he also knows a lot about stone masonry and renovation, either from having done it himself or from writing about it as a how-to columnist for several publications. I gravitate to a task that seems well suited to my own skill set: digging deep holes with a hand auger to accommodate the tall wooden cradle on which Miss Edna's air conditioner will soon sit. Task two is to drop into the holes the four legs of the cradle, make it level and plumb, then secure the footings with poured concrete.

Tom and Allegheny work a miracle inside, organizing a hodgepodge of cabinets still in their packing crates on the floor and installing them adroitly on the kitchen walls. The rest of us form small units: a stair crew, a spindle crew, a trim crew, a soffits-and-vent crew—the last a crew of one, and that is Stu. With every passing hour, my affection grows for these eleven eager and affable compatriots. In the evening, over deep-fried shrimp, jambalaya and Abita Amber beer (brewed at Abita Springs, fifty kilometres north of New Orleans), we tell the stories of our lives. We hoot a lot.

Alex and Allegheny tell me, "We've kind of adopted this place. We hope to come back every year." They were here as recently as May, working on another Habitat project in the parishes. They describe the exhilaration of going from a concrete foundation to roof rafters in a single day.

DURING A tour of the Camp Hope facility, one of its staffers remarked on the help that had come from Canada. Standing in the hallway outside one of the bunk bed–filled dorms, he told us that a week before Christmas 2007 there were 832 young volunteers staying here—five hundred of them college students from north of the border.

Ken Meinert, the Canadian interim executive director of Habitat for Humanity in New Orleans (he was filling in for someone recovering from a heart attack), made the same point when he met us in the lobby of our hotel the first night. These waves of young volunteers, along with greybeards like me, do a great deal in New Orleans, not just in actual reconstruction but in lifting the spirits of the locals. Such contributions were everywhere acknowledged.

A pattern to our days and our nights soon emerges. We work all day, and the evenings see us hosted somewhere for a meal. Two nights it is a restaurant. One is a step up from a greasy spoon where we are offered monstrous portions—my spaghetti came with meatballs almost the size of baseballs. The other restaurant is more upscale, a neighbourhood hideaway called Elizabeth's down by the Pauline Street Wharf and the rail line. On the two other nights, we find ourselves guests in the homes of local individuals who are spearheading reconstruction projects.

Three nights out of four there are speeches of introduction and of thanks. Ken Meinert, who has his own design firm back in Oakville, Ontario, believes passionately in the work of Habitat for Humanity, as does Sandy Berg, who leads our group so enthusiastically. Both believe in the good that volunteers do, so the gratitude bestowed on us is sincere and heartfelt. But I also feel uncomfortable accepting thanks for being "part of the solution." The solution? Not really. I am one band-aid in a first-aid kit, and the solution to New Orleans' problems demands so much more than first aid.

There is an undeniable discordance between our days and nights. By day, we work on modest little bungalows in lower middle-class neighbourhoods, with a shrimp boat in the front yard or oil refinery stacks close by emitting suspicious odours. The neighbourhoods are tight (Miss Edna knows every person on her street), and the people next door are always friendly and happy to let us use their water and electricity hookups if need be.

But at night we sleep in splendid three-pillow beds at the Hilton. Allegheny had been put to the task of finding cheap hotel accommodation and had managed to secure our $365-a-night rooms for $59—a testament, I suppose, to her powers of persuasion, to it being off-season and to Habitat's reputation in these parts. In the hotel lobby there are always a well-stocked fruit bowl and gourmet cookies under glass. At the end of every working day we help ourselves to both while the desk clerk smiles approvingly. In the French Quarter, where we sometimes dine, it is hard to imagine that flooding had ever taken place. It had, but nothing to compare with the levels in the hardest-hit parishes.

Once out of the central business district, we enter a world of abandoned houses and businesses, of entire malls stripped bare like ghost towns. Black men sit in chairs in front of their wooden houses and stare at traffic. Poster art on the street-facing wall of one house depicts a man sitting in a rocking chair while waving an American flag. A railway crossing all week flashes red, and we dutifully stop, look and listen before braving it every time, though there is never any train to be seen.

Still evident in the parishes are the stamp of the hurricane and its aftermath: high-water marks on buildings;

spray-painted codes on houses that alert emergency staff to what had been found inside (the date, number of persons found dead or alive, pets found dead or alive, the military unit leaving the message); and everywhere are concrete steps in the middle of vacant lots, all that remain of houses.

SEPTEMBER 30. Most of the day is devoted to making Miss Edna's sidewalk. Haul forty-kilogram bags of cement, drop their contents into the wheelbarrow, use a shovel to mix the powder and stone with water until it forms a thick stew. Then pour the concrete onto the framed stretch of ground where the sidewalk is forming, with Tom deftly using a board to make the top smooth. Haul, drop, mix, pour; haul, drop, mix, pour. Grunt work. We go through several dozen bags of cement.

All of us make mistakes and learn as we go, and we pick up from David, the North Carolina judge, a useful southern expression: "That dog won't hunt." It means that something is not going to work.

AT A seniors' centre under construction in the parish, we meet David Dysart, a colonel in the U.S. Marine Corps who is now director of Homeland Security and Recovery in St. Bernard Parish. He has a shaved head, a firm handshake and a taste for the limelight, as if he is always on stage, before an audience, with a microphone at his lapel.

Dirty and sweaty from a day at Miss Edna's, "Team Canada," as we are introduced, eagerly accepts the bottles of cold water he lobs to us from the fridge. We gather in a meeting room where Colonel Dysart shows us a video that was taken the day after Katrina struck the parish. Where we are sitting was that day under water, and municipal staff escaped the building by punching a hole in a window (now covered by drywall) in that same room. The video shows images of people scrambling into boats, dazed men and women waiting, always waiting under a blistering sun, and a Taco Bell restaurant with only the red roof showing, the rest under water.

"One of the things to note," Colonel Dysart tells us as the video rolls, "is that the first rescue unit to come into St. Bernard was Canadian." He reminds us that it wasn't the hurricane that flooded the parish, but the catastrophic failure of the levees. The "rescue" in those first hours was a failure, almost comic. Six thousand refinery workers, he says, were moved on huge barges to the other side of the Mississippi, but then ferried back when it was discovered that there were no resources to evacuate them. Parish councillors tried to commandeer Jet Skis to rescue citizens. One civic official went on the radio and urged those in danger of drowning to tie themselves to trees. The messages relayed to parish residents were sometimes inane, and often conflicting. Some six thousand residents of St. Bernard Parish eventually had to be evacuated.

The dead numbered 135. The tally was originally posted, with names, as 136, but one of them actually lived and he apparently makes a point every year of visiting just to see his name on that list. Asked if the man ever thought of having his name removed, Colonel Dysart says, "No, he thinks it's bringing him good luck."

Colonel Dysart has some knowledge of post-disaster reconstruction. He oversaw the rebuilding of Fallujah, in Iraq, after "hostilities" ceased in late 2004 and early 2005. That city had been almost levelled by the U.S. Marines. But the destruction of St. Bernard Parish, he says, was of another order.

"It was the most amazing thing I have ever experienced," he tells us. Only by helicopter was he able to get into the parish, which was drained and dry within ten days of Hurricane

Katrina, then flooded again by Hurricane Rita. "Four cata-strophic events occurred," he says, "in a thirty-day period." The first was Hurricane Katrina. The second was the failure of the levee system. Third, barges came loose and battered, then broke, the levees. And fourth, four million litres of crude oil were released into the water—the largest residential oil spill in American history.

Sandy Berg told me later that what struck her about coming to the parishes on her first post-Katrina visit in 2006 was the pallor that hung over the place. Nature had, for all intents and purposes, died there—or at least gone into hiding. There were no leaves, no grass, no living green plants of any kind, no birds or insects, no animals.

Colonel Dysart minces no words about the Federal Emer-gency Measures Agency (FEMA), which he claims "destroyed the recovery process with its bureaucracy." Three years after the hurricanes, FEMA is still regarded as ineffectual, even obstructionist. The federal bureaucracy would attempt to pay as little as possible at every stage of reconstruction. Battle-weary residents had fought the flood, now they were pit-ted against a more formidable foe: recalcitrant Washington nitpickers.

Colonel Dysart saves his biggest darts for what might be called the debris befuddlement.

"I'll tell you exactly how absurd this became," he begins. "We had pre-existing Katrina debris that was left to be picked up. We had Gustav debris. And then Ike came through, and it also blew up debris." What FEMA suggested was that dif-ferent contractors be hired to pick up debris from each hurri-cane, and they proposed bringing down "debris monitors" who would determine which debris in someone's front yard could be charged to which hurricane. The contractors would, of course, squabble with the monitors in order to maximize their profits. Dysart called it "an absurd game. And you wonder why it takes three years to recover."

Colonel Dysart's end piece is a story he apparently tells all teams of volunteers. In between hurricanes, residents were allowed to return to their houses for what was called a "quick look and leave." During past evacuations, they had returned with trailers to take clothes and treasured possessions, but Katrina was different. This time the water damage was so severe that most could put what was salvageable into a shoebox.

Worse, each resident was supposed to be wearing PPE (protective personal equipment) gear, since the flood material was a toxic mix of water, chemicals, human waste, crude oil and whatever else the flood had grabbed in its headlong rush. Colonel Dysart drove up to one house and there stood an elderly man "with a dust mask, short sleeves, cut-offs, flip-flops and that's it. 'Perhaps you didn't get the memo?'" the colonel asked him, and reminded him that he really shouldn't be walking around as he was. The colonel asked the man if he had sufficient food and water, and if there was anything he could do for him.

The man desperately wanted help to locate something in his kitchen, which happened also to be the repository of a great deal of detritus as the waters withdrew from the house. Down in the mud, he hoped to find his dentures.

His dentist had assured him that if he soaked them in bleach for thirty minutes, "they'll be as good as new." He had paid $3,000 for those dentures, and the last time he saw them—just before Katrina hit—they were on top of his refrigerator.

After fishing in the mud for a few minutes, Colonel Dysart found the bottom plate and, a few minutes later, the top plate.

"Katrina," the old man declared, "took everything else I own, but at least she didn't get my smile."

Then the colonel thanks us and reminds us again that the sight of volunteers from elsewhere in North America tells people in the parish that they're not forgotten. "They have a huge struggle," he says, "with a federal government that was supposed to make sure that none of this ever happened to them. That's why they pay their taxes, that's why they're good residents." He becomes emotional just briefly as he describes how St. Bernard Parish firefighters were offered to other parishes after Hurricane Gustav in 2008, three years after Katrina. That, he says, is how it's supposed to be: we're supposed to help each other. "Not a hand out," he emphasizes, "a hand up."

Then he invites everyone back to his house for fresh oysters and beer.

OCTOBER 1. Miss Edna's porch is almost finished, and the sidewalk is half finished, but a thick and wide mass of dumped concrete near the road still stands in the path of our new walkway. The concrete island must be broken up and tossed aside. Three of us take turns with the sledge. "Sweat equity" is what Habitat for Humanity asks of those who benefit from its housebuilding and interest-free loans, and sweat is what flies as we make a prolonged assault on the concrete and the day heats up. When, after many blows, a small tectonic rift appears in the block, the other two cheer its maker. I start singing that old Sam Cook song from 1960: "That's the sound of the men workin' on the chain gaaaaaang..."

The shower at day's end is the best thing I have experienced in a long time.

ONE MORNING before work we stop at Tennessee Street to admire some brand-new, ecologically advanced houses that had been built by the Make It Right Foundation, the creation of actor Brad Pitt. He came down to New Orleans after the hurricane and one resident urged him to "make this right." Pitt challenged a team of thirteen American architects to come up with affordable "green" designs. His foundation aims to build 150 such houses in the Lower Ninth Ward.

It seems an odd marriage: cutting-edge green technology and affordable housing. These ultramodern structures would stand out in any neighbourhood. In the Lower Ninth, they scream "Look at us!" And we do.

"When you're thinking about constructing affordable housing," Sandy Berg says as we stand on the sidewalk and gawk at one of them, "it isn't just the upfront costs of building it—you want to keep those low—but it's also the after-move-in costs for the families themselves." In Canada, heating is the bigger cost. Down here, it's cooling.

Just then, the site coordinator walks by. Jon Sader is a third-generation contractor and developer from Michigan and among the first contractors to come to New Orleans after the floodwaters receded.

My first question to him is the obvious one: what's green about these houses?

"Everything," he replies. The concrete is recycled and pervious, so water can run through it. They used "blue wood"—lumber taken from trees killed by mountain pine beetles. Solar panels, of course. Cisterns under the house catch rainwater from the gutters for use in watering the lawn or flushing the toilet. All the houses are at least four feet off the ground, some a great deal more. The one I looked at most closely had an two-metre elevation, allowing its owner to park a car underneath in the shade. And the windows are high-impact and designed to withstand a two-by-four travelling at 210 kilometres an hour. Mind boggling.

Families are chosen for these houses through a selection process not unlike the one used by Habitat for Humanity. Each family picks from thirteen different models, and each house is built to suit its requirements. The crew members who built these six houses are highly trained professionals. They broke ground early in July, and by October, when we visit, they are on their "punch list," the last few details.

Only late in my conversation with Jon Sader do I discover that the house we are admiring at 1720 Tennessee Street has been built by Mike Holmes, the Canadian home renovation specialist with his own television show (*Holmes on Homes*). His motto, to which he owns the trademark, is "Make It Right." As I understand it, the first communication between Holmes and the other Make It Right was from Holmes's lawyer, advising the foundation to think about another name because "Make It Right" was taken.

Holmes apparently softened that stand mightily when he learned more. In a two-hour television special on the Tennessee Street project—*Holmes in New Orleans*—the burly contractor is seen joking with Brad Pitt about the two Make It Rights. Pitt observes that Europe was completely rebuilt within four years following the Second World War. New Orleans remains unfinished. We also learn that the new owner of 1720 Tennessee Street is a grandmother, Gloria Guy, who needs the space to look after the six grandchildren in her care.

The house is spectacularly green, but its neighbours may be green with envy. In the Lower Ninth Ward, many people still live in so-called shotgun houses—tiny and narrow clapboard homes. The origin of the name has many explanations, but one is that because all inside doors are on the same side of the house, you could fire a shotgun through the open front door and the pellets would emerge out the back door without hitting a wall or door.

Many of those shotgun houses sit vacant or were washed away in the flood. The Lower Ninth once housed 18,000 people; only 1,200 live there now. Gloria Guy is one of the lucky ones. She's back in her old neighbourhood where she wants to be and in a splendid house, a "Brad Pitt house," as people here call them. The other 16,800 people, dispersed all over the United States, are still waiting.

OCTOBER 2. Miss Edna's "hurricane protection kits" are put in place. One piece of fibreboard, about two metres high and one metre wide, with precut holes at the four corners, is set up over each window. Alex holds the heavy fibreboard piece in place from the ground, while I scurry up a ladder and drill the screws through the holes and into the house's siding. The white "anchors" are ingeniously designed: one half is a wood screw allowing it to penetrate wood, the other outer half is threaded to accommodate a wing nut, and with a five-cornered head so my drill's driver can turn it. The four anchors will stay in place on the corners of each window, and the boards will be stored in the crawl space under Miss Edna's house, awaiting the next big hurricane. When it comes, and it surely will come, I will think of her. Hurricane "protection" in a kit; if only it were that simple.

Near the end of the day, I find in the dirt on the path of our new sidewalk two objects sacred to Miss Edna: the faux marble bases of her husband's bowling trophies and, attached, a twisted remnant of each top. Miss Edna grows misty-eyed at the sight of the first one, and cannot bear to look at the second. She holds up her hands and shields her eyes, as if the thing I hold in my hand emits a cruel light.

The people of St. Bernard Parish and the Lower Ninth Ward have been traumatized. What I have read about—unspeakable loss, deprivation, anarchy—they have experienced first-hand. I imagine it's why the sight of mangled trophies can bring back a flood of emotions. In the end, Miss Edna likes my suggestion that the items be entombed in the concrete of her new walkway.

BEFORE I left for New Orleans, I raised $4,500 for Habitat for Humanity through a letter I wrote to family and friends. Like the eleven others on my reconstruction team, I also contributed $500, as Habitat requires of everyone wanting to participate in what it calls "a team build." So Habitat received from me alone $5,000 plus the names of seventeen individuals who will now go on the Habitat mailing list. We all believed we were doing good, and we were.

But were we also propping up the status quo?

My friend Jamie Swift, the most ardent social activist I know, sent me a cheque and reminded me of a passage in Naomi Klein's book *The Shock Doctrine,* the section on New Orleans.

The passage starts with a quote from Harry Belafonte, the American musician and civil rights activist. "Katrina was not unforeseeable," he said in September 2005, just after the hurricane hit. "It was the result of a political structure that subcontracts its responsibility to private contractors and abdicates its responsibility altogether."

Klein was in New Orleans during the second week of September 2005, shooting footage for a documentary film. She describes navigating dark streets without streetlights, seeing hurricane debris everywhere and then getting involved in a nasty car accident that landed her in hospital. Klein ended up at the Ochsner Medical Center in downtown New Orleans, where she was given prompt, even first-class, medical attention.

Charity Hospital, meanwhile, the one that catered to the poor of the parishes, was flooded.

What Klein argues in her book is that disasters like Katrina are not universally regarded as an occasion for everyone to put their oars in the water and pull together. No, disasters are viewed by some as opportunities for private enterprise. She cites the example of how FEMA paid one company $175 a square foot to cover damaged roofs with blue tarps—tarps provided by the government. By the time the contractor and subcontractors had hived off their cuts, workers installing the tarps were paid as little as $2 a square foot.

MIDWEEK, MISS Edna approaches me (I wear a tool belt and may look like I know what I'm doing) and asks if I would go with her into the house. She says once more how much she appreciates the work we have done, work that she has often witnessed herself. Her habit was to stand on the perimeter of the lot and watch with her right hand raised to her chin and the right elbow cradled in the palm of her left hand. Occasionally, she would intervene.

One morning, for example, Miss Edna said she wanted to speak to "the carpenter" who had installed a piece of trim by the back door. I had not nailed it all the way in. It was the last thing I had done the day before, and I simply wanted to set it into place while we worked on the other pieces. Well, I had installed *wood* trim and she had bought herself some *faux wood* trim that was meant for that door. She wanted the trim switched, and we did that.

But this morning she has a more serious request. She loves the work that Tom and Allegheny have done with the cupboards, but there is one ("all by its lonesome") that she wants moved.

My first response to Miss Edna's entreaty is not the kindest one. I think she is looking a gift horse in the mouth, and Tom thinks much the same when he hears of it. But later, we both reject that interpretation. We decide we like the fact that she has spunk enough to say what she wants. We lack the time to fulfill Miss Edna's request, but maybe she will implore the next crew.

Peter, a Habitat contractor who sometimes comes around when we need guidance (the tricky math and carpentry involved in making stringers, or stair supports, presented one such occasion), says he has been approached many times by neighbours who have an irate response to a Habitat crew descending on their street. "Where the hell," they ask, "is *my* house?"

Good question.

OCTOBER 3. On to a new site, the house of Miss Janet, a red-haired Lucille Ball look-alike. Much like Miss Edna's, the shell of this house is up, the roof is on, but there's a lot of finishing work to be done inside and out.

I put up more hurricane kits and cut more vinyl siding to make way for door trim. My power tool is a grinder, a small circular blade with a horrible whine and a menacing feel. "Scary tool," says Tom, before counselling me in its safe use. The best approach is the one used by anyone wielding a chain saw: hold the saw off to one side, so that any kickback projects harmlessly into the air, and not into, say, your jugular vein.

KEEPING US hydrated is Sandy's biggest concern in the oppressive heat: "Are you drinking lots of fluids?" is always her question. I go to the back of a seafood diner where we had enjoyed a shrimp lunch midweek, and two workers there help me refill our water cooler. At one point, the cooler lid hits the dirt and one of them warns me to wash it off. "No tellin' what's in that ground," he says.

The two men thank me (another round of thanks) for coming to help with reconstruction and one jokingly suggests that I come back in July when the heat and humidity soar. Later, I think about what he has said. He was grateful but he was also scoring a small point: all volunteering drops off in midsummer, and he knows it.

STU HAS met a lot of people on his volunteer forays to New Orleans. He finds he can go into bars in the parishes and strike up a conversation with just about anyone, some of whom later become friends and e-mail correspondents. Being a volunteer down here means you carry a special passport.

"There's someone you might want to talk to," Stu says to me over lunch at Camp Hope. It is always the same lunch: multi-coloured pasta, diced olives and tomatoes, thick chunks of canned ham, a salad, and peaches, likewise liberated from a can. Everything is set out in metal containers under an aluminum canopy, cafeteria style, and all washed down with a Kool-Aid-like orange drink I can't seem to get enough of.

The woman he introduces me to is from outside San Diego, and she is no volunteer passing through for a few weeks or even months. Crystal Wells has turned the reconstruction of St. Bernard Parish into a calling. After seeing the images on television in February 2006, she dropped everything and came to New Orleans.

I want to know the impulse behind her move, one that has changed her life.

"A lot of people ask me that," says Crystal. She owns a salon and retail store back home, and the plan was to "break away" for a week or two, something she says she could well afford to do. What made her want to stay was the starkness—the emptied parish, the dearth of every service from electricity to running water to food.

"I was really angry," she says.

"Angry with whom?"

"The country, the government."

"For abandoning these people?"

"Yeah. I just wanted to tell everybody. Please, come down, we need help."

"It's like I have the gene, the gene to help," she says later, and a few others clearly have it too. In the early days of Camp Hope, seventeen-year-olds mixed with retired men and women who had arrived with their church groups. "The common denominator," says Crystal, "is that there was no doubt in anyone's mind that they should be here."

She kept going back to California, then returning to Louisiana, and finally she told her salon staff that they would have to run the business themselves for a while. Crystal has since bought a house in New Orleans and set down roots. "I believe in this place," she says.

For Wells, the impulse is not religious. She wonders if it stemmed from parents who made helping others a priority in their lives. Now a full-time volunteer, she finds the work has slowed the pace of her life in a way she likes. She no longer puts in the ninety-hour weeks she used to, but she helps Camp Hope's director, assists with special projects, works in the kitchen, conducts orientation sessions for new volunteers. The normal distance that exists between strangers doesn't apply to volunteers who come here, she says, and I can attest to that.

And the people who live here? "Salt of the earth," she pronounces. "I've never met people like them, and it's one of the reasons I wanted to stay here." Crystal was raised in a small coastal community of six thousand people in San Diego County, and when it grew and the price of property soared, it drew people with no sense of community. "Not-in-my-backyard types" is how she describes them. She finds the people of the parishes almost their opposite. "They're survivors," she says, "and the kind of people I want as neighbours."

"I can tell you," she concludes, "that what's lacking in our society is a sense of community." We are cut off from each other, she says, by our cars and our office cubicles.

At the far end of the cafeteria where we sit, someone has arranged a giant mural of one-metre-by-one-metre pieces of art, maybe sixty pieces in all. Their creators had spent time volunteering at Camp Hope and the one that catches my eye is from a fraternity, Alpha Phi Omega. Over a red heart, someone has written the words of Mahatma Gandhi: "The best way to find yourself is to lose yourself in the service of others."

That message, in Crystal's opinion, hasn't made it to San Diego. The reaction of her family and friends to her work in New Orleans was supportive at first, but as the weeks stretched to months and then years, they became baffled by what she is doing. She invents a story that no doubt was familiar in her previous life, about a young woman in tears because her wedding plans are in disarray—the flowers don't match the bridesmaids' dresses and "how dare they treat her like that after all the money she spent." Crystal doesn't want to hear about such things. "I don't want to be in a community where that matters."

Where she lives now, true celebration is when a neighbour calls to say that they're finally putting up drywall in her house, or a school has opened and the kids are back in class. "Do you know how meaningful and powerful that is? That, to me, is living."

OCTOBER 4. Our last day. Construction sites produce an enormous amount of scrap, and I spend the morning with a crew loading the big black trailer, riding to the dumpsters and flinging in the debris. Another job well suited to my skill set.

I'm nailing in a final bit of door trim that afternoon when the call goes out for a farewell photo. Someone drapes a Canadian flag over Miss Janet's new railing, as Team Canada (the Yanks have been adopted as honorary Canucks) poses on the porch. I unbuckle my tool belt and toss my hammer in the back of the van. We're done.

OCTOBER 5. We cross the border.

"What were you doing in New Orleans?" the Canada Customs official asks.

"Volunteering with Habitat for Humanity."

"Was it fun?"

"Yes," I reply. "Yes, it was." And she waves us on.

Part of me agrees with Siobhan, a nineteen-year-old woman from Oakville, Ontario, whom I met at Camp Hope and who had come down for a three-month stint. For her, "this whole thing can be reduced to its simplest form: it's one human being helping another." I will cherish my experience in New Orleans, and I would do it again.

But another part of me wonders why we as a society can't do better for folks like Miss Edna and Miss Janet, never mind the thousands whose uninsured homes remain abandoned and shuttered. One of the community papers in St. Bernard Parish, a satirical weekly I read one morning over eggs and sausage in a diner, asked why the government bailed out Wall Street while continuing to turn its back on the people in the parishes.

Those American citizens are entitled to a fair shake and what they're getting is hit-and-miss charity—for which they never cease to offer profuse thanks. I thought of that Leonard Cohen song, "Bird on the Wire," in which a beggar counsels not to ask for so much, while a pretty woman urges, "Hey, why not ask for more?"

Tom has the same thought afterwards. He remembers how John Kenneth Galbraith likened the trickle-down theory of economics to feeding a horse a lot of oats while trusting that a few grains would pass through and onto the road for the sparrows.

I try to imagine what might have happened had such a calamity as the levees failing occurred in, say, an old Connecticut neighbourhood. Mostly white, educated, politicized and affluent, the residents would have demanded, and received, instant government assistance. Mostly black, uneducated, apolitical and poor, the people in the hammered parishes of New Orleans have come a long way, and I admire their spirit, but I wish they didn't have such a long way still to go.

OCTOBER 27. The trickle-down theory comes up in conversation at a fundraiser held by the local Canadian Cuban Friendship Association. Three hurricanes in succession had battered Cuba in the fall, causing billions of dollars in damage and taking down half a million homes.

Over beans and rice and chicken, and while wet snow swirls outside, Paul Gervan and I get into an animated discussion about philanthropy. Paul is a contrarian who operates with a healthy dose of cynicism, but he has a smart and lively mind, and when you take him on you're in for a tussle.

His argument, in a nutshell, is this. Maybe it's smarter to let entrepreneurs like Bill Gates and Warren Buffett turn their billions into gazillions and trust that they will share their fortunes later in life. The more wealth they're allowed to accumulate, the greater the chance that they will turn those golden eggs into a baker's dozen. Paul points to the corruption that siphons off huge amounts of government-to-government aid money.

I trot out my usual objections to trickle-down philanthropy: too much power in the hands of a few, the risk of lousy decisions, the tail wagging the dog. "You're not talking about philanthropy," he counters. "You're talking about changing the way the world works. Ain't gonna happen, my friend."

Paul is on his high horse, so I get on mine. I tell him he's fatalistic. The Shah of Iran had his secret police and American military backing, and yet he was deposed. The Berlin Wall fell. Apartheid in South Africa ended, and Nelson Mandela overcame twenty-seven years in prison to become president and a winner of the Nobel Peace Prize. The world does change, and sometimes for the better. Ten months in the trenches and thinking about the current system of sharing the wealth have led to convictions I did not possess when I started down this road.

I pointed to all the silverware on the table. The current system allows one of us, perhaps the one endowed with the greatest determination or the most intelligence or the most charm, to gather up every knife, fork and spoon. And after the meal, his pockets heavy with silver, he may decide to give one among us a spoon.

Is it so outrageous to imagine a world in which everyone not born with a utensil is given one? What is wrong with sharing? Any chance we can make sharing as sexy as accumulating?

We are just a week away from the American election, and Republican John McCain's pitch sounds like base greed to me. "Barack Obama wants to spread the wealth," he says. "I want to create wealth." So his message is clear. Amassing wealth is a good thing, sharing it is not.

HURRICANE KATRINA offered a lesson, if we needed it, in the power of the sea. Might ocean societies have something to teach us about sharing? On the remote islands of Fiji, most people live by fishing and farming. I was there in 1985, and I remember how serene and stress-free the people were. If a fisherman caught, say, five fish, three would go to the person's family and close relations, the other two would be given to those in the village most in need of them. This custom is not called "generosity," and certainly it demands no gratitude. Sharing the wealth is so ingrained in the social fabric that it's done without thinking. One day, illness or old age will lay low that fisherman and help will be forthcoming. He paid, and now he is owed.

In Newfoundland, the tragedy of 9/11 forced many New Yorkers into billets around Gander. Somewhere I read about a man—a black man, a minister from Nigeria—being approached on the streets of Gander by an eight-year-old boy. The boy, it being a small town, had come to know the man's name, and he went up to him, took his hand and asked him if there was anything he needed. That man, and those New Yorkers, will remember the generosity of Newfoundlanders—who took them in, washed their clothes, fed them and in every way treated them as kin—for the rest of their lives.

But here's what I want to take from the tale: how the Newfoundlanders did what they did almost instinctively, without expectation of thanks or reciprocity. The Newfoundland writer

Michael Winter puts it well in his novel *The Big Why*. A New-foundlander, he says, "gives a hand and he gets a hand, and hardly a nod of the head to either." The outport tradition of hospitality, especially to those shipwrecked and washed up on shore, and of looking out for one's neighbour, lives on.

. . .

[A NEW ROOF FOR CHARLIE]

THOUGH I live in Kingston, I play old-timer hockey in Picton most Monday afternoons between September and April. We call ourselves the SELF—the Self-Employed League of Friends—and we are a far cry from the National Hockey League. We are writers and musicians, artists and contractors, truckers and entrepreneurs, and while some can claim to be in their thirties, most are in their forties, fifties, even their sixties. Play is slow but sometimes edgy, and from such heat and the barroom chat that follows, forgiveness is forged and affection blooms.

Late in January 2007, we learned that our oldest player, a retired lawyer and science teacher named Charlie Publow, had a problem. Charlie's roof leaked badly and he had no money to fix it. Every cent he had went into the stray cat sanctuary (close to a hundred felines) he operated from his house and various outbuildings on a ramshackle property north of town. Worse, Charlie had cancer and the outlook was grim. One of the players, a retired engineer named Dale Hicks, approached John McKinney, one of the musicians and SELF's organizer, and together they quietly put out the word: what say we put a new roof on Charlie's house?

So we did. Dale is connected with Habitat for Humanity (he has volunteered in New Orleans), and he called in a local farmer who also supports that organization. ("I don't mind roofin'," Allen Koopmans told me when I asked him why he was helping a man he had never met.) About eight guys from the team showed up one morning at Charlie's. He had been forewarned we were coming, but surprise and delight still registered on his face.

Up went the scaffolding, off came the old roof. I remember the pinging sound, like that of rifle fire in old Westerns, as our flat shovels got under the roofing nails, and, with a flick of our wrists, the stubby pale-grey nails popped skywards. Ping! Ping! Ping!

Another farmer down the road loaned us his tractor and forklift so we could heft flashing and shingles up on the roof. We were like ants crawling over that house, and each of us gravitated to specified tasks, as if we'd been doing this all our lives. The whole event had the rugged good cheer of a barn raising. It was actually more work than anticipated, since the wood below was rotten in places. Dale, especially, logged several days at Charlie's house installing new plywood, flashing and just generally making it right.

But what could be better than putting a roof over another man's head, a man you call a friend? My soreness at the end of the day actually felt good. And while we were up on the roof hammering, Charlie—I heard this later from his sister, Margo— was inside weeping. Then he went to town and bought us food and drink: Tim Hortons donuts and cold Coronas.

We all liked Charlie. A wiry man with a lopsided grin, helter-skelter hair and sad-sack green eyes under bushy eyebrows, he was bright, sometimes cantankerous, frequently mischievous, always irascible. Humankind often irked him, but Charlie thought animals—cats especially—were kindred spirits.

After he died in Picton Hospital, in March 2007, we gathered at the Acoustic Grill following Monday afternoon hockey, as is our custom, and someone put a rum and coke, Charlie's poison, on the bar. One by one, we clinked his glass and told Publow tales. The time he lost a high school golf tournament and tossed his clubs in anger off the bluff. His proclivities as a hockey player—at sixty-four, slow but sneaky, a dipsy-doodle dandy who didn't mind, and clearly enjoyed, the odd collision.

His quick demise was a blessing, all things considered, but so too were those days of hammering on Charlie's roof under a cold winter sun.

ENGLISH
Class on the Rez

"TELL ME about the lip ring," I ask Cindy. She is seventeen and I am fifty-nine as I write this, and it is the first thing that strikes me. The difference between us, captured in a pierced mouth. What is mere fashion for her seems curious and alien to me.

"It goes with the style and the clothing," she says, a style she defines as "emo" (she pronounces it ee-moe). I have never heard of emo, have no idea what it means. Again, I am reminded of the canyon between a white male soon eligible for the Canada Pension and a tawny stripling on a Mohawk territory. Cindy explains, patiently, that emo stands for "emotional" and that the fashion is marked by dark colours and bold designs, with one eye often covered by hair that falls over the face like a curtain, as Cindy's jet-black hair does. A curtain to peek out of, or retreat behind, as need be.

Cindy says that to have the piercing done professionally would have cost her $40 or $50, money she didn't have. So she sterilized an earring and did the job herself.

What has brought Cindy and me together is my desire to teach Aboriginal youth. After hearing Karihwakeron Tim Thompson,

---

the principal of First Nations Technical Institute (FNTI), speak on CBC Radio, I made a few phone calls, and here I am. Cindy dropped out of high school, but she has returned to FNTI, located some twenty-eight kilometres east of Belleville in southeastern Ontario. Diagnosed with attention deficit disorder and saddled with both long-term and short-term memory problems, she could use tutoring as she pursues her diploma, and I offer my services.

As an exercise, I suggest we interview each other and then write a short profile of the other. This is a lesson in listening, in taking notes, then coming up with a piece of writing based on what we have learned.

My impression of Cindy is that she's quiet but forthright, and very proud of her Mohawk heritage. A shawl dancer at powwows ("You move your shawl around like an eagle," she explains), she's learning Mohawk and teaches me hello ("say-go" is how you write it phonetically) and thank you *(ne-ow-ah)*, and informs me that she hopes one day to teach her children, if and when they come, the language. Cindy hopes, too, to write and illustrate kids' books. This is a lofty goal for someone who finds reading difficult. The only thing I know about writing, I tell her, is that before writing comes reading.

Cindy is slight, almost tiny, like a bird. After leaving school ("I was skipping classes and mouthing off at teachers"), she lived on the street for a while.

"Is there anything good about living on the street?" I ask her.

"No," she says flatly. "It's a terrible way to live." Street life taught her only one thing: to be kind to street people.

Cindy earlier showed me a piece she had written about how she is moved to tears at seeing starving children on television and how she wishes she could help them. "I hate seeing people on the street with no food or proper clothing," she tells me. "Those people need help." Helping is a powerful instinct with Cindy.

Later, I ask her if she believes that life on the rez is any different from, say, my life in midtown Kingston. "No," Cindy tells me. "We're both human."

Cindy has a dog at home, "a rez dog," as she calls the mix of husky, shepherd and Lab who follows her around the house. I am left with two conclusions: first, the dog has good taste in humans. Second, there is more that joins Cindy and me than divides us.

I write my profile of Cindy. I'm still waiting for her profile of me.

NOVEMBER 6. I sense exasperation in Tracy Maracle, principal at the Ohahase Education Centre, which is a part of FNTI. She is also responsible for the HOPE program: Haudenosaunee (meaning "people of the long house") Opportunity for Personalized Education. Tracy Maracle, in effect, runs an alternative school, one that operates thanks to a partnership involving three others: a high school in Belleville, the local county school board and the Mohawks of the Bay of Quinte. Programs are individualized for students who, to put it mildly, have not done well in traditional educational settings. Ohahase means "new road" in the Mohawk language.

The First Nations Technical Institute has been offering educational programs for twenty-four years and is the oldest Aboriginal post-secondary institution in Ontario. The Ohahase Education Centre is housed in an old building at the airport in Deseronto (one of the diploma programs offered by FNTI trains pilots to fly single-engine airplanes). Everything possible is done to celebrate and restore, if it's missing, the students' sense of Mohawk heritage and history. In Toronto, where racial violence has marred some high schools, several black educators have argued for segregated high schools where black history would be a core subject. Here, Mohawk history is front and centre.

The good news at 3 Old York Road in the Tyendinaga Mohawk Territory is that students at the educational centre come here every fall determined to earn their high school diplomas. But like the building's aging single-hung windows that struggle to keep out the cold, some students are ill-equipped.

I'm to give a nuts-and-bolts talk on writing next week. "You may have eight students in your class," Tracy tells me. "You may have two. You may have none."

Like Cindy, many students here have learning difficulties, many have dropped out and returned after being chastened by a year or so of working in fast-food joints. Some are young mothers, and are finally making time for themselves. But noble aspirations in September often fall prey to circumstance by November.

Tracy Maracle's task as their English teacher is to give them tools so they can read a piece of writing, process it and allow it to inspire writing of their own. But many of these students are as frightened of words as I am of numbers. She tries to give them works written by Native writers: Drew Hayden Taylor is a favourite because of his comic edge, but Joseph Boyden, the rising CanLit star with Métis and Mi'kmaq blood flowing in his veins, is a bridge too far for most of them.

I know that Joseph Boyden has done a lot of teaching on reserves, and knowing this helped push me in the direction of the Mohawk First Nation. This is the place where enraged protesters parked a bus on a main rail line to drive home their points in a land claims dispute in the summer of 2007. My guess from talking to people here is that the reserve is divided between those who found the protest excessive and those who deemed it entirely fitting.

NOVEMBER 12. On the morning after Joseph Boyden is awarded the prestigious Giller Prize for *Through Black Spruce,* I mention his win in the English class at FNTI. There are only four students this day, and one of them produces from her bag—with a little flourish—a copy of the novel. I am quite sure she struggles to read a book at that level, but I admire her pluck.

She is a woman in her mid-twenties, a few years older than the others and with a child at home, and a burning desire to get her secondary school diploma. Her name is Laurel and, like her classmates, she is intimidated by the writing process. Organizing the ideas, writing that first sentence, are major feats for all of them.

At the end of the class—an introduction to the tools commonly used in writing—I give them an assignment. Write three hundred words on interacting with an animal. They groan. You would think I had said "lift a three-hundred-pound weight and carry it three hundred yards."

THE NATIONAL high school dropout rate in Canada has been falling in recent years and now stands around 14 per cent. Among First Nations youth, however, the overall figure is more than 50 per cent and even higher among youth living on reserves. Aboriginal students who graduate are twice as likely as other Canadians to drop out of college or university or never pursue a post-secondary education.

Those are grim figures, but the situation seems worse the closer one looks at life for young Aboriginal people. According to figures from the First Nations Child & Family Caring Society of Canada (FNCFCS), one in ten First Nations children (27,000 in total) are in care outside the home, compared with one in two hundred for the rest of Canada. The Society also argues that the agencies assigned to help Aboriginal children are woefully underfunded by the government, so much so that they launched a formal complaint with the Canadian Human Rights Commission in 2007, arguing discrimination. As I write this, the complaint has yet to be heard.

Meanwhile, some $5.6 billion is spent by government, ostensibly to make life better for Canada's 1.2 million First Nations people. But serious doubts have been raised about whether that money is being spent wisely. The Congress of Aboriginal Peoples, which represents 800,000 Native people living off reserves, published a major report early in 2008 called *Where Does the Money Go?* It noted that "a crisis of confidence" surrounds public funding of Aboriginal programs and services in Canada.

A book published the month before I signed on at FNTI went even farther. Written by Frances Widdowson and Albert Howard, *Disrobing the Aboriginal Industry* argues that in the absence of any requirement to account for spending, vast sums of money are going into the pockets of band council members and their families or to the many non-Aboriginal lawyers, anthropologists and others who are paid as consultants during land claims settlements.

One bit of good news is that educators have become convinced that immersing First Nations children in their ancestral languages, cultures and customs is a way of both restoring pride in these young people and keeping them in school. What FNTI does is supposed to work, and Tracy believes that it does. The dropout rate locally is much lower than on reserves as a whole.

NOVEMBER 17. The classroom is bright, with a blackboard and whiteboard at the north end. Over the blackboard is a horizontal poster featuring the phrase I had seen at Vinnie's: "No act of kindness, however small, is ever wasted." The walls are an aqua blue, and as I stand by the blackboard I face a long single line of desks running left to right. Behind the students are pine bookshelves, home to a collection best described as tired. I would call this a spartan classroom.

"Compared to what's available elsewhere in this region," Tracy tells me, "this pales. We feel fortunate to have what we have, but educational funding for schools on reserves is one-sixth what it is in the rest of Canada. It's very disheartening."

The books on the shelves hardly constitute a library. "They're donated," says Tracy. "'Give the poor Indians some books to read.'" FNTI does have computers on site, but there is no money for computers in the classroom, educational assistants or speech pathologists. Any magazines or newspapers are brought in by staff. The 120-year-old building is drafty in winter, and when windows break or light bulbs go, they are slow to be replaced.

THE FIRST boy into class this morning says he didn't get his assignment done. "I had a rough weekend," he says. "A very rough weekend."

He looks at me as if I should know what he means simply by looking at his face, as if the evidence is there should I care to see it.

"Is your eye swollen?" I ask finally.

"My nose is broken," he says.

It seems he was staying at a friend of a friend's house on Saturday evening and awoke to find someone straddling him in bed and raining blows down on his face. My student knew his attacker and knew the reason for the assault. "A girl," the student shrugs. All's fair in love and war.

Of the four students who were given the animal interaction assignment, one doesn't come to class and two fail to accomplish the task. But Laurel has written a page and a half about an encounter with a horse. It is a lovely piece of writing, full of colour and detail and imagery. Too shy to read it herself, she wonders if I would. I am so impressed that I later ask her to send it to me via Tracy's computer so I can lay on spit and polish and show her how basic editing and rewriting can take her essay to the next level.

For this class, I have brought with me a basket full of props: an Indonesian wooden statue of a prancing horse on a pedestal, a heavy blown-glass paperweight that bears the features of a giant marble, the horsehair fly whisk I use when riding my horse in summer, a wooden carving of a turtle (an animal sacred to Mohawks) and several other items. These are meant to help overcome my pedagogical challenge: how to break through the students' writer's block. It was as if the flow of a creek had been arrested by a beaver lodge, so that downstream only a trickle of water ran while upstream a small lake had formed.

I had told them, "If you can see, you can describe. If you can speak, you can write." But none believed me. Then an idea came. What if I brought two students up before the class, blindfolded one and made him or her the poser of questions while the other held an object in his or her hands and described it in response to the other's queries? I would take notes of each response, put those words on the blackboard, and have the class use those words as the basis of a sentence or two.

If I could make them comfortable with the process of writing, which is often nothing more than responding to the world, the act of putting pen to paper would seem less frightening. Fear of writing, I had told them, is a form of self-induced blindness. By taking away one sense, that of sight, my hope was that the others would rush in to compensate. That the colour, texture, feel, weight and heft, dimensions, smell and whatever thoughts the object provoked would all be grist for the writing mill.

The exercise proves to be a great success. It forces the students to find the words to capture the essence of the object, and sometimes the images that emerge are exceptionally vivid. My paperweight reminds one student of a fortune teller's ball. Another observes that the bubbles frozen inside the blown glass bauble remind her of the action in a glass of 7-Up or of candy cooking on a stove.

I tell them that the types of images they conjure have a name, and that each one is a writer's tool, that these tools have a place in the writer's kit in the same way that hammer and saw belong in a carpenter's wooden box. "Like a fortune teller's ball" is a simile. Bubbles in a glass of soda or candy cooking on a stove are metaphors.

The dam, I hope, is broken and the creek is flowing again.

NOVEMBER 19. The students, says Tracy, are really enjoying my classes, but enjoyment has come my way too. I may have engineered a minor breakthrough the other day with the blindfold game. Today, I have another such moment.

I have been asking questions as a journalist and writer for thirty-six years, and it's become second nature to me. One question invariably leads to another and, with luck, follows naturally from the one before. I have two lists of questions in my head: the ones that I bring to the interview—the who-what-when-where-why questions that are the bedrock of any story—and the questions that are provoked by what my subject is saying. Often, the follow-up question is *why*.

Today, the class helps a student named Claire with one of her writing assignments, a personal essay that is almost a psychological profile of herself. And it occurs to me that her fellow students hardly know where to begin with a line of questioning. They are more inclined to offer answers or stories than questions. Laurel, for example, remembers the kindness of Claire's mother, who once showed up at Laurel's house, unbidden, with a stove and fridge and furniture because the need was there. You, said Laurel, looking at Claire, are cut from the same cloth.

Eventually the questions do come, questions designed to reveal character. What are you afraid of? someone asks Claire. The dark, it turns out, stemming from a time when an older sister locked Claire in a closet and then told her there was someone in there with her. What do you find funny? Who do you admire? Why?

I SPEND the lunch hour working privately with Tom. He tells me that he has been living in Toronto the past year with an older sister. He was sixteen and only saw her—I presume owing to conflicting schedules—about once a week.

Tom, with his Snoop Dogg white baseball cap set on his head at a rakish angle, strikes me as a complicated guy, and remarkably self-aware. He wants his essay to establish his character against the backdrop of the reserve—as it is now, and as it was, say, in his mother's time. But his mother apparently has no appetite for that discussion (a privacy issue, possibly), so Tracy has agreed to be interviewed by Tom about her childhood on the rez. Their conversation will be part of Monday's class.

In the meantime, Tom is one of those who doesn't know where to begin in writing about himself. So, in an office at FNTI, I interview Tom while eating my noodles and cheese. I learn that he's a capable hunter and spear fisher, that he's confident he could survive in the bush, that he has a ritual of going to the nearby Shannon River most clear days to watch the sun go down, that after his mother and father split up, his mother connected with the father of his best friend—"who can always put a smile on my face. Don't know how he does it, but he can."

I discover that Tom has soured on love and is convinced that boy-girl relationships always end badly. The quiet and seclusion of the reserve are the things he both loves and hates about the place. The rez's boredom means that personal news spreads like wildfire, but like that circle game we played as children— a secret is whispered on and becomes distorted by the time it returns to you—no one has the facts straight.

And yet, Tom loves the bush and how the seasons are more deeply felt here. He loves his Mohawk culture and is immensely proud of it. And for all the nosiness and intrusiveness of life on the rez, he knows he could knock on many doors here and be welcomed. Tom, at a tender age, understands that two sides of a story can both be true.

We talk for about an hour. At first, Tom thinks that he has too little material. Then he thinks he has too much, and how is he going to organize it all?

For some reason, perhaps because I have asked him to name his favourite things, the song from *The Sound of Music,* "My Favourite Things," comes into my head. I sing the chorus aloud and Tom recognizes it: "When the dog bites," etc.

It occurs to me that Tom could open his essay with those lines and launch into his own favourite things. We're letting a song act as a structure for a self-portrait. The reader of the piece has a signpost to show the way forward. Like a sign at the entrance to a village, except this one doesn't say "Welcome to Deseronto," it says, "Welcome to Tom-land."

NOVEMBER 24. My plans for the class on the art of interviewing are sidelined when Tracy isn't able to come.

For his self-profile, Tom still needs the experience of an older reserve resident that he can compare with his own. Though not even ten years older than Tom, Laurel has seen a lot and she agrees to be interviewed by the class for the purpose.

First, students pair off and create the off-the-shelf questions they will ask her, the basic questions that journalists always ask, in one form or another. But I want them to listen deeply, to be alert to possible follow-up questions. I am thrilled with how honest our subject is, and how carefully the others listen and formulate their queries.

Laurel comes from a large family with a past so catastrophic that her optimism and good cheer are astounding. Named after a cat her mother once owned, she had a sister who was raped and murdered out west. Laurel and her family fled their father only to be tossed, frying pan to fire, into the hands of an alcoholic stepfather, who later became what she calls "a dry drunk"—sober but hostile and resentful about being deprived of his stimulant. Have I mentioned the crack cocaine–addicted uncles? How this young girl, at the age of seven, was "a mother to my siblings"? How she left home, a two-bedroom cabin without running water, when she was fifteen?

And yet, Laurel says, "I love the territory," meaning the reserve. "I feel connected to the earth here. It's mine. I would never leave here." She is, though, alive to the place's contradictions. Laurel describes how, on the one hand, many young people strive for spiritual connection, yet on the other, how light-fingered some are.

Tom asks her to name the top ten things that would define the rez, and she lists them, all of them positive. Laurel cherishes the tranquility, the spiritual questing, the powerful sense of family, the drive to do something with one's life, the compassion everywhere in evidence, how safe she feels here, how accepting people are, how unaccepting the outside is, the beauty of the place, its history.

When I ask Laurel to show proof of the "unaccepting" outside, she urges me to walk out the main door and look up at the broken windows of the old hangar from which this school is carved. This rez school looks nothing like a mainstream school. She's asking that all-important question: why?

All in all, a dynamic class, at least from my perspective.

To make it all the sweeter, Cindy, who pointedly and almost rudely shuffled papers for most of last class, shows up this morning with an eight-page essay on her *tota ma,* her Mohawk grandmother, and it is good, very good. It reads like a kid's book.

NOVEMBER 26. The last class, as expected, features several no-shows. Two mothers had warned me. One is taking her son to a local production of *The Velveteen Rabbit,* and, since she is the one with the wheels, the other has no transportation.

Another student simply doesn't show. Another slips in late, having missed the bus. So the class begins with just Cindy and me. That's fine. I want to go through her essay, show her what I've written in the margins and suggest ways in which a very good piece can become an excellent piece.

What I love about the essay is how it reads as if spoken. At one point, Cindy wants to make the point that her *tota ma* ("duh-duh ma" is how it's pronounced in Mohawk) makes the best moose stew. The author has simply inserted mmmmm-mmm-mmm into the middle of a sentence. This is a fresh, original touch, and she does something similar four times in the piece.

What is missing, I think, is a visual picture of her grand-mother. By now, Tom has arrived, and since he has met this woman, we are able to draw a picture of her. The cascading brown hair, the dark eyes, the ever-ready smile, the proper, never casual, style of dress. Cindy's *tota ma* runs a catering business and can, with help, provide for up to four hundred diners. I ask Cindy about the "comfort food" her grandmother makes for her. Turns out, an Indian taco is what she loves, and Cindy describes how these are made.

AFTER CLASS, I help Tom structure and write the personal pro-file that has eluded him for several days. After our talk the week before, he has the raw material, along with the information he has gathered after questioning his older, fellow student. Now, how to organize it? "My Favourite Things" becomes the starting point. Then we go on to further divide his material into black and white elements, positive and negative, with little bridge sentences to link it all. It will be a fine piece. He had started to write it but went too deep into his past, and the emotions that rose in him stayed his hand. So many of these students have endured suffering.

There were moments during my time at FNTI when my world and this world seemed all of a piece. I remember sitting in Tracy's office, which though small, seems well-enough appointed—not so different from my own at home. But as soon as you delve into the home circumstances of many of these students, you are reminded just how complicated and often fractured their lives are. I had the same sense of entering alien territory as I did on my first days at Vinnie's or Place of Hope in San José. I got just a peek into what some of them have been through, and I am astonished at their resilience.

THIS HAS been an immensely rewarding experience. My task was to make the thought of writing a little less daunting, and I think, I hope, I have made a little headway.

"You got Cindy to produce a piece of writing!" Tracy enthuses as we part. She hands me a few souvenirs: a handsome Ohahase Education Centre pen and pencil and a suede-bound day planner for 2009. I tell an old friend, a retired English teacher, about my time at the school. She seems genuinely interested and promises to send Tracy a note. Maybe the tutoring will continue.

How many other retired English teachers are out there? Or retired writers and journalists? Teaching those young people was a great gift. I wasn't helping out in any way I could; I was passing on skills and knowledge that are central to me, that have defined me for all of my working life. This kind of volunteering has the potential to be the most rewarding of all, and I didn't have to get on a plane to do it.

Most of the volunteers who come through FNTI are Aboriginal, though I know of another white writer who taught some classes there. They would be most welcome, Tracy says. "They just don't know about us."

First Nations kids, especially those living on reserves, could use a leg up. Why are we so blind to needs in our own backyards?

JUST AROUND the time I was finishing my stint at FNTI, I went to a talk at Kingston City Hall to mark the thirteenth anniversary of a silent vigil held every Friday at noon on the steps of city hall to call attention to the forgotten poor. For thirteen years, the nuns of the Sisters of Providence of St. Vincent de Paul and like-minded folk have stood silently facing Ontario Street wearing placards.

I've gone to a few of the vigils, mostly the ones to mark an anniversary. Except for a few occasions (when Christmas fell on a Friday, or severe weather blew in, or once when a film was being shot on those same city hall steps), the vigil has continued. Some Fridays it draws but a dozen souls, though one time, in 2005 when the Make Poverty History cry was in the air, some of the nuns stitched sheets together and there were enough to circle the entire block.

Sister Pauline Lally, the General Superior of the order, recalled coming to the vigil with a fellow nun then in her eighties, Mary Hamilton. "You know," Sister Mary told Sister Pauline, "I almost didn't come today with my old bones, but I'm awfully glad I did." They talked about how they felt better afterwards, and Pauline wondered whether it was the fresh air or, more likely, "the solidarity of silence."

Before the talk began that night in the Memorial Room, the hundred of us in attendance had taken candles, strung the ready supply of placards around our necks and walked slowly around city hall. My placard had read: "Poverty Does Not Take a Holiday."

Later, in her address, economist Armine Yalnizyan—the first winner of the Atkinson Charitable Foundation Award for Economic Justice—set the occasion in context. Thirteen years before, then premier Mike Harris had campaigned on a "common sense" revolution that slashed social welfare spending, presented tax cuts to the rich and middle classes and downloaded the problem of the poor onto city budgets.

There was a dustup at a Kingston golf course when Harris came around to spread his gospel, and the nuns—who were there but uncomfortable with in-your-face protest—decided that a silent vigil was a good way to remind everyone who passed them every Friday at noon that "there are poor among us."

Yalnizyan urged her audience to battle poverty on two fronts. Continue the vigil but ratchet up the pressure on senior levels of government. Victory goes, she said, to the ones with the strongest lobbies. Yalnizyan pointed out that while the nuns' vigil in Kingston is evocative, it is also silent. (Though that's not quite true: on several occasions, the protestors have gone straight from the silent vigil to the offices of local provincial and federal parliamentarians and given them an earful. And the nuns continue to speak in public and contribute op-ed pieces on the suffering that stems from inequality.)

Jamie Swift, in his introduction, had quoted Jane Addams, the first American woman to win the Nobel Peace Prize. "The good we secure for ourselves is precarious and uncertain until it is secured for all of us and incorporated into our common life."

All over the world, the great divide goes on widening. About 1.1 billion people live on less than what one dollar a day would buy here in Canada. At the other end of the spectrum, the world now counts 587 billionaires with a combined wealth of

$1.9 trillion. In the meantime, the ratio of CEO income to aver-age worker income has skyrocketed from 45 to 1 in 1973 to 500 to 1 today. In the United States, the richest 1 per cent now pos-sess more wealth—at least $2 trillion more wealth—than the bottom 90 per cent of the population.

Some historians have argued that gross inequalities in cer-tain societies have led in the past to revolution, the rise of fas-cism and the rise of communism. Poverty fuels crime, violence and war. The greater the gap between rich and poor, the greater the risk of systemic collapse (there is ample evidence from the robber baron literature of Andrew Carnegie's day that fear of social unrest fuelled that first golden age of philanthropy). Food banks and soup kitchens may keep the poor from starving, but they undermine whatever dignity the poor still possess.

The impulse to action is sometimes a mystery, and the nuns' vigil has for thirteen years been issuing a constant reminder to me—like a sonar blip from the depths of the ocean. Maybe the blip is getting louder? Never underestimate the power of nuns.

. . .

[FREE LUNCH]

THE PUREST form of generosity, it seems to me, is the quiet kind. In Kingston, there is a wildly colourful restaurant at the bottom of Princess Street called The Sleepless Goat. It's run as a workers' co-operative—one that is explicitly anticapitalist. Staff call themselves "goats" and all make the same minimum wage—$10.25 an hour. The fare is largely vegetarian, the teas are many, the coffee strong.

The Sleepless Goat is also the only restaurant in town where there is, indeed, a free lunch. Each month, the downtown eatery gives away five hundred to six hundred servings of its homemade soup of the day and vegan whole-wheat bread to anyone who asks for it. The charge is $3.90 for those who wish to pay. This is a boss-less workplace run by idealists and everyday philanthropists.

"Our soup program," says Daniel D., a member of the co-operative, "was conceived originally as an expression of solidarity between the goats (who occupy a very low income bracket) with other poor and marginalized people in Kingston and not simply as an act of charity."

89.4
on the FM Dial

DECEMBER 5. We have logged more than ten thousand kilometres in the air, from Toronto to Paris, then Paris to Dakar, and can feel the stamp of that journey in our bones. We left home Thursday at noon and now, thanks to crossing time zones and a twelve-hour layover in Paris, it's late Friday evening. Air France Flight 718 touches down. Paris was chilly and wet, and as I walk down the stairs from the plane and my foot touches Senegalese soil, I welcome the warm, dry air of West Africa.

The mostly Senegalese passengers spent much of the flight from Paris visiting with each other, some standing in the aisles and draped over seated passengers, the whole cabin abuzz with their chatter and laughter. Many were going home for the holidays and they were getting a head start on their socializing. Family and faith are two pillars of Senegalese society, and we were approaching an important time for both. At the end of the flight, a flight attendant strode down the aisle looking beseechingly into each row and holding aloft a woman's silk scarf: a diaphanous mauve *foulard* left behind by a wanderer.

Ulrike and I have the usual jet-lagged passenger's desires: checked bags nicely circling on the carousel, a successful rendezvous in the terminal with our hosts and a bed, the sooner the better. But now comes a snag.

The world-weary Senegalese immigration official is not satisfied with our claim that we are staying "with friends" and that said friends are here at the airport to meet us. He wants an address or proof of these friends' existence. Without glancing up, he invites us to cast about for our contacts and then he pointedly, and wordlessly, deposits both our passports in the corner of his booth and goes on to process the next arrival. I feel a rush of emotion: anger at the intransigence and arrogance of bureaucrats, a kind of nakedness upon being so summarily deprived of my passport minutes after arriving in Senegal and a vague disquiet. The mission is so young and already off the rails.

In the next room is gathered a thick and boisterous soup of milling travellers, hotel greeters holding signs, porters with trolleys, and soldiers with rifles and red berets—while the carousel is slowly spinning. Roped and plastic-wrapped suitcases are heave-hoed off and taken away, but there is no sign of Ulrike's sturdy new grey number or my old black backpack. Neither is there a smiling man holding a white sign with "Laurent et Ulrike" written on it. While I will our bags to appear, Ulrike presses deeper into the bowels of the airport, past the X-ray scanners, and then outside the terminal where she at last finds Amadou Pouloh, chauffeur for the women's radio station in Dakar where we will volunteer for the next four weeks.

His sign reads simply "Manooré FM" and on hearing of our little contretemps at Customs, offers it as proof for the immigration official. The latter's scepticism does not immediately vanish when Ulrike shows him the crude sign. She goes back a second time to Amadou, who writes down the phone number at Manooré. Finally, our passports are stamped and returned. Meanwhile, our luggage has arrived. Crisis averted.

I am prone to the pushing of panic buttons, and I always feel foolish later when things work out. My experience has been that things usually do, eventually, so what's with the sky-is-falling response at times like this? Perhaps I am an optimist in theory only, and a pessimist in practice.

We haul our luggage to the spot outside where Pouloh has instructed us to station ourselves while he gets the car. A tall, T-shirted young man now approaches, Pouloh's younger brother evidently, and he assures us that Pouloh will be along shortly. Charming and confident and ever helpful, he warns us to be vigilant about our bags, he directs Ulrike to a bank machine to procure some Senegalese francs, then he calls Pouloh to see what is causing the delay. More assurances follow, along with the news that his calling card is now running on empty, and can we advance him a little cash to top up the account? Ten thousand francs to be exact (about $24).

I am sure that Oumy Cantome Sarr, the radio station's director, has told us in an e-mail that we will be met at the airport and that we will settle up later with the chauffeur. Even in my travel-induced stupor, my antennae go up at this upfront cash request, and so do Ulrike's.

Another man, this one in a wheelchair, approaches wanting to know our nationality, and on hearing it, reports how generous Canadians have always been when he asked them for money. Yet another man insists on helping us with our bags and reaches for the handles, despite my repeatedly declining his offer. A third young man wants to shake my hand and feigns hurt when I keep my grip on our bags. "In Senegal," he chides me, "this is how we greet each other," implying that whatever my home country, it knows nothing of manners.

In Senegal, French is the national language that many speak and write, but Wolof is the one regional language that almost everyone speaks or at least understands. The Wolof word for white-skinned person, I will soon learn, is *toubab*. The assumption, rightly so, in this black African country is that whites have money. The trick, the livelihood even, for some Senegalese is to get at it. Pouloh's "brother" soon vanishes when we balk at his request, as do the others once Pouloh and Oumy arrive on the scene.

I had wondered what it would be like to have the tables turned, to be for once in the minority. What hits me is how visible we are, how separate, how white our skin and how black everyone else's. We may see ourselves as volunteers from afar, here to help and armed with good intentions, but most Senegalese assume we are either tourists or with NGOs, in any case white and moneyed non-Muslims who speak not a word of Wolof. Will it be like this for the duration of our stay? Or can we close those gaps, even if just a little?

EACH YEAR, according to Canadian Crossroads International (CCI), three thousand Canadians participate in development projects abroad. In December, Ulrike and I join that number.

The trip to Senegal is the most exotic of my twelve volunteering endeavours and took the most planning. Karen Takacs, the Toronto-based executive director of CCI, and her staff in the Montreal office were extraordinarily quick in finding a fit for us. I wanted Africa to be part of my experience for reasons I can only describe as instinctive and intuitive. I was originally drawn to two independent charitable endeavours, both with Kingston connections. One was in Kenya, a school in Nairobi called Sud Academy for orphaned Sudanese children who have fled war at home. The other was in Tanzania, the school/ orphanage run by a former teacher in the shadow of Mount Kilimanjaro, which had been suggested by Dr. John Geddes and his CanAssist African Relief Trust. For a time, one or the other looked to be our destination. But in the end, the idea of working in French and in radio to try and help women in West Africa was simply too appealing.

Among our preparations for Senegal was a visit to the local health unit to get booster shots, acquire anti-malarial prophylactic medication and antibiotics in case of travellers' diarrhea, and to receive practical health counsel. I had taken chloroquine to combat malaria during the trip to Costa Rica, but I reacted badly to it, so I was anxious to hear about alternatives.

Told the reason for our trip, the nurse observed that she had been seeing a dramatic increase in travellers coming into her office with volunteering abroad in mind. Some, she said, were my age and older, and occasionally they took on more than they could chew. "They're not going to Barbados or sitting on beaches," she said. "They're going off the beaten track." I took her to mean that some of the more venerable participants come back with medical scars.

The nurse was also seeing very young and idealistic individuals, some travelling with church groups, who wanted to blend exotic travel and the rewards of volunteering. But many of them, too, she warned us, come back very ill.

Both Ulrike and I had returned from Costa Rica with unwanted passengers in our gastrointestinal tracts. We lived on rice, toast and bananas for almost fourteen days. I asked the nurse about acidophilus, a bacterium used in the making of yogurt and to supplement intestinal flora. We had taken these pills (available at any health food store) prior to a trip to Brazil in 1999 and suffered no illness at any time during that trip. The nurse kindly suggested that expecting friendly bacteria to fend off their hostile cousins in West Africa is a quaint, even laughable, notion.

Neither did we want malaria, especially because the disease rampant in Senegal is nastier than the strain in Costa Rica. So the nurse offered us a choice of three drugs: one plays havoc with the bowel, another triggers nightmares and the third, the one she called "the Cadillac" of anti-malarials, has the fewest side effects but is pricey. She neglected to say how pricey.

For the anti-malarials for two, for the antibiotics, and for several booster shots, the fee was $854. "Can you repeat that?" I asked the receptionist as I handed her my credit card. Ulrike's drug plan at work will cover the lion's share of that cost, but I was reminded once more of why the pharmaceutical industry ranks among the most profitable on the planet.

OUR FIRST meeting with Madame Oumy Cantome Sarr was in Montreal in early November. She had flown in for a ten-day visit to reconnect with officials at Crossroads, to seek out support from other NGOs and to check out the two new recruits.

Oumy Sarr is wide-eyed and light-skinned, her hair arranged in tiny corn rows, and there is a particular set to her jaw, somewhere between taking the world very seriously and being amused by it. She speaks fluid French and in her opening remarks talked at great length about the radio station she directs, the plight of women in Senegal and the ongoing struggle of the station to secure funding.

We met in the modest Montreal offices of Canadian Crossroads International on rue Saint-Denis. Crossroads is a fifty-year-old NGO that fights poverty and promotes human rights, especially the rights of women, all over the world. CCI works with twenty-eight partner organizations in eight countries in West Africa, southern Africa and South America. Crossroads has a special interest in skilled volunteers and in radio as a tool for change. More and more, given my past as a producer with CBC Radio, going to Dakar to teach radio journalism felt right to me. Ulrike, who teaches English to francophone cadets at Royal Military College in Kingston, will do the same sort of work at the radio station where, Oumy said, the reporters are keen to improve their basic command of the language.

There is state radio in Senegal and there are private stations, dozens of them. But Manooré FM is a community radio station uniquely designed to give voice to women, their rights, issues and concerns. The reporting staff comprises nine women and three men, all paid, but a number of the hosts of hour-long programs (on music, women's health, the world of the disabled, sport and religion) are volunteers. Madame Sarr looks to me to continue the education of her staff. Some reporters have both training and experience; others are amateurs learning on the job.

One of Oumy's first requests from our meeting in Montreal was that I create and send her a *guide de formation,* an outline of what I hoped to teach her reporters. This got me thinking about the art of the interview on radio, the importance of brevity in writing for radio, and it sent me searching for teaching materials. Maybe I could offer my thoughts on structuring an interview, the importance of sound (and not just talk) in radio, and where to look for ideas and subjects. This could all be a lot of fun, and it would certainly present a huge challenge: I must do all this in French.

Every week that fall, I had sought the company of francophones. I studied French at university thirty-six years ago, and trips since to France, North Africa and Quebec meant that any facility I possessed with the language never entirely disappeared. But it needed reviving if I had any hopes of teaching in Senegal.

Through contacts at Queen's University, I tracked down a Senegalese family in Kingston, likely the only one, in preparation for our trip. I wanted to hear the accent, to learn something of Dakar and the Senegalese culture. And so began a friendship with Serigne Dieng and his wife, Aïssatou, and their children, Saliou, Mame Diarra and Cheikh. We had dinners at each others' homes, and later while in Dakar, I contacted their families who showered us with kindness.

Aïssatou spoke little English and admitted to us that the move to Canada had been gut-wrenching. Serigne had his studies (he's pursuing a doctorate in geology at Queen's), his teaching and his colleagues, but Aïssatou felt imprisoned in their rented duplex, cut off from the usual supports of family, friends and neighbours—an isolation that worsened as the temperatures dropped and the snow started falling. Only when I lived in Dakar and saw how families and neighbours interact and rely on each other did I truly understand the magnitude of Aïssatou's deprivation.

So I did a "good thing," as Ulrike and I would later term it. Shortly after first meeting Aïssatou, I sent a note to Immigrant Services, wondering if one of the francophones on staff could call her and tell her what programs were available. Every week thereafter, she walked a kilometre or so to the Immigrant Services offices, had coffee with new friends from all over the world and practised her English while others looked after Cheikh. She got a much-needed break. By spring, perhaps cheered by warm weather and blossoms, her outlook had marvellously brightened.

Pound for pound, my phone call made more difference to one person's life than some of the other "good things" I did in 2008 that may have felt more significant at the time. I cast my mind back to that sign on a cupboard at Vinnie's about no unimportant acts of kindness.

Before we left for Dakar, the Diengs taught us a little Wolof. *Asalamaleykum* is not Wolof but Arabic, and it's used commonly as a secular greeting in Senegal. It means "Peace be with you." And the reply is *maleykumsalam,* which means "And with you, too."

Na nga def means "How are you?" And if you're fine, you say, *Maa ngi fii.*

Dieureudieuf means "thanks."

ULRIKE DISCOVERS by reading Lonely Planet's *West Africa* travel guide (the bible that many travellers carry in Senegal) a film called *Mooladé*, about female circumcision. The director is Senegalese, the late Ousmane Sembene. Released in 2004, three years before Sembene died in Dakar at the age of eighty-four, the film tells the tale of a woman who has herself been circumcised as a girl but who refuses to have her daughter cut. Now four other young girls have come to her for protection (*mooladé* means "sanctuary"). This provokes tension in the village. Though the country is never named in the film, it was shot in Senegal and the characters speak Wolof. The film explores the conflicts that arise when modern and traditional views clash.

Mooladé is the second in a trilogy of films by Sembene that examine heroism in daily life. There's a note from him on the back of the DVD cover: "Female genital mutilation is practised in 38 of 54 states of the African Union. Whatever the method used (traditional or modern), to excise is a violation of the woman's dignity and integrity. I dedicate *Mooladé* to mothers, women who struggle to abolish this legacy of bygone days."

At one point in the film, men in the village who are angered at this threat to traditional "purification" toss about thirty radios onto a pile and set them on fire. Radio, the men believe, has filled these women's heads with nonsense.

The first pan-African meetings to discuss excision, a centuries-old practice that was largely hidden from Western view until the latter part of the twentieth century, took place in Dakar in 1984. The cutting is done by women, and the pressure to conform remains high. Why it's done seems clear: with the clitoris removed, a woman's ability to experience sexual pleasure is much diminished, and in traditional, paternalistic societies men don't want women to be tempted by their libido into wandering from the marital bed.

That some girls (four to twelve is the typical age) die from these amateur surgeries, that the mutilation is horribly painful and may lead to difficulties with intercourse later on, seems not to matter to its proponents. In *Moolade*, a girl does die from being cut. At the end of the film, the women who do the cutting are forced by other women to toss their red-handled knives onto a blanket on the ground. The knives, what we would use to peel potatoes or slice carrots, make a thin metallic sound as one strikes another.

DECEMBER 7. Manooré FM's car resembles most cabs in Dakar. Rumpled and dimpled and dented on the passenger side, with a cracked front window, the aged Toyota generally bears the look of a vehicle fresh from a battle with rock-throwing children. A bold Manooré FM sticker high on the driver-side window is Amadou Pouloh's attempt to discourage harassment from policemen. Cops in blue uniforms routinely and randomly pull over drivers, ostensibly to check licences and registration and nab illegal aliens but often just to collect small bribes. Later on, I will see it for myself. My "taxi-man," as cabbies are called here, is given a choice: pay the fine for not wearing a seat belt (which almost no one does) or slip the copper a thousand-franc bribe (about $2.40 Canadian) to look the other way.

I will not see one stoplight in all of the four weeks I am in Dakar, although I am told they exist. Roundabouts manage the choked traffic, more or less. Each small or large circle, each intersection, presents an occasion for a game of chicken. Cabs in Dakar may have faulty headlights and taillights, the dashboards may not illuminate at night and the shocks have almost surely succumbed to the potholes, but the one essential piece of equipment is the horn.

As we drove on that first night from the airport in west Dakar to what we would call our *quartier* (Liberté Quatre, in north-central Dakar), what struck me most was the sheer number of creatures in this city of several million. Often the streets are divided by treeless wide islands of earth or concrete, but those islands housed thousands and thousands of sheep—rams tethered to stakes, ewes bunched behind crude fences. Their shepherds manned fires, more for light than heat. Even with the windows rolled up, I could hear a cacophony of bleating.

We are, it turns out, just days from La Fête du Mouton, or Tabaski, as the Senegalese call it. In the rest of the Muslim world, it's known as Eid-el-Kabir. Imagine Thanksgiving and Christmas rolled into one feast. Tabaski honours that moment, described with some variations in both the Quran and the Bible, when Abraham has his faith tested by God, who commands him to sacrifice his son. At the last second an angel intervenes, and a ram caught in nearby bushes is slaughtered instead as an offering to God. Every family in Dakar that can afford to buys at least one sheep for Tabaski. In the morning at Oumy's house, I meet the three sheep they have bought and are keeping in the courtyard.

Almost all those rams and ewes clogging parking lots, soccer pitches and boulevards will be gone in four days' time. I have brought with me to Senegal my tape recorder as well as my camera, and right from our first hours in Dakar I begin to collect this place's singular soundscape: the holy men calling the faithful to prayer at dawn from loudspeakers atop mosque minarets, the sounds that women make with their short wide brooms whisking dirt from flagstone paths, the slap of their plastic sandals on the tiled courtyard floor outside our room. And the sound I will hear increasingly in Liberté Quatre as Tabaski draws near: the grinding sound of butcher knives being sharpened on round whetstones.

DECEMBER 15. This is the lay of the land. Our bunk is a tidy bedroom, plus toilet and cold shower, part of a three-storey apartment complex. For the time we are here, we will displace Coumba, a sister-in-law of Oumy's, from her usual lodgings. In this room we will eat our breakfast (tea or coffee we make ourselves and a baguette with Vache Qui Rit cheese or jam bought daily at one of the hole-in-the-wall stores that dot the neighbourhood) and eat our other meals with Oumy and her family at their house around the corner. The equivalent of about $40 Canadian a day, shared between Oumy's family and Coumba's, will give us our meals and lodgings.

Another CCI volunteer, a Quebec filmmaker named Olivier, had enjoyed a similar arrangement a few months back. I guess we *toubabs* all look alike, for the kids of the *quartier* gleefully shake my hand and call me "Olivier!" every time I pass them on the way to and from the radio station.

The station is a fifteen-minute walk away. The house that Oumy shares with her extended family—niece Anta, brothers Alioune and Ndiaga, sister Fatou and husband Modou and their sons Pa doudou and Papi—is pretty much like others here. A 2.5-metre-high brick-and-stucco facade with a heavy metal door, open-air courtyards fore and aft with the larger one at the back ideal for hanging clothes and washing dishes (and a temporary home for the three tethered sheep), three ample bedrooms, a large salon and a small TV room on the main floor, and, upstairs, another bedroom plus rooftop patio where a local teacher conducts private classes for children struggling with schoolwork.

The door to Oumy's house features bolts top and bottom, but during the day only the high bolt is ever in place and I just reach over top and gain entry. Oftentimes the door has been left ajar. This was my first lesson in Senegalese hospitality and casual sense of security, a far remove from the high gates and barbed wire of Costa Rica.

Neighbours and friends here don't call ahead or even knock on doors as they do in Canada. They just waltz in and they may stay a few minutes or a few hours. They may sit in for a meal, or maybe not. The coming and going is spontaneous, never orchestrated or planned. Only old outport Newfoundland offers comparable hospitality in Canada.

Hospitality, though, doesn't really describe what Fatou does at mealtimes. What I observe is sharing in a manner so unremarked, so unconscious, that it allows any recipient of this largesse the one thing that most other forms of human help swallow: human pride.

The rooftop teacher, for example, receives only a small honorarium for his work. He eats with us. The *domestique* (servant girl) eats with us, and once a week Fatou's hired washerwoman and her helper eat with us. Fatou's door is always open, and everyone who saunters down her hallway at meal time is invited to join the family. One day, nine gathered for dinner; as one rose to leave, someone else dropped down to take his or her place. In her own way, Fatou feeds the world.

We eat in the Senegalese manner, communally, sitting on plastic chairs or low wooden benches around a rough wooden table covered by a grey plastic tablecloth. The food comes in one huge round plate with a five-centimetre-high lip. The meals are often the staples of fish and rice (including the national dish—*tiéboudiène,* as it's called in Wolof), sometimes with baguettes, and with Fatou acting as a kind of culinary cop throughout the meal, making sure that guests and children get their share of fish or meat. She uses her right hand to dole out these portions, and, to serve herself, she forms a small ball of fish and rice in her hand and pops it into her mouth from a discreet distance so that hand and mouth never make contact.

Every meal is a small miracle. Spices and peanut sauces—some sauces learned from Fatou's Moroccan mother and many featuring onions—ensure that while fish and rice are dominant choices, I never feel like I am eating the same thing twice. The colours, the textures, the degree of spiciness change with every sitting. There is *yassa* (grilled chicken marinated in lemon juice and onions), *mafé* (a meat and peanut stew) and *thiakry* (a delicious "rice" pudding made from couscous). I like how eating at such close quarters brings everyone together. It must be hard to hold grudges or harbour ill feelings against a brother or a neighbour when you're shoulder to shoulder like this.

There are grave problems in Senegal: poverty, untimely deaths from malaria and malnutrition (life expectancy here is fifty-nine years, compared with Canada's seventy-nine), a crumbling infrastructure, corruption up and down the line, constant interruptions in the supply of both electricity and water, an on-again off-again rebellion in the southern region of Casamance. Yet the Senegalese have much to teach the world about getting along.

By any standard, certainly African standards, theirs is a peaceable kingdom. The Muslim majority happily coexists with the Christian minority, and each celebrates the other's feasts. Among the rituals of Tabaski are these: some of the meat goes to Christian families in the neighbourhood, and at Christmas, when fowl are slaughtered, that favour is returned. Each family also shares its meat with neighbours; in the densely populated *quartiers,* it's well known where the need is greatest. Finally, each person knocks on the door of a neighbour and asks forgiveness for any harm or slight inflicted in the past year. A handshake in Senegal involves a soft touching of the hands, not those vice-grip exchanges that some North American men deploy. In Senegal, a handshake is a sign of peace.

It probably helps the cause of peace in Senegal that this country has few raw materials to offer the world. There are no oil or gas deposits, nor gold or diamond mines to tempt warring factions or invaders, as there are in the tortured Democratic Republic of Congo, for example. Senegal has fish to sell to the world—and peanuts. Another ubiquitous sound of Senegal is that of women on the streets cooking peanuts in sand-filled pots over charcoal stoves, their spatulas making a scraping sound as they turn the nuts lest they burn.

DECEMBER 19. The studios of Manooré FM, 89.4 on the Dakar dial, lie due south from our digs in Liberté Quatre. "La voix des femmes" reads the multicoloured sign that hangs outside the station's third-floor window overlooking the always busy street, Alleés Khalifa Ababacar Sy.

In the patriarchal Senegalese society, where polygamy is common and female circumcision is still practised in the countryside, women need reminders of their rights. Oumy and her staff all agree on that. One of my assignments at Manooré FM is to listen every day to the half-hour noon-time program, *Le Journal*, which offers a blend of Africa-wide news with local items generated by Manooré's nine reporters. The items are typically several minutes long, though more extensive pieces, which they call *dossiers*, could be six minutes in length. What all the items share is their perspective. These are the voices of Senegalese women, expressing their worries and world views. My job, in part, is to suggest ways that each piece might be better produced.

Often I go out with a reporter and watch her or him conduct interviews, and later offer feedback both on the approach and the finished news item. One morning Jupiter investigated conditions for the forty thousand students at the University of Dakar. One room (I walked it off at seven metres by three metres) is home for eleven female students. Though they lamented the cheek-by-jowl lodgings, and said so for the record, they were still thrilled to be there, in part because a degree from this university is widely respected all over Africa. Ironically, the sound Jupiter used to "illustrate" her piece on bursting dorms was that of young women laughing.

Another reporter, Mame Nar, one day missed the boat, or so it seemed to me, with her coverage of an international festival that gathered disabled artists from all over Africa and even Canada. Along with Oumy and Ulrike, I attended that festival, which was charged with music and dance and colour (including dancing on the ground by some profoundly disabled dancers). I thought Manooré's reportage was flat and uninspired, and Oumy agreed with me during the post-mortem back at the station. Glaringly absent was any attempt to gather ambient sound (*bruitage,* they call it). Mame Nar said nothing in the piece's defence; case closed.

Yesterday, Mame Nar came to the regular morning story meeting with an idea for interviewing women who work as hotel maids and who face, she knows, constant sexual harassment from hotel guests. Other reporters scoffed at the idea, not because it lacked merit, but because, they said, the maids would not speak for fear of losing their jobs, nor would their male bosses let them. Mame Nar thought it was worth a try, and I wholeheartedly agreed with her.

DECEMBER 20. The hotel maids reportage is perhaps the best I hear in my weeks at Manooré FM. Not only does Mame Nar find a sympathetic hotel manager, a man who talks openly about how male guests solicit young female maids, but she also interviews a maid who speaks with great dignity about how she values her work, how pleased and proud she is to contribute to her family's household income, and how she has to quietly, persistently and always politely discourage guests who proposition her.

This is pure gold, I tell the reporters during my next class in journalism (Ulrike and I alternate, with me teaching radio skills one day and her teaching conversational English the next). This particular *domestique* is honest and courageous, articulate and smart, and I am very moved by her testimony. The story almost certainly could have been longer, and I urge the reporters to keep this woman in mind for future broadcasts. Unfortunately, Mame Nar is not there that day to hear me sing her praises, but word does reach her.

The transmitters at Manooré FM have a range of one hundred kilometres, putting their potential audience at some three million. But no one can say for sure how many tuned in today to hear that maid speak so eloquently and affectingly about her life. I know only that whenever I mention the station to people I meet in Dakar and beyond, they seem to know it.

The station was created in 2002 by L'Association pour les femmes et la communication alternative (Altercom), a Senegalese women's organization. Altercom, which is funded in part by Canadian Crossroads International, believes that community radio stations can be agents for change, and that change is overdue. Only 29 per cent of women in Senegal are literate, and 60 per cent of the population lives on a dollar or less a day. Violence against women, I am reminded almost daily at Manooré, remains a major problem.

DECEMBER 22. I have come to feel a great sympathy for Manooré's reporters, all of them. Last week, Amadou, one of the men on staff, kindly invited us to a prenuptial party for his sister, thus giving us not only an unforgettable ride to Pikine, an eastern suburb, in a rented *car rapide* (one of Dakar's signature, and miniature, tin-can buses) with the other revellers, but a glimpse into wedding celebrations in Senegal and the highly erotic dancing that marks them.

After the expenses of Tabaski and his sister's wedding, Amadou is flat broke. He strikes a deal with Oumy to wash her heavy blankets, the ones she sometimes lays out on the rooftop courtyard for late-night chats. Ulrike teaches Amadou a new word in English class: moonlighting.

Prisca, a female reporter, is studying at a journalism school, plus she has a house to clean and a husband and a mother-in-law to feed, and her home is ninety minutes' and several bus rides away in Pikine. Jupiter is pursuing a master's degree in sociology and is the single mother of two preschoolers. Only with the help of her family is she able to survive. Cheikh is the self-described loner on staff, the philosopher and resident intellectual. One evening he invited me to sit in the studio and observe as he conducted a live interview with a guest. I heard Cheikh quote Rousseau as a counter to the guest who quoted Machiavelli.

DECEMBER 24. We gather in the meeting room at Manooré FM. Overhead is a rusty white fan that is never used. On the south wall and keeping time is a large white clock with black numbers and a serious crack running across the dial from the 9 to the 1. Posters adorn every wall: one is from Oxfam, declaring the rights of citizens in the face of mining. An oversized postcard that Oumy had sent back during a visit to Montreal showing St. Urbain Street under a thick blanket of snow is taped to a glass partition. Lighting in the room comes from one long fluorescent light tube, a testament to the price of electricity here.

Every day between 3 p.m. and 4 p.m., this meeting room becomes a classroom. Ulrike and I tape a fresh sheet of plain brown paper to the glass partition and use felt markers as chalk. In the journalism class, we discuss the challenges of writing for radio (keep it simple), the art of the interview ("The host steers, the guest paddles," is how the doyen of Canadian radio interviewers, the late Peter Gzowski, once put it), how to separate wheat from chaff (I give the reporters ten details from an imagined news story and they write a lead sentence that captures its essence).

By and by, I have picked up their radio vocabulary. *L'attaque* is the first question in an interview. *Le chapeau* is the opening line in a report, *la chute* is the closing one. *En boîte* describes an edited item, "in the can" and ready to roll.

They are good students, most of them keen, as Oumy promised. They are all paid, albeit badly. One day, Ulrike summoned the courage to ask one of the reporters about her wages. Her monthly salary, she said, was fifteen thousand francs (about $35 Canadian). To put that in perspective, Ulrike and I spent ten thousand francs for a dinner at a very modest Senegalese restaurant in downtown Dakar.

Only one reporter has a computer at home, but he has no Internet connection. Only a few own digital recorders, and when one machine breaks, that reporter is out of commission—like a journalist without a pen. The rest use cassette recorders, so quality of sound can be a problem. Oumy has a computer and printer, likewise the station's administrative assistant has a printer, but the rest of the staff share one Internet-connected desktop computer. Announcers gathering news and headlines for *Le Journal* corner it most of the time. The result is that scripts have to be handwritten by reporters, meaning that legibility becomes an issue. The engineer's room has one set of headphones, but only one earphone functions. In the absence of headphones, communication between a studio and the engineering room may be a knock on the window between them or the wave of a hand.

Manooré once possessed other headphones, but reporters were in the habit of taking them from the technicians' room and using them elsewhere in the office to edit their gathered tapes. There is no space at the cramped office, let alone quiet space, and pretty soon the headphones were damaged by heavy use.

DECEMBER 27. Just as I am about to start a class one afternoon, I get a reminder—if I ever needed one—that I am in Africa, where the modern and the primitive coexist. The window overlooking the street is wide open and I hear a commotion outside. Two people died in a demonstration near Dakar a few days earlier in a protest over unemployment and other discontents, and I assume this is another.

What I see below me is a crowd perhaps forty-strong, loud and agitated and spilling from the sidewalks onto the street. They are heading north, determinedly so. What has happened, apparently, is this: the crowd has apprehended two older men, wise in *grigri*. The word actually means "amulet" or "charm," but it's also used to describe a kind of hypnosis that some thieves use to separate victims from their valuables. These men were seen approaching people at a bank machine across the street, uttering incantations and persuading their targets to hand over their cash. Word of the thefts spread, and the two accused were surrounded and were being marched to the nearest police station.

I later put that story to a smart, well-educated Senegalese I come to know in Dakar. I also tell her that one of the Manooré reporters interviewed sellers of amulets, mysterious powders, animal fur, bones and leather, one of whom freely admitted that he was a charlatan and that the amulets possessed none of the powers he claimed for them.

"Do you believe in *grigri*?" I ask my friend.

"No," she replies, but then adds that it isn't that simple. She tells the story, sheepishly and laughing, of her handing over cash and jewellery one time to someone who pulled the wool over her eyes.

I have the sense that religion is a force in Senegal, and largely a force for good. Directing it all are the *maribous*, the holy men who head the all-powerful brotherhoods. Their paintings and photographs are ubiquitous—on the walls of houses inside and out. I see the same painting of one particular holy man outside our door, on a high wall around the corner, and in the living room of Serigne's brother, Cheikh, where we had dinner one evening with him and his wife, Anna. These holy men act as brokers in family disputes and at the highest political levels, but sometimes they lead protests too. By most accounts, the *maribous* are level-headed and often wise, and they push government at least in the direction of honesty.

And yet some of them deploy beggar boys in the streets to collect money for them. Barefoot and shabbily dressed, the boys set out every morning in crews of three and four begging for change with a coffee can. Their families give the boys over to these teachers, ostensibly so the boys can be educated in the teachings of the Quran. The begging is supposed to offer them lessons in the harshness of life, but it also exposes the boys to all the dangers and health risks of the street.

We follow the advice of our Senegalese friends who suggest that we refrain from giving the boys money. Give them bread, instead, we are told. They are always very grateful to get an edible offering.

JANUARY 3. Have I imparted anything of value to the reporters at Manooré FM? Is their conversational English a little better? Perhaps so. We have performed one other task before leaving: Ulrike has translated into English and I have fine-tuned documents that Altercom will use in its fundraising.

Today, Ulrike and I agree to a forty-minute interview with Lamine, who hosts an hour-long program for Manooré FM on civil society. He is seeking our impressions of Senegal and Manooré and the status of women as compared, say, with Canada. And among his most pressing questions is this: how will you maintain your contact with Senegal and with Manooré FM? Will we be remembered, he is asking, or forgotten? I think instantly of what Mirna in San José wrote on the back of the photo she gave me of her son, Carlos, who has been staring at me from my desk since the spring of the year: *Para que me recuerden siempre y no me olviden.* So that you will remember me and never forget me.

To those in impoverished countries who make contact with NGOs, people like Ulrike and me are lifelines. Sometimes, a way out. We offer at least the possibility of help.

Lamine knows that help is unlikely to come from the state. One could argue, and many do, that volunteers and NGOs—that whole sprawling global network of well-intentioned individuals and organizations—simply let governments off the hook, in the way that food banks do a job that government should rightly be doing itself. One could argue too that my flights to Africa devoured ozone and thus hurt mankind more than my stint at Manooré FM helped it. My defence is that I learned about Africa, and about Senegal in particular, things I could never have learned in any other way than by going there. I now know about the work that Manooré does, and I know exactly what they need. In my last class, this afternoon, I ask the reporters to draw up a wish list.

They need ten laptop computers, one for each of them, though even a few would make a substantial difference, and at least one more printer. They need ten digital tape recorders, they need several CD players, better microphones and a good French dictionary. There is one parked in the smaller studio, but the cover is long gone and now it's shedding pages, so that anyone double-checking the meaning of *abandonner* is out of luck. Finally, they need more landline telephones. The only phone available to reporters is in the cramped technician's room centred between two studios, and I once looked on as Jupiter pre-interviewed someone for a taping while a technician played music, two other reporters chatted and cut tape behind her, and a fourth reporter, rather boisterous, periodically ran down the hallway to join them, like some loud and errant pinball.

Luck will play a part in determining if their wish list is ever fulfilled. In the meantime, those who need help are not shy about asking for it, and who can blame them? In Dakar, we looked up relatives of our Senegalese friends in Kingston, and out of that came several fabulous dinner invitations and even a weekend trip north to a remarkable bird sanctuary called Djoudj near the old Senegalese capital of St. Louis. Anna Coulibaly, the architect of that latter trip, made a point of telling us about a women's collective she helps to manage in Pikine. Called Femmes, Actions et Développement, it uses micro-credit loans from its partners to allow poor and often illiterate women to participate in a co-op that offers them a measure of independence and financial security.

Through the co-op, the women may be given sewing lessons or start-up money for rooftop gardens, fruit and vegetable pickling enterprises and other small business ventures such as fabric dyeing. Once their enterprises are up and running, the women put back into the collective a small portion of their profits, with the benefits enjoyed by all women in the co-op. They receive mosquito nets for their families and medical consultations meant to reduce the incidence of malaria, an annual scourge that comes with spring rains and flooding (a huge problem in Pikine especially). We were much taken with the idea, told one of the reporters at Manooré about it, and, within days, Anna and several other members of the collective were describing their operations on the radio.

We saw Anna and her colleagues afterwards in the hallway. Following introductions, one woman turned to me, then to Ulrike, and said, "Laurent et Ulrike, nous comptons sur toi." We are counting on you.

WE WERE back from Senegal only weeks when I wrote a piece in *The Whig-Standard* describing our experience and pleading on the radio station's behalf for assistance. I then sent the piece to family and friends, and it was the latter who responded most vigorously. Through connections at work, my sister Rosemarie, my sister Karen and her husband, Mike, and Ulrike's sister Karen mustered eight fairly new laptop computers. My friend Michael Cooke, who helped facilitate our trip to Senegal, offered a cheque, a digital camera and a digital tape recorder. Ulrike and I kicked in three new digital recorders, a good-quality microphone and a big bag of jelly beans, remembering how one day someone brought in candy and we feasted on them. Finally, someone came to my house with a brand new hardcover French dictionary. It wasn't on the reporters' wish list, but it was on mine.

The whole package was delivered in three installments by CCI staff and their allies over the course of several months. "I wish I had a camera to film the response," Oumy wrote when that first box arrived.

WAS THERE Strindbergian humiliation in any of this charity? Only to this extent: what had spurred me to act was not just the wish list that I myself had helped compile, but an e-mail from one of the reporters asking me for a laptop. She had an ambition to write a book about women who had made a difference in the political life of Senegal.

Later, after the shipments had arrived, the custodian at the radio station, who also does a tiny amount of reporting, wondered in an e-mail if he, too, might be sent a computer. Then, chums of a Manooré reporter who work at a private radio station likewise sent a note hoping to be added to our list. In Senegal, the high cost of shipping computers, the devalued Senegalese franc and the fact that a third of the people live below the poverty line all conspire to put a laptop beyond most people's reach. So they feel they have no other option but to ask a *toubab* like me. And that, I think, is demeaning.

. . .

["A PLACE THAT CAN BE DONE TO"]

IN HIS book *The Uncertain Business of Doing Good: Outsiders in Africa,* award-winning author, journalist and filmmaker Larry Krotz sifts through his experiences of spending some twenty-five years off and on in Africa. He has thought a great deal about why certain forms of help work and others don't. What he bristles at ("I have fought this all my life," he says) is the superior attitude that mostly white and Western governments bring to Africa, a legacy from missionary and colonial days which, he says, we have yet to renounce.

Larry Krotz told an audience at the Winnipeg International Writers Festival in the fall of 2008 that the notion persists of "Africa as a place that can be done to." In any contact between those who come to help and those who actually live in Africa (though the lesson applies anywhere in the world), Krotz stresses the importance of humility and communication, relationships and solidarity. "It's not a power thing," he said, adding that the thought of Madonna going to Malawi and adopting black children makes him feel "icky."

He cited two examples of help, one that backfired and one that is still working. In the 1990s, said Krotz, "structural adjustment guys" came to Zimbabwe and told the government to cut the public service, which was once highly regarded. These cuts were to pave the way for foreign aid from the World Bank. So the government let go huge numbers of teachers and nurses, and the loans came—but at a huge cost to the country's independence and well-being.

In the same country, meanwhile, there is a project called Campfire, run by Zimbabwe's own wildlife department. This program takes a percentage of profits from safari tourism and big-game hunting and compensates farmers when, say, their maize fields are trampled by elephants. If you can keep villagers from killing elephants, and protect the environment and wildlife at the same time, the tourists and hunters will keep coming and locals will have jobs. Even better, the dignity of those people is maintained.

Krotz talked about the American writer Paul Theroux going back to Malawi forty years after he had worked there as a CUSO teacher. He complained that everything was worse than it had been, and that a culture created around self-sufficient enterprises had collapsed. The feeling in Malawi was that there was no need, for why bother when American aid is pouring in? "This is not abling," says Krotz, "but disabling."

It's a sentiment echoed by Dambisa Moyo in her book *Dead Aid: Why Aid Is Not Working and How There Is a Better Way for Africa*. She argues that aid to Africa (more than $1 trillion dollars in the past sixty years) is patronizing, kills entrepreneurial spirit, invites and sustains corruption and offers a good living to half a million westerners employed by NGOs. The Zambian-born economist has striking credentials: with degrees from Harvard and Oxford and experience working at Goldman Sachs and the World Bank, she was named in April 2009 by *Time* magazine as one of the world's 100 most influential people.

The book's call for ending all aid to Africa within five years predictably sparked controversy. Moyo makes most sense when she celebrates micro-credit financing (the Grameen Bank, for instance) and less sense when she suggests that African countries cozy up to China as a trading partner. Moyo argues that the Chinese don't come to Africa with all the missionary and colonial baggage that Westerners do, but she seems to forgive China's horrendous human rights record and backing of an odious regime in the Sudan.

When Larry Krotz says, "It's not easy to receive charity," he's expressing a profound truth. Build a house for a hurricane victim in New Orleans, and the neighbours will indeed rightly ask, "Where's mine?" When I bought reading glasses for Yanci in San José, Orlando warned me that unless I made it clear to everyone, including Yanci, that this was no gift but payment for translation services, I would only sow jealousy in that little community.

It's no easier dispensing charity. Anyone able to help must decide who will be chosen, to what extent and for how long. Like those unfortunate women on *Queen for a Day,* one will see her wishes come true and three others will get nothing.

We can do better than this, a lot better.

EPILOGUE

AT THE end of this year-long odyssey—my "radical sabbatical," as someone put it—I did not at first feel changed in any fundamental way, just a few illusions shorter perhaps. What I felt most powerfully was anger at the disparity that I witnessed first-hand, gratitude for my own health and good fortune, and a conviction that even a small act of kindness can profoundly affect both giver and receiver. That "kindness begets kindness," as Sophocles put it, is well documented: those helped are often inclined, once on their feet, to become helpers themselves.

On reflection, though, I realized that I had changed. I'm more comfortable now around homeless people, more likely to talk to them and put myself in their corner. I'm less conscious of skin colour but more conscious of black history. One of the haunting images from our time in Senegal was the museum on Ile de Gorée, off the coast of Dakar, a stepping-off point to the slave ships. The dungeon-like cells where Africans were jammed often for months before departure and the Door of No Return, the last homeland portal they walked through, left a

304

deep impression. Africa is on my radar now, and I'll go back. Being in New Orleans reminded me that the state may care little for the poor, even less for the black poor.

Thanks to Lake Ontario Waterkeeper, my faith was bolstered in the law and seemingly innocuous and quasi-judicial bodies. My experience in Costa Rica offered me a rare glimpse into the world of transvestites, sex-trade workers and people with literally nothing, yet who struggle mightily and often nobly to survive their pasts. Orlando Navarro and June Callwood, it turns out, were saying the same thing: one of the greatest gifts you can offer someone else is to listen to his or her story. My time in prisons showed me what a determined individual, with support and encouragement, can overcome. Spending weeks with physically and intellectually challenged people, with immigrants struggling to adapt to a new country and with Aboriginal teens striving to acquire a high school diploma was never dull and, to my surprise, often enjoyable. I am glad of all the people I met, the places I saw, the kindness I was repeatedly shown. The experience was far richer than I could have hoped for, and I would do it again.

Anyone who volunteers knows the rewards. The sense of connectedness that I felt in 2008 was out of all proportion to the modest help I offered. I learned lessons that are available only to those who go inside. My time at Hospice Kingston, for example, taught me how it's possible to maintain one's dignity and sense of humour while confronting one's own mortality. In Dakar, from Fatou, I learned the wisdom of turning kindness into a quiet and routine gesture—out of respect for the recipient. Every volunteer shift taught me something different.

I've had a year to think about Strindberg's line, that "all charity is humiliating." That view, I came to realize, is too strident, but more than that, too sweeping. As I write this, just weeks before Christmas in 2009, my siblings in Toronto are returning from a shopping spree. One of my sisters, Rosemarie, suggested a different gift-buying arrangement this year, and my siblings and I all agreed: instead of each of us picking a name from a hat, we would pool the money and buy gifts for another family, a single mother and her two children who get by on very little. A downtown church gave us their first names and their modest wish list. The mother hoped for cooking pots, a kettle and a toaster; her son, a skateboard, shoes and snow boots; her daughter, some toys, shoes and a ballet costume. My brothers and sisters and their children had fun purchasing and wrapping those gifts, knowing what joy they would bring. I didn't regard this as charity, but more like the tiniest of transfers—our version of the Tobin Tax. We will never meet this other family, but a link was made between us and them.

A second link followed. On December 4, I was in a prominent Toronto eatery with Rosemarie and my father, enjoying a meal and looking forward to a show later in the evening. That plan went up in smoke when Rosemarie's purse was stolen in the restaurant; she and four other patrons found themselves in the manager's office frantically cancelling credit cards. Two days later, though, a man who bunks at the Gateway Salvation Army Hostel—the same one I had visited in February 2008—chanced upon my sister's wallet and keys. The man was scrounging for beer cans near city hall when he found a black bag containing five wallets, my sister's included. The cash was gone but all her credit cards and identification were still inside. The man, Tom Kapansky, called every theft victim to report his discovery.

Rosemarie had never been inside a men's hostel before, but when she met Tom to retrieve her wallet, she brought with her a dozen donuts and a cash reward. He had made her day and she wanted to make his. Part of Tom's reward was used to purchase a bus ticket to the alcohol addiction treatment centre in northern Ontario where he's headed in March. And because I said I would drop off a box of books for the Gateway library, he feels pleased to be helping an organization that helped him. All of us involved in this confluence of strangers now have a story to tell—about the cleverness of a thief and the honesty of a homeless man. Mostly though, this is a story about hope. The words *charity* or *humiliation* crossed no one's lips.

That said, I don't reject Strindberg's idea entirely. I developed an antipathy to the word *charity* (as those at Vinnie's loathe *soup kitchen*), and I came to understand the anger and resentment that recipients of charity, especially chronic charity, sometimes feel. In such anger there is at least a spark of pride and self-respect, which charity can kill. It may be that the word *charity* has suffered the same twisting of meaning that *philanthropy* has. What seemed to make more sense than either of those words was the plain and simple phrase *helping the less fortunate*.

Chance is a major determinant of circumstance, so those born unlucky will soon discover that help is slow in coming and may not come at all. I was forced to think more about what passes for social justice in this country and around the world.

THE ECONOMIST, in a summer 2004 issue, featured a special report headlined "Doing well and doing good. Why a new golden age of philanthropy may be dawning." The word *golden* stuck in my craw when I read it, and it irritates all the more now with its rosy hint of huge problems solved and satisfaction achieved, simply by rich folks digging into their pockets.

The Economist described how latter-day Carnegies such as Bill Gates; Pierre Omidyar, founder of eBay; and George

Soros, who made a fortune as a currency speculator, have rebranded themselves as imaginative philanthropists. The article described two major developments: the staggering rise in the number of philanthropic foundations on both sides of the Atlantic (in the U.S., the number has gone from 22,000 in the 1980s to 70,000 today), and the unprecedented intergenerational transfer of wealth now under way. In the U.S., between 1998 and 2052, anywhere from $41 trillion to $136 trillion will change hands.

The first development suggests that many millionaires and billionaires—no doubt spurred on by charitable instincts as well as the counsel of tax lawyers—are following the lead of Gates and the rest. Foundations, which are essentially privately run charities, can do a world of good, and many do. But the heady growth of foundations also means a massive tax-enabled shifting of funds from public coffers to private ones, where the agenda may be supporting the public good—or the status quo.

George Soros once said, "The truth is I am not a humanitarian... I detest foundations in the conventional sense. My motive has never been charity. You could even say it was self-interest. I wanted to further those societies where people like me could live in peace." How many foundations fund research into the kind of radical structural change and income redistribution that would actually end or diminish the need for foundations and philanthropy? Precious few.

The second development—all that money passing hands from mothers and fathers to sons and daughters with some going to charity along the way—suggests a shining future for charity brokers, those who help affluent clients find that perfect philanthropic fit. There is an enormous opportunity here for doing good; let's see what comes of it. But whether spent wisely or not, that money likewise will be controlled by individuals. Society has no say. This sets the table, once more, for private hit-and-miss philanthropy. (Studies show, incidentally, that when it comes to philanthropy, the poor punch above their weight and give more than the rich do.)

My initial response to the generosity of Gates and Buffett et al. had been admiration, pure and simple. Better to have them engaged than not, it had seemed to me. And I could understand that it would be fun, and uplifting, to give away buckets of money and watch it go to work. Indeed, the literature on philanthropy offers numerous and compelling examples of people who amassed a fortune expressly to give it away.

Pitting Gates and his billions against malaria may well be the best use of that wealth. Some 244 million cases of malaria were reported worldwide in 2006, and 880,000 people, most of them poor, die each year from the disease. The Gates Foundation's approach includes research to develop a malaria vaccine, along with money for mosquito nets, educational awareness programs and new treatment regimes. But if this isn't the wisest deployment of that money, there's no easy way to steer this private body in a new direction. Many are loath to criticize Gates for fear he'll fold his mammoth tent, but there are growing concerns. Some question whether vaccines are the best way to defeat malaria. Think of the challenges in refrigerating such medication in equatorial countries prone to power outages or in delivering it to remote villages. Very often what villagers need more than anything is a new well or a water filtration system.

The other worry has to do with changes of heart. Diana Leat, director of creative philanthropy at the Carnegie UK Trust, told *The Guardian* in 2007, "If Gates wakes up tomorrow and says 'I am bored with HIV/AIDS research now,' there is absolutely nothing to stop him pulling his entire budget out of it, which would have a catastrophic consequence on that whole field. At least with government funding, there is a mechanism for kicking up a fuss."

Melinda Gates, for one, understands that governments have to be on side. She told *The Wall Street Journal* in 2006 that beating HIV/AIDS, tuberculosis and malaria around the world will not be achieved by the Gates Foundation alone. "It's going to take the involvement of governments," she said. "These are enormous, intractable problems. It takes governments."

Stephen Lewis has long advocated that position, most recently as United Nations special envoy for HIV/AIDS. If the leaders of the G8 countries were to make good on their promises to devote 0.7 per cent of their gross national product to fighting world poverty, he says, the magic figure of $200 billion could be raised and the world's poor would indeed have the food, water and shelter they need. New trade deals and debt forgiveness, also promised by the G8, could wrest poor nations from poverty's grip. But, as Lewis told me, "it's one sham meeting after another."

For Lewis, the answer to world poverty is government action, and he offers a little math as proof. Bill Gates, the richest man in the world, can offer only 2.5 per cent of what's required each year to end global poverty. Lewis has travelled in Africa with Gates, and he has seen first-hand his passion and thirst for knowledge. "I'm very glad he's on our side," says Lewis, but adds that it's naive to think that a few deep pockets will break the back of global poverty.

"Poverty," says Lewis, "bedevils everything. It's at the root of hunger and disease and sexual violence and conflict as people squabble over resources. It is possible to overcome poverty, but it will never happen without a grand coalition of governments, non-governmental organizations, international financial institutions and devoted community activists in country after country."

VOLUNTEERING RATES in Canada have dipped lately, and I wonder if there is a connection with all this high-profile philanthropy. Perhaps people think, "they don't need little old me; Bill Gates is on the job."

Michael Hall, vice-president of research for Imagine Canada (formerly the Canadian Centre for Philanthropy), told me in 2008 that he was shocked by a study in 2000 that documented a 31 per cent nosedive in volunteerism in Canada and the loss of a million volunteers during the previous three years. He speculated that time pressures on families were to blame. The most recent polling done by Imagine Canada (released in the summer of 2009) shows that 12.5 million Canadians volunteer, and the numbers are up slightly in recent years. But a few volunteers do the lion's share: 10 per cent put in 54 per cent of the 2.1 billion hours worked.

In 1999, Ontario began requiring high school students to perform forty hours of volunteer service in the community as a condition of graduation. British Columbia, the Yukon, the Northwest Territories, Nunavut and Newfoundland soon followed with similar programs. According to the Laurier Institute, the Ontario program was initiated "to address declining civic engagement within society." It's too early to tell whether these programs actually make students more likely to volunteer later on as adults, but early analysis suggests that the more positive the experience, the greater the impact. And there is one bright spot amid the data: teens in general volunteer far more than the general population.

A four-year study published in 2004 of Canada's nonprofit and voluntary organizations turned up some impressive numbers and some worrying trends. (The survey was called Cornerstones of Community and drew on the resources of Statistics Canada and the Canadian Centre for Philanthropy.) On the one hand, this sector lists 161,000 organizations, with revenues (in 2003) of $112 billion and paid staff of two million men and women. Ours is the second largest such sector in the world; the Netherlands is in first place, with the U.S. in fifth. On the other hand, more than half the organizations polled in the study report problems with keeping volunteers and board members, and with funding; reductions in government financial support pose a major problem for them.

Volunteers are the heart and soul of Canada's charitable and non-profit service organizations. For them, our time is worth more than our money. There's a mad scramble on for both, with winners and losers. Mike Meadows, director of resource development with the Boys and Girls Clubs of Canada, told me that smaller charities—without websites or professional fundraisers—are fighting for their lives. "It's an enormous concern," he said. "The question is how to level the playing field."

Imagine Canada numbers support his fears. Some 21 per cent of donors account for 82 per cent of donations, and the 1 per cent of charities and non-profit organizations with revenues of $10 million or more are grabbing 60 per cent of available donation dollars. Meanwhile, the 42 per cent of organizations with revenues under $30,000 share just 1 per cent. Charitable donation totals, thanks to the largesse of some wealthy donors, stand at record highs, but smaller charities aren't seeing a benefit. Moneyed donors are inevitably drawn to prominent children's hospitals, to national and provincial art galleries and to their alma maters, not to the local food bank, the John Howard Society or any of the less sexy and low-profile charities.

IN 2001, John Ralston Saul gave a talk to a national forum in Vancouver on volunteerism. The Canadian author and philosopher argued that it's extremely dangerous to the health of a democracy to treat volunteering as somehow separate from the normal obligation of all citizens to participate and contribute (he bristles, for example, at the phrase "the volunteer sector"). Saul wondered where it came from, this notion that governments are ponderous or lack the means and wherewithal to fund a civil society, that wealthy individuals, corporations and volunteers must now see to the public good, and that it's better this way. Noblesse oblige has returned with a vengeance. There is room, Saul told his audience, for "a more specific, personality driven, sometimes more innovative layer of individual giving. But it cannot and must not be conceived of as replacing the universal, egalitarian concept of social justice."

In 2006, the Canadian Institute of Chartered Accountants published a book called *Registered Charities Guide*. The Introduction reads in part: "Over 80,000 registered charities operate in Canada today, helping to provide funding and delivering a wide range of health, social and other services to improve our society. They play an increasingly important role by undertaking a wide and growing range of social tasks that are beyond the ability of government to perform."

There it is, in a nutshell. Governments can't do those "social tasks" any more. Indeed, governments exempt charities and non-profits from taxation, thus encouraging charities and non-profits to do the job and sparing themselves the bother. (There is a difference between charities and non-profits: the former are exempt from most taxes and may issue tax receipts, while the latter may enjoy the first privilege but not the second, although there are exceptions.) There's no need for governments to feed their poor citizens when food banks will do it for them. So much activity is being privatized and outsourced: there are private armies, private police, private schools and private health care nipping at the heels of the publicly funded system. Small wonder that poverty, too, has been privatized with nary a squawk from voters.

For decades, all in the name of fighting debt and deficit, the Canadian government has cut back on its societal obligations in health care, post-secondary education, legal aid, the arts and culture, and the non-profit organizations that rely heavily on government support. *Taxes* has become a dirty word, with governments cutting taxes at every opportunity, then bragging about it to voters. After the G8 summit in Italy in July 2009, Prime Minister Stephen Harper opined, "I don't believe that any taxes are good taxes." *Globe and Mail* columnist Jeffrey Simpson rightly called it "one of the most stunning, revealing and, frankly, ignorant statements ever made by a prime minister... very, very scary socially and politically."

Ideology drives some of these tax cuts, but maybe they seem more tolerable to those making them when private money appears to be filling the void. In Western society, we hold dear an individual's right to create wealth. Sharing that wealth is the tricky part. Simply put, we can tax the rich and let elected officials decide how that money should help the dispossessed (while risking corruption and mismanagement), or we can keep taxes to a minimum and let the economy roll on unfettered in hopes that some tycoons, sooner or later, will "give back" (though some tycoons may just keep it all for themselves).

The first option strikes me as a place to start. Former NDP leader Ed Broadbent wrote an op-ed piece in *The Globe and Mail* on November 23, 2009. The headline read: "How to End Child Poverty: Tax the Rich." Broadbent asked this question: "Why is it that Finland, Sweden and Denmark have almost wiped out child poverty, and we have not?" He argues that deregulation, globalization and income tax changes have all favoured upper-income Canadians. A mere six-point increase in income tax on those earning more than $250,000 a year, Broadbent argued, would create a $3.7 billion nest egg to boost in a dramatic way the National Child Benefit Supplement. The timing for the piece was darkly apt: in Broadbent's last speech in Parliament, he had introduced a motion to end child poverty in Canada, and everyone clapped and agreed that this was a good and eminently attainable goal. That was in 1989.

THE POLITICAL process can be excruciatingly slow, and it's become popular to discount it altogether. I recall then Prime Minister Paul Martin responding in 2005 to a question from a high school student in Kitchener, Ontario, on the dearth of women in politics.

"I'm not sure that Parliament is all that functional a place," he said, before praising the good work that women can accomplish in non-governmental organizations.

That year, former U.S. president Bill Clinton made similar points about the frustrations of political office, and how comparatively easy it was using his name to raise $2 billion for the anti-AIDS effort. Individual social activism answers an immediate need with immediate benefits. If you want to effect change, the thinking goes, don't run for political office. Form a foundation for your favourite cause and run it as you see fit.

At the moment, it seems, we love philanthropists and we loathe politicians. Some wonder if we are returning to the days of the Medicis in Renaissance times, when the rich acted as patrons to science and art. Jeffrey Brison, a professor of history at Queen's University and the author of *Rockefeller, Carnegie, and Canada: American Philanthropy and the Arts and Letters in Canada,* points to an optics problem for governments. When the state does the right good thing—builds a library, say—the act is either invisible or taken for granted. Private philanthropy, in contrast, is celebrated, and we give it more weight than it warrants. The state has more clout, the philanthropist gets more credit.

But, argues Brison, "It's a lousy system. And it's inefficient. People assume that because the rich are good at making money, they're good at solving the world's problems. It's a spurious assumption."

Michael Hall at Imagine Canada agrees. "Philanthropy is an important part of the human spirit," he says. "But philanthropy is not a panacea. There are many things it can't address."

"Philanthrocapitalism" is the new buzzword to describe harnessing the power of business to achieve social change. Books such as *Philanthrocapitalism: How the Rich Are Trying to Save the World* (2008) by Matthew Bishop and Michael Green heartily endorse the phenomenon. But in his book, *Just Another Emperor? The Myths and Realities of Philanthrocapitalism* (2008), Michael Edwards offers a history lesson. He notes that "systemic change involves social movements, politics and the state, which these experiments [meaning the work of Gates and others] generally ignore."

Edwards, who has worked as a senior manager for Oxfam, Save the Children, the World Bank and the Ford Foundation, has written widely on civil society, often with a refreshing sense of humour. He quotes Mexican philanthrocapitalist Carlos Slim: "Wealth is like an orchard. You have to distribute the fruit, not the branch," to which Edwards has penned this addendum, "presumably because the branch, tree and forest all belong to [Slim]."

Edwards argues that the civil rights movement, the women's movement, the environmental movement and the New Deal were "all pushed ahead by civil society and anchored in the power of government as a force for the public good."

This is a message we seem to have forgotten. In his book *Letters to a Young Activist* (2003), Todd Gitlin, a leader of the Students for a Democratic Society (SDS) in the late sixties and now a professor of sociology and journalism at Columbia University, describes how today a "realistic spirit of service" seems to hold sway: plant those community gardens, feed the homeless, tutor the illiterate. "The emotion: compassion. The slogan: make a difference." The sixties, however, were all about sit-ins, protest marches, confronting authority. "The emotion: anger. The slogan: We want the world and we want it now."

Gitlin concedes that such analysis is simplistic, and yet there's truth in it. The idealist has given way to the pragmatist. Much of that energy and activism that once went into political and economic reform has been diverted to non-profit agencies.

I was a university student in the sixties—not nearly as radical as the SDS in my leanings, but I read my Herbert Marcuse (his *One-Dimensional Man* was the bible of the student left) and I marched in protest. My own trajectory fits the one that Gitlin describes. In the early seventies, I walked the odd picket line as student left and labour left flirted with each other. But I also headed up charity fundraisers on campus, so the non-profits already had me in their sights. In the eighties, I felt both political and non-profit tugs equally: walking in anti-nuclear protests and volunteering in that movement, while also sitting on committees and raising money for the community school in my village. By the nineties and into the twenty-first century, my overt political engagement was dwarfed by my involvement with non-governmental organizations, volunteer teaching and a host of other causes. I had been conscripted into the volunteer ranks. It's an army I'm happy to serve in and will go on serving in until I am no longer able. I believe in benevolence.

That acknowledged, I have to say that the status quo stinks. Volunteers alone, magnanimous philanthropists alone, are not the answer.

What if, for starters, all the money sheltered in private foundations were to be taxed and placed in public coffers—and dedicated to social justice? What if all the tax breaks given the non-profit sector were to be revoked, forcing non-profits to rely solely on fees and donations? These are questions that a professor of sociology and social work at the University of Southern Maine, David Wagner, asks in his book *What's Love Got to Do With It? A Critical Look at American Charity* (2001).

Wagner calculates that the tax subsidies given U.S. non-profits amount to $220 billion—about twice what his government spends on poor and jobless people. (I consulted a Toronto tax lawyer who estimated that subsidies given Canadian non-profits are likely in the $22 billion range.) Wagner finds the American model of philanthropy paternalistic and given to self-congratulation. Charity, he says, "is a moral enterprise with a clear social script. It produces heroes and model citizens who give, and deferential and meek citizens who accept." Out the window, in this script, goes the notion of such amenities as housing, health care and civil society as basic rights.

Wagner, Gitlin and Edwards all agree. The major advances among the disenfranchised have come not from charity but from social struggle: people organizing and mobilizing to stage civil rights marches, protests, strikes and walkouts, to write letters and petitions, to make angry phone calls to constituency offices, to exert pure and unrelenting political pressure.

IN 2005, the World Health Organization formed a blue-ribbon panel of policy makers, academics, former heads of state and former ministers of health to consider the role that inequality plays in determining human health. Their report, released on August 28, 2008, concluded, not surprisingly, that "social injustice is killing people on a grand scale."

There is no point in throwing modern medicine at illness, the nineteen commissioners argued, unless underlying structural problems are addressed first. The solutions are those that many governments once embraced and that some still do: affordable housing, a fair minimum wage, a safety net such as welfare, redistribution of wealth through taxation, and universal access to health care. The report, called *Closing the Gap in a Generation: Health Equity Through Action on the Social Determinants of Health,* praised the Scandinavian countries, where policies encourage equality of benefits and services, full employment, gender equity and low levels of social exclusion. This, said the commission, is an outstanding example of what needs to be done everywhere.

Ronald Labonté, who holds the Canada Research Chair in Globalization and Health Equity at the University of Ottawa, told *The Globe and Mail,* "There is nothing terribly magical about these approaches, but the commission provides compelling evidence that they work."

Monique Bégin, professor in the School of Management at the University of Ottawa and a former federal health minister, was one of the commissioners. "Canada," she said, "likes to brag that for seven years in a row the United Nations voted us 'the best country in the world in which to live.' Do all Canadians share equally in that great quality of life? No they don't. The truth is that our country is so wealthy that it manages to mask the reality of food banks in our cities, of unacceptable housing, of young Inuit adults' very high suicide rates. This report is a wake-up call for action towards truly living up to our reputation."

The Scandinavian and Nordic countries being held up to us as ones to emulate have very high rates of taxation, among the highest in the world. But when the Organisation for Economic Co-operation and Development surveyed people in thirty-one countries prior to releasing its study on life satisfaction in the spring of 2009, Denmark, Finland and the Netherlands ranked first, second and third. Maybe it is possible to pay high taxes and be happy. Maybe the Danes, Finns and Dutch worry less than we do. Canada, by the way, came fifth. If you believe this survey, we Canadians are still fairly happy with our lives, but less than we were. The U.S. ranked eleventh. The northern European countries have more or less agreed, as societies, as a matter of public policy, to share.

And the evidence is piling up that inequality is bad for our health, as individuals and as nations. The spring of 2009 saw the publication in Canada of a very important book. Called *The Spirit Level: Why More Equal Societies Almost Always Do Better*, it looks at a wide body of data from Western democracies to bolster the argument that the greater the income gap between rich and poor in a society, the worse off that society is. The authors, Richard Wilkinson and Kate Pickett, both epidemiologists, examined rates of infant mortality, illiteracy, teenage pregnancy, homicide, incarceration, mental illness, obesity and many other indices. The more pronounced the inequality, the less trust, the more violence. Norway, Japan, Sweden and Finland fared well in this analysis; the U.S., less so.

This is a book that points fingers: "Nor should we allow ourselves," the authors write in their conclusion, "to be cowed by the idea that higher taxes on the rich will lead to their mass emigration and economic catastrophe. We know that more egalitarian countries live well, with high living standards and much better social environments... Rather than adopting an attitude of gratitude towards the rich, we need to recognize what a damaging effect they have on the social fabric."

Finally, researchers at Statistics Canada recently examined the impact of poverty on life expectancy. What they found is that only 51.2 per cent of Canadian men in the bottom 10 per cent of income can expect to live to age seventy-five; but 74.6 per cent of those in the top 10 per cent of income can expect to live that long. For women, the gap is almost as large.

Reporting on the study in November of 2009, *The Globe and Mail*'s public health reporter André Picard asked a pertinent question: "Why is tackling poverty not a health priority?... the data tell us that the most powerful tool we have in our health care armamentarium is income redistribution. The most powerful drug we have—money—is pretty plentiful in Canada. But it is not being prescribed to everyone who would benefit."

THERE IS a parable I often encountered while reading the literature on development. Imagine this scene: you're by a river, enjoying the view from the bank on a warm summer day, listening to the water gurgle and eddy and maybe thinking about going in for a dip. Out of the corner of your eye, you catch sight of something floating in the water upriver. It's a basket and—can this be right?—there's a baby in the basket. You can see tiny fists waving; you can hear the child's cries.

Of course, you wade into the river. You're waist-deep, you get to the basket, you swing it to shore. You call to your friends and announce your discovery. And while you're all gathered round, someone shouts, "Here comes another one!" So you and your friends and neighbours rescue that infant too. But then another one comes, then another. And pretty soon you are fully occupied rescuing babies. Too busy, perhaps, to ask the all-important question: who in the world is throwing babies in the river, and what can be done to stop this despicable practice?

In 2000, Statistics Canada calculated the annual worth of human kindness in this country. In other words, if all the candystripers at hospitals, Meals on Wheels drivers, hockey and soccer coaches, hot-lunch servers, door-to-door canvassers and their counterparts with all other charitable organizations were paid even a minimum wage for their volunteer labour, the tab would be $17 billion a year.

All well and good. But what about those babies floating down the river? Volunteers should feel pride and satisfaction, knowing that the volunteer work they do does make a difference. But let there be no smugness. There is something profoundly wrong with a system that allows for such a cruel gap between the rich and poor in my city, in my country and all around the world.

The nineteenth century gave birth to people like Andrew Carnegie, men who were convinced that giving back to society—always at the end of their lives—would save it from the riots and revolution they very much feared from the poor and downtrodden. I guess it never occurred to Carnegie and those who followed in his footsteps to share their wealth earlier on, in the form of higher wages and benefits to those they employed. Leo Tolstoy, both a writer and a philanthropist, put it well: "I sit on a man's back, choking him and making him carry me, and yet assure myself and others that I am very sorry for him and wish to ease his lot by all possible means—except by getting off his back."

In December 2009, I read about two disturbing and recently published reports suggesting that social justice remains an elusive goal in this country. HungerCount, the national survey of emergency food programs conducted annually by Food Banks Canada, recorded an alarming 17.6 per cent surge in demand between 2008 and 2009. Some 800,000 Canadians visited food banks in March of 2009, 120,000 more than the same month a year earlier. In the twenty years such data have been kept, that's the biggest jump on record. Also released were Statistics Canada data revealing that less than a quarter of citizens taking home salaries of $80,000 or more donate to charity. Those who do offer, on average, a paltry $250 a year. Charitable donations in Canada in 2008 fell by $400 million, just when charitable foundations saw their invested funds shrivel in the plunging stock market and governments contributed less and less to their social service budgets. "What a perfect storm of parsimoniousness," a *Globe and Mail* editorial lamented.

WHAT DOES one do in the face of human suffering and need? All I know is this: what one should *not* do, is nothing.

What I learned during these twelve months was something I think I already knew. The point was simply hammered home. There is a price to be paid when you immerse yourself in dark issues, when you are up close with desperate conditions, chronic poverty or environmental degradation. Those on the front lines of such work must feel some days the great weight of hopelessness and despair, especially when it seems like nothing ever changes but for the worse. Yet there are victories and there can be real, even transformative, joy in service.

There are no magic wands to end poverty and inequality (though the Scandinavians come as close as anyone on the planet). I would love to wake up and read that the Tobin Tax has been implemented by every country in the world, that a $200-billion war chest has been established to combat hunger and housing woes in every corner of the globe, and that wise women and men were overseeing the fund with no hint of corruption anywhere down the line. That day will almost certainly never come.

In the meantime, keep on volunteering, keep on giving. Do not stop, and in fact do more. Weave generosity into your daily life: I found that stopping in at Vinnie's regularly kept me in touch and more inclined to help. Hanging a picture of young Carlos on the wall behind my computer meant he stayed in my thoughts. When Patricia Rebolledo told me she was going to Costa Rica at Christmas, she took with her a gift from me. My sister and I took an interest in Tom Kapansky, and through the contacts we've made at his hostel, we'll follow him on his journey. And we'll be richer for it.

But marry that individual giving with political engagement. Pressure politicians at every level—municipal, provincial and federal—and join forces with those who advocate for the poor, those in your community and those who are oceans away. Be less the avid consumer and more the engaged citizen. Show empathy as a volunteer, show passion as an activist. Get angry, get informed, go upriver.

.   .   .

[POSTSCRIPT]

AS I WRITE THIS, in December of 2010, the demand on services at the St. Vincent de Paul-Loretta Hospitality Centre in Kingston has never been greater. The numbers are staying the same for clients coming for meals but are increasing for groceries, and the warehouse is often extremely crowded.

Big Gord, the agency's volunteer truck driver, died of a heart attack a year and a half ago while shaving as he prepared for another day at Vinnie's. Jenn has moved on, so Sully is the chief cook now. Thelma still serves every day.

Next year is Vinnie's fortieth anniversary, and they are applying to foundations to enable some much-needed renovations, especially to the warehouse. "Hopefully," says Deb, "it will look more welcoming and less garage-like."

When Vinnie's applied to the United Way for funding, Deb asked one of her clients, John Dickson, to write something. What she loved about his statement is how it "blows away" stereotypes about what it is to be poor. Here is what he wrote:

Despite mental health challenges and a very limited income, I wish to flourish, not just survive. An empty room with bare walls can be a relief from even worse circumstances, but it takes small (and large) comforts to make any place a home. Through their mind-boggling array of donations, St. Vincent's makes available not only the staples such as food, diapers and clothing, but one might also acquire a nice art reproduction, or an armload of great books, glassware/dishes, jigsaw puzzles or a board game.

With the help of St. Vincent's, I have for the first time in a decade been able to create a peaceful, attractive and edifying environment absolutely singular to me and, most importantly, one in which neither I nor my company are confronted by my poverty. This is simply because St. Vincent's works so hard to re-route quality items that others don't want. They Reduce, they Reuse, they Recycle and, in turn, I and others feel less . . . poor. Feeling poor is worse than being poor.

THE TORONTO Disaster Relief Committee has fallen on hard times. Gaetan Heroux, who had accompanied me on my tour of men's shelters, has been unemployed for a year. On the other hand, when City Hall tried to bar him from the premises, he sued, and after no one from the city showed up in court, he got an early Christmas present late in 2010—a cheque in the mail for more than $5,000. Cathy Crowe ran for office as the NDP candidate in a provincial by-election in a downtown Toronto riding early in 2010. She came second and put up a fine showing. Beric German was on medical leave for a while, but he's back to work at Street Health now. "He's hanging in there," says Cathy, who is also unemployed but remains the volunteer executive director of the TDRC.

In October of 2010, the TDRC ran out of funds. Unable to afford staff or office rent and expenses, they moved out and are now what Cathy calls "homeless." "Twelve years of our materials, files, photos, films, press releases, etc. (or, as the City of Toronto Archives described it, 'nine metres of textual records') have been accepted into the archives," she says. "The remaining catalogue of newsclippings covering the early 1990s to today have been taken to York University's Homeless Hub."

Cathy told me that the TDRC is partnering with other agencies to hold a public inquiry into hunger. The TDRC is also a founding member of a coalition of community agencies that has filed a constitutional charter challenge on the right to housing. Finally, the TDRC co-produced (along with Mike Yam) a film called *Unheard Voices*, which chronicles the experiences of seven homeless people.

"It shows," says Cathy Crowe, "how the city of Toronto's Housing First policies have not improved their situation. It is a very dark and sobering film."

Cathy says, "We respond as we can to other issues, but these are very, very difficult times for us. I'm relying on speaking engagements to keep up the TDRC funding so we can do events. The only thing that makes me smile about our situation is that someday a researcher will get his or her hands on our materials and photos in the archives that show the activism that did result in so many victories."

The TDRC still has a mailing address. It's PO Box 662, 31 Adelaide Street East, Toronto, Ontario, M5C 2J8.

AT HOSPICE KINGSTON, eighty-three-year-old Ron passed away, but the others continue with their euchre and lunches. The major change is that Hospice has moved to a new location thanks to a $500,000 donation from a local philanthropist.

AT IMMIGRANT Services Kingston and Area, I am sad to report that Carolyn Davies, ISKA's head, died of a coronary in March of 2010. ISKA, meanwhile, moved to a new location on Princess Street in Kingston.

AT HOGAR de la Esperanza in San José, most of the people we met are doing well. Marlon, though, who walked with us in the May Day parade, was in jail for a time; Yanci contracted meningitis and was doing very poorly but has since rebounded; Kyra has another baby. So does Mirna, who now lives with her family near San Isidro. Carlos is doing fine. Mario is thriving. Jimmy, Luis Martin and Lucrecia have left Hogar.

Horizons, after a long and nervous wait, finally received approval in January 2010 from CIDA for its new five-year program (2010–2015). Among the many challenges facing Horizons is that of raising the funds required to match the CIDA grant (they must raise more than $800,000 each year to get the equivalent amount from the government).

AT THE John Howard Society, Lisa Finateri shocked everyone by announcing her resignation and moving back to her hometown of Ottawa, where she coordinates rooming house services for the city. The four ex-convicts I interviewed are all still out and doing well.

The new executive director, Debbie Woods, tells me that the JHS is in the process of building nine bachelor units in the basement of its building on Montreal Street in Kingston.

AT DARE TO DREAM, Charmaine Green is acquiring formal certification in riding instruction for the disabled. She's also looking to move the operation closer to Belleville, Ontario.

LAKE ONTARIO Waterkeeper wishes it had better news to report on Lynne and Sanford's battle with Cameco. "The saga goes on forever," is how Mark Mattson put it.

Much has changed in Port Hope. The pipe that stirred Lynne Prower to make her Application for Investigation has been replaced with two new, bigger pipes running from the dump to Lake Ontario. The dump has been transferred from Cameco to Atomic Energy of Canada Ltd. (AECL), so the dump is now owned by the federal government again. "The AECL," says Joanna Bull (no longer a law student but LOW counsel), "plans to expand the dump to include much of the waste that is currently scattered around the town and sitting in barrels on Cameco's property. In the summer of 2009, AECL tried to get a licence to start building this dump, but the plans they submitted to the CNSC were sorely missing important details (i.e., a water treatment plan or contaminant discharge limits). They will have to go back for another hearing before any construction can start, and that is where we are now. In the meantime, the two new pipes have been seen floating on the surface of the lake. They don't seem to work any better than their predecessor."

In other Waterkeeper news, Lafarge seems to have abandoned completely its plan to burn tires upwind of Kingston.

In December of 2010, Lake Ontario Waterkeeper and Lafarge announced what both called "a landmark agreement" on environmental changes to a landfill site at the cement plant in Bath, Ontario.

ONGWANADA CONTINUES apace, but Dusty will make no more rounds there. She died June 4, 2009, at the age of thirteen and is buried near our cabin in Prince Edward County. Dogs, I think, have much to teach us about unconditional love, affection, gratitude and, yes, generosity.

SOME OF the builders on the New Orleans trip have gone on to work with other Habitat for Humanity reconstruction projects in the far north of Canada and in Cambodia.

When I got in touch with Sandy Berg (now a Kingston city councillor), she wrote: "I can remember each street, each sweaty water break, each conflicted, frustrating moment when Miss Edna implored us to perform another house repair project when we should have moved on to another family in need. I remember the joy of seeing a butterfly in a flower-covered lot, which had been devoid of all living things two years earlier."

THE STUDENTS of First Nations Technical Institute continue their studies. Cindy, nineteen as I write, now has a baby, and the father is younger than she is. Still, she seems determined to get her diploma.

AT MANOORÉ FM, there's been some turnover, as expected. When my father died of heart failure on December 19, 2009, at the age of eighty-three, he was running an office out of his room in a seniors' wing at Providence Healthcare in Toronto. He was a volunteer writer and editor with the in-house newsletter, a job he did well and took seriously. J.B. Scanlan had two printers (one new colour model and a smaller black-and-white one), a laptop computer and a tape recorder.

On his death, those of his sons and daughters interested in this equipment drew from a deck of cards. One of my brothers turned up a king, and that, we thought, was that. Ulrike, picking for herself and me, drew an ace. And so it is that Manooré FM and Vinnie's ended up sharing the reporters' tools of James Bernard Scanlan.

When I contacted Canadian Crossroads International late in 2010, I was told that Manooré FM was not broadcasting, owing to a broken transmitter. They did manage to get back on the air, but funding is extremely precarious and they will need help to continue. Anyone able to help may contact CCI.

I WOULD be grateful to know if this book has influenced readers in some way, perhaps sparking interest in volunteering, in greater civic engagement or in donating to any of the twelve organizations profiled. All of them are easily found on the Internet, as are the other organizations I mentioned here: Dr. John Geddes's CanAssist African Relief Trust and Sud Academy (the school in Nairobi for Sudanese refugees). Anyone wishing to help the women's collective in Pikine, Senegal (Femmes, Actions et Développement), may write to acdev@telecomplus.sn.

Or write to me—at qareview@queensu.ca—and I will connect you with any of the above.

ACKNOWLEDGEMENTS

I AM indebted to Steven Burkeman, who delivered the 1999 Allen Lane Foundation Lecture in London, England. That thoughtful essay, titled "An Unsatisfactory Company?", shaped my thinking on philanthropy.

For letting me into their world, and for their kindness, my thanks to everyone at the twelve organizations profiled in this book. They are too numerous to name, but they know who they are.

In Costa Rica, Carlos Minott and Arthur Samuels were the most affable of hosts. Space wouldn't allow for a description of their laudable work with Asociación Proyecto Caribe, but I do want to mention it here. APC tries to raise awareness and pride among black Costa Ricans. I won't soon forget chatting with a young American ESL teacher in Cahuita who was appalled that some of her Costa Rican friends would head to the capital with green or blue contact lenses in their eyes to mask their black ancestry.

Special thanks to Doña Esilda, who housed and fed us in San José and made us feel so welcome. Her little dog, Venus (which in Spanish sounds like *Bay*-nus), would scrap every day with Creto, her cat, who had come to the house as one of two kittens. When the two kittens began to tug at Venus's teats, she abided this. And when her milk came, she let them suckle. The story struck me as a marvellous metaphor for generosity—of the short-lived kind.

In Senegal, Oumy Cantome Sarr and her family showed us the meaning of hospitality. A highlight of every evening was playing with her young nephews, Pa doudou and Papi. Karen Takacs, the executive director of Canadian Crossroads International, facilitated our connection with Manooré FM, and I'm grateful to Michael Cooke for paving our way to Karen and for his ongoing interest in my project. The French in my *guide de formation* (an outline of what I planned to teach at the radio station and sent before our departure) was immensely improved by Bianca Côté, who helped me at the busiest time of her teaching year.

Two books proved indispensable to my teaching in Senegal: *Le Journalisme Radiophonique* by Dominique Payette (a former CBC Radio host who now teaches at Laval University), and *CBC Radio Skills*, produced by CBC Training and Development (and written by a long-time friend, Marilyn Smith, who still works at the CBC in Toronto).

Family and friends took a special interest in this book and I am indebted to them. They financially supported reconstruction work in New Orleans, they mustered computers and other equipment for the radio station in Senegal and they helped me in other ways. Special thanks to Selby Martin, the Sisters of Providence of St. Vincent de Paul, Frances Itani and Ted Itani.

Jan Walter edited this book and sharpened it immensely by her intelligence, her instincts and her uncompromising standards. Ruth Wilson made some nice catches as copy editor, as did Douglas & McIntyre's associate editor Lara Kordic, managing editor Susan Rana somehow kept us all on schedule, designer Heather Pringle created a simply perfect cover, Jessica Sullivan produced a pleasing design, and marketing director Emiko Morita and publicity manager Corina Eberle spread the word. The entire team at Douglas & McIntyre deserve my thanks, and especially associate publisher Chris Labonté, and Scott Steedman before him, both of whom encouraged me from the earliest days of this undertaking.

Jackie Kaiser, my agent, came up with the structure for this book and has long been its champion. Ulrike Bender was, as usual, the manuscript's first reader and my partner in Senegal and Costa Rica. Her facility in French and Spanish helped me immensely. This book and this author owe much to her.

SELECTED BIBLIOGRAPHY

Adamson, Gil. *The Outlander*. Toronto: House of Anansi, 2007.

Bishop, Matthew and Michael Green. *Philanthrocapitalism: How the Rich Are Trying to Save the World*. New York: Bloomsbury Press, 2008.

Brison, Jeffrey D. *Rockefeller, Carnegie, and Canada: American Philanthropy and the Arts and Letters in Canada*. Montreal: McGill-Queen's University Press, 2005.

Carnegie, Andrew. *The Gospel of Wealth and Other Timely Essays*. Garden City, New York: Doubleday, 1933.

Commission on Social Determinants of Health, World Health Organization. *Closing the Gap in a Generation: Health Equity Through Action on the Social Determinants of Health*. Geneva: World Health Organization, 2008.

Crowe, Cathy. *Dying for a Home: Homeless Activists Speak Out*. Toronto: Between the Lines, 2007.

Dyer, Geoff, ed. *Selected Essays of John Berger*. London: Bloomsbury Publishing, 2001.

Edwards, Michael. *Just Another Emperor? The Myths and Realities of Philanthrocapitalism*. New York: Demos: A Network for Ideas & Action, 2008.

Endicott, Marina. *Good to a Fault*. Calgary: Freehand Books, 2008.

Furey, Robert J. *The Joy of Kindness*. New York: The Crossroad Publishing Co., 1993.

Gitlin, Todd. *Letters to a Young Activist*. New York: Basic Books, 2003.

Grady, Wayne. *The Great Lakes: The Natural History of a Changing Region*. Vancouver: Greystone Books, 2007.

Grandin, Temple. *Animals in Translation: Using the Mysteries of Autism to Decode Animal Behaviour*. New York: Scribner, 2005.

Hawke, Whitney, Max Davis and Bob Erlenbusch. "Dying Without Dignity: Homeless Deaths in Los Angeles County, 2000–2007." Los Angeles: Los Angeles Coalition to End Hunger and Homelessness, 2007.

Jordan, Mary, and Kevin Sullivan. *The Prison Angel: Mother Antonia's Journey from Beverley Hills to a Life of Service in a Mexican Jail*. New York: Penguin, 2005.

Klein, Naomi. *The Shock Doctrine: The Rise of Disaster Capitalism*. Toronto: Knopf Canada, 2007.

Krotz, Larry. *The Uncertain Business of Doing Good: Outsiders in Africa*. East Lansing: Michigan State University Press, 2008.

Laird, Gordon. "Shelter: Homelessness in a Growth Economy: Canada's 21st Century Paradox." Calgary: Sheldon Chumir Foundation for Ethics in Leadership, 2007.

Luks, Allan, with Peggy Payne. *The Healing Power of Doing Good: The Health and Spiritual Benefits of Helping Others*. New York: Fawcett Columbine, 2001.

Maskalyk, James. *Six Months in Sudan: A Young Doctor in a War-Torn Village*. Toronto: Doubleday, 2009.

Milanovic, Branko. *Worlds Apart: Measuring International and Global Inequality*. Princeton: Princeton University Press, 2005.

Moyo, Dambisa. *Dead Aid: Why Aid Is Not Working and How There Is a Better Way for Africa.* Vancouver: Douglas & McIntyre, 2009.

Newman, Paul, and A.E. Hotchner. *Shameless Exploitation in Pursuit of the Common Good.* New York: Doubleday, 2003.

Orbinski, James. *An Imperfect Offering: Humanitarian Action in the Twenty-First Century.* Toronto: Doubleday, 2008.

Payette, Dominique. *Le Journalisme Radiophonique.* Montreal: Les Presses de l'Université de Montréal, 2007.

Phinney, Richard. CBC Radio "Ideas": The Kings of Philanthropy. Two-part series, August 8 and August 15, 2007.

Pizzigati, Sam. *Greed and Good: Understanding and Overcoming the Inequality That Limits Our Lives.* New York: The Apex Press, 2006.

Shields, Carol. *Small Ceremonies.* Toronto: McGraw-Hill Ryerson, 1976.

Simonds, Merilyn. *The Convict Lover.* Toronto: Macfarlane Walter & Ross, 1996.

Smith, Marilyn E. *CBC Radio Skills.* Toronto: CBC Training and Development, 1999.

Wachtel, Eleanor. *Random Illuminations: Conversations with Carol Shields.* Fredericton: Goose Lane Editions, 2007.

Wagner, David. *What's Love Got to Do With It? A Critical Look at American Charity.* New York: New Press, 2001.

Widdowson, Frances, and Albert Howard. *Disrobing the Aboriginal Industry: The Deception Behind Indigenous Cultural Preservation.* Montreal: McGill-Queen's University Press, 2008.

Wilson, Brian, Nancy Bullis and Gwen Benjamin. *Canadian. Registered Charities Guide.* Toronto: Institute of Chartered Accountants, 2006.

Wilkinson, Richard, and Kate Pickett. *The Spirit Level: Why More Equal Societies Almost Always Do Better.* London: Allen Lane, 2009.

Winter, Michael. *The Big Why.* Toronto: House of Anansi Press, 2004.